OVERLAND TO INDIA

An 8,400 mile adventure on a 55-year-old motorcycle

GORDON G. MAY

Editor
JANE GREGORY

Rixon Groove

First published in 2008 by
Rixon Groove
PO Box 153, Stockport,
Cheshire, SK6 2EZ

Printed in England by Rixon Groove

ISBN: 978-0-9561168
www.overlandtoindia.co.uk

Thank you to the following for kindly allowing the use of their photographs:
Tony Henry. Photograph of Gordon departing Folkestone, Page 127
Csaba Szikszai. Photograph of Gordon and Ferenc, Bekescaba, Page 127

Acknowledgements

First and foremost, my thanks to the quite incredible Andy Berry whose skills made my motorcycle so exceptional. He not only created a superbly reliable engine, but crafted many other parts on the bike including the front forks. He also gave constant advice and unflagging support throughout the restoration and the ride itself.

When things looked precarious in the last few weeks before departure, Derek Thom stepped into the breech, truly saving the day. He did a fantastic job of making brackets, fixing the pannier carriers and sorting out my carburettor. On top of that I will always be indebted to him for the much-needed moral support he gave me.

Many companies also offered valuable support and provided some excellent equipment which I used on the ride. I was both surprised and pleased by how well these people responded to my plans to use such an old motorcycle and their backing was invaluable. By means of a thank you I've included a list of them in the final pages of this book.

My utmost thanks go to Jane Gregory, who has born the brunt of my wanderlust for several years, wonderfully looking after our son, Jacques, together with his sister, Surya, single-handed for months on end. What's more, on my return Jane offered to help by editing this book, and I'm very grateful for her hours of hard work as well as her skill. She says it's been worth the effort for the laughter that the excessively high number of (now modified) Freudian slips have given her.

While I was on my journey, I received countless messages of encouragement and support from people following my ride online. Because of the pressures, mainly time, of riding up to ten hours a day, I just wasn't able to reply to the hundreds of emails and blog posts I received, but they did mean an awful lot to me.

What will I remember most about the experience? Much as I loved riding my motorcycle and seeing some of the exquisite places I passed through, it's the people I met along the way that made the journey so special. Strangers unfailingly offered me assistance, hospitality and a generosity of spirit that was heartwarming, uplifting and reaffirming of the goodness of human nature. I hope the pages in this book reflect my appreciation of them.

Gordon G. May
November 2008

Start
1
2
3
4
5
6
7
8
9
10
11
12
13-14
15
16
Start Manchester, UK
1 Oxford, UK
2. Folkestone, UK
3 Mainz, Germany
4 Hahnbach, Germany
5 Cesky Krumlov, Czech Republic
6 Hustopece, Czech Republic
7 Szarvas, Hungary
8 Truckstop west of Sibiu, Romania
9 Giurgiu, Romania
10 Kazanlak, Bulgaria
11 Edirne, Turkey
12 Izmit, Turkey
13-14 Safranbolu, Turkey
15 Amasya, Turkey
16 Erzincan, Turkey
17 Dogubayazit, Turkey
18 Maku, Iran
19 Zanjan, Iran
20 Saveh, Iran
21-22 Esfahan, Iran
23 Kuhpayeh, Iran
24 Rafsanjan, Iran
25-26 Bam, Iran
27 Mirjaveh Border, Iran
28 Dalbandin, Pakistan
29-31 Quetta, Pakistan
32 Sukkur, Pakistan
33 Bahawalpur, Pakistan
34 Lahore, Pakistan
35 Amritsar, India
36 Ludhiana, India
37-39 Delhi, India
40 Agra, India
41 Orchha, India
42 Khajuraho, India
43 Seoni, India
44 Adilabad, India
45 Warangal, India
46 Vijayawada, India
47 Nellore, India
48 Chennai, India

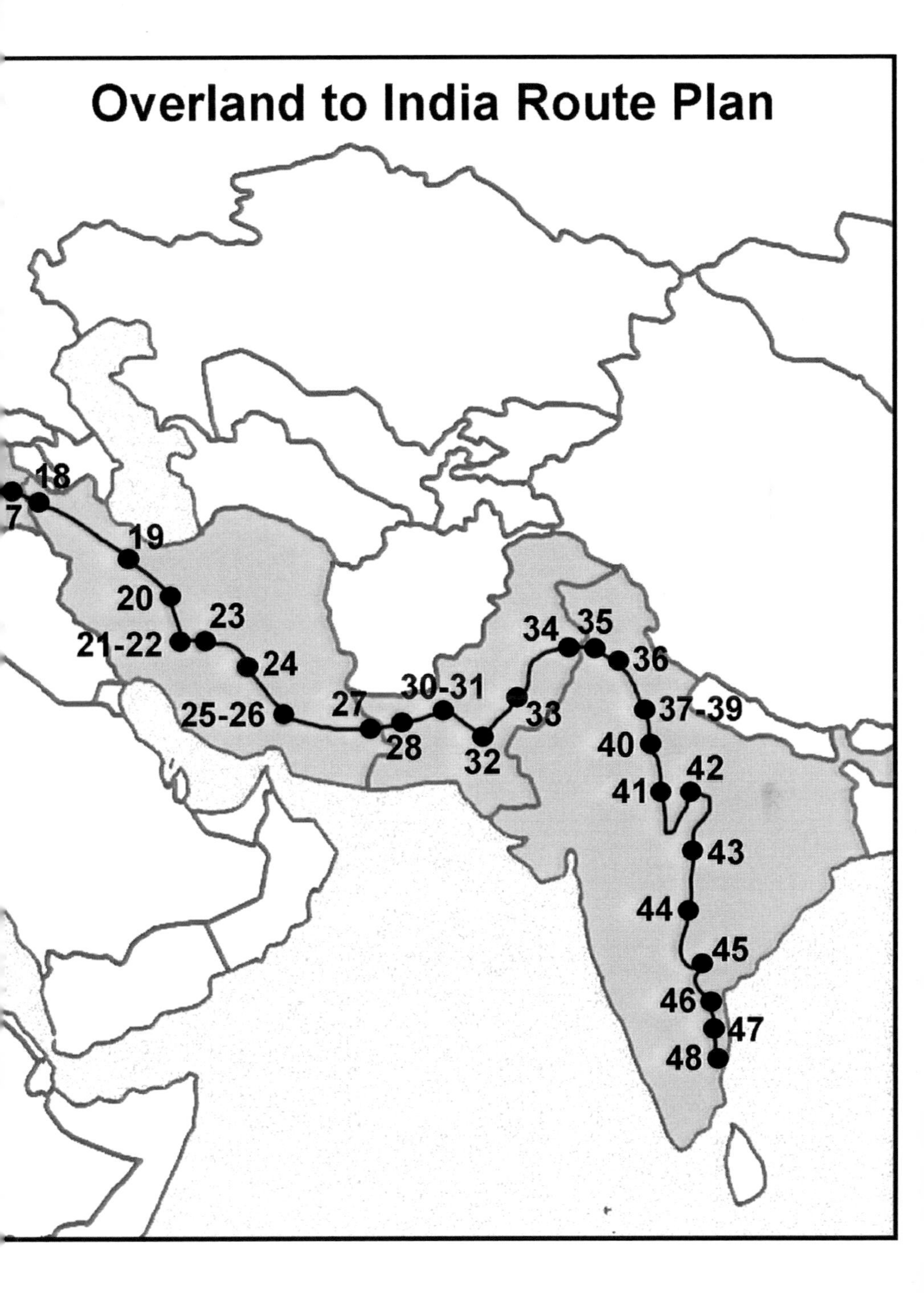

Overland to India Route Plan
18
7
19
20
23
21-22
24
25-26
27
30-31
28
32
33
34
35
36
37-39
40
41
42
43
44
45
46
47
48

The source of inspiration. 1956, Redditch, Alfred Barboza (left) and John Noronha (3rd from left) rode their Royal Enfield Bullet from India to the UK, "From East To West With India's Goodwill". They are met by Enfield managers Major Vic Mountford (2nd from left) and Jack Booker (right).

Introduction

Early morning, one balmy October day, 1988. I ride a post-office red 350 cc Royal Enfield Bullet Deluxe, resplendent with rich chrome that glistens in the glow of the still rising sun, through the empty streets of Kathmandu, Nepal. The exhaust note makes a heavenly-sounding deep boom that rebounds off the ancient white stone buildings, crumbling stupas and flag-topped temples that grace the streets.

On the back sits my New Zealand girlfriend, Jude, the book *Birds of The Indian Subcontinent* in one hand, folded map in the other. She taps my shoulder for me to turn right and we finally pull up outside a small guest house with a courtyard that offers secure parking. We've been on the road for seven intensely satisfying days, having left Delhi, where we bought the bike some weeks earlier, with a rough plan to ride to Nepal and leave it safely locked up while we go trekking. We've ridden from dawn to dusk most days and slept at a diverse range of accommodations, including on a rope bed in a Hindu temple and a spare room in a Christian missionary hospital. We've had the time of our lives.

This charmed existence continues for another four months. We sell the bike in January, ready to fly onwards to Bangkok and ultimately, New Zealand. It's heart-wrenching to part with the trusty friend that's carried us over seven thousand kilometres with little more than a snapped clutch cable. I have another Royal Enfield stored away in the UK, a 1963 250 cc Crusader in need of re-commissioning, but it will never be the same as the wonderful motorcycle we have just amassed so many vivid memories on.

Fast Forward to 1997. Standing in a New Zealand stationers, I pick up a copy of *Beaded Wheels*, the bimonthly magazine for New Zealand's Classic Car owners. I can't help myself casually scanning its pages as there are occasionally old bikes listed for sale. Nestled amongst adverts for a Nash Standard Six convertible, an Alvis Drophead coupe and an MG-A, is a small advertisement with no photograph:

1953 Royal Enfield Bullet in need of restoration. Many spare parts collected over years including 2 sets of crankcases. New Plymouth.

I 'phone the advertised number and speak to a very amiable man who admits to not having enough time to restore the bike. He'd like to see it bought by someone who'll actually do something with it. Photographs arrive in the post a couple of days later, showing a loosely assembled machine painted a motley collection of colours: chipped burgundy, rust-resistant bright orange and undercoat grey. But the bike itself looks pretty much original.

"Come on, let's go and see it," says my partner, Hilda, committing us to a four hour drive that will take us around the lower slopes of the stunning, cone shaped volcano, Mount Taranaki. As chance would have it, this allows her to drag me through a series of blooming rhododendron gardens en route... the method in her madness. It's a small price to pay.

Seen at close quarters, the bike is in a sorry state of repair, but the collection of spares, which fills three banana boxes, looks promising to my inexperienced restorer's eye. A deal is struck.

The Bullet arrives at my clothing manufacturing factory in Wellington the following week, courtesy of a furniture removal company I persuaded to pick it up. Two burly Samoans untie it from the back of their van, and in response to my offer of a cup of coffee and a healthy tip, wrap a couple of piano straps around the forks and haul it up a flight of stairs to my workshops. How little did I know to what degree this was a prelude of things to come. The bike sits untouched in my office for the next two years, making a somewhat unusual talking point for first-time visitors.

Four years later, I find myself living in England, the Bullet secure in a storage unit fourteen thousand miles away in the southern hemisphere. I decide to ship it to the UK. Hilda responds to my request for help, meticulously freeing it from under the piles of household belongings that are stacked on top, then hands it over to an international freight company. Somewhere in the region of forty eight years after first being exported from England as a brand new motorcycle, it returns, arriving at Felixstowe docks

Over the following few years, its restoration nearly costs me my home when I'm caught red-handed by my landlord smuggling it piece by piece into a London flat. The frame lives in a camper van for eighteen months while the cycle parts reside in a less than salubrious garden shed and it is eventually assembled slowly in my present first floor flat. It's a small miracle nothing major has been lost along the way.

Now I have to confess at this point that I'm a bit of a Jeremy Clarkson when it comes to mechanics. I laugh at myself every time I see him on *Top Gear* undertaking a project that requires some engineering finesse. Give him a hammer and chisel or chainsaw and he's happy. Ask him to do something that demands delicacy or mechanical aptitude and just watch the wheels come off.

The difference between us, however, is that I do have rather a lot more patience. I may bodge something once, or even twice, but like a dog at a bone I keep going back for more until I finally get it to fit. At that point, the perfectionist in me kicks in and I send the several times bodged part away to be re-welded, repainted or re-polished before its final fitting. This serves to make the restoration of my Enfield a somewhat protracted process.

In 2001 I get incredibly lucky when I meet a bright and chirpy Northerner called Andy Berry, who is, in my mind, unquestionably the best engine builder and tuner of Royal Enfields. Andy and I are of similar age, sharing a deep passion for these bikes, which means we talk endlessly about them. Where our motorcycling conversation diverges is when Andy's technical knowledge is tapped... it's immense. He manages to make unwaveringly accurate mental calculations of tolerances, ratios and balance factors at lightning speed. I just nod and agree, happy he doesn't expect the same back from me.

Once he has the Bullet, Andy completes the engine's restoration first. At one point I visit him and am asked to feel the flywheels turning round.

"Feel that?" he asks. "It's not a hundred percent smooth. I'm going to strip it down and do it again." he adds.

This is why I trust Andy so much. He's simply not content to build an engine that's 'good enough'. It has to be 'absolutely right', period.

In 2002 I write an article about an Englishman called Greg Staves, who, in remission from cancer, rode a late-model Indian 500 cc Bullet from the Arctic Circle in Alaska to Tierra Del Fuego, the southernmost region of South America. The tale of his journey inspires me so much that I keenly decide to emulate him.

On my next visit to see how things are going, I somewhat tentatively say to Andy,

"Um... can we start again with my Bullet, making it as tough as possible so I can ride fifteen thousand miles on it, including over the Andes?"

Thankfully, he's a pretty stable character and never seems to be put off his stride by whatever hair-brained scheme I might come up with. The conversation immediately turns to the procurement of parts, including a set of similarly aged 500 cc crankcases we can start afresh with, concluding that the already assembled engine will keep for a future restoration project.

One of the many good things about riding Royal Enfields is that numerous after-market parts have been developed to make them go faster. Because these components are made inherently tougher to cope with the strain of speed tuning, they're an ideal way to make a de-tuned engine tougher; even, dare I say it, bullet-proof. A Midlands based business, Hitchcocks Motorcycles, have developed such a wide range of performance parts that I'm like a child in a sweet shop as I browse through their catalogue.

Over a period of six months, Andy painstakingly assembles the new touring engine, using a completely new Hitchcocks crankshaft with a needle-roller big end as the basis. Added to this is a top-of-the-range American forged steel piston and, in place of the usual Enfield wet clutch, a race-tested belt drive kit. Andy donates an original 1960's Redditch barrel and I buy a rare early cylinder head from a fellow Royal Enfield Owners Club member, Mark Mumford, at a club rally.

With the engine complete, Andy delivers it to my home and together we bolt on the frame complete with forks he specially built to accommodate a later, but stronger, double-sided front brake. From here on in, it's up to me finish the bike.

Without specialist skills and a workshop full of engineering equipment to do a lot of things yourself, restoring an old bike is a bit like throwing money into a bottomless pit. Furthermore, every spare part seems to need reworking to make it fit and function correctly. It's an exasperatingly slow job. Six months ahead of my planned departure for the Americas in January 2006, I accept I haven't a chance of making it on my motorcycle. I decide to change tack, undertaking the journey by train as much as possible and resorting to buses and jeeps only when there are no rail tracks.

The bike languishes in my flat for three months while I explore the Americas, and its restoration only slowly inches forward in fits and spurts after my return. New inspiration, thankfully, comes from a photograph in one of my books.

In 1955, Alfred J Barboza and John J. Noronha, two university students from Madras (now Chennai), bought the first motorcycle to be assembled at the new Royal Enfield factory in Thiruvottiyur. Together they made an adventurous journey across eleven countries, including Pakistan, Iran and Turkey, before finally rolling up at the gates of the Royal Enfield factory at Redditch in 1956. The photograph of their arrival clearly shows pannier boxes painted with a map of their route and the words, *East to West with India's goodwill.*

The notion of doing a similar ride, but in reverse, on my old Royal Enfield starts to grow in my mind. I realise that in 2008, it will have been twenty years since I first rode there, which seems like a pretty good kind of anniversary to celebrate.

The idea for Overland To India is born.

Preparations

Once committed to the project, I set about planning the ride in detail. In his motorcycle epic, *The Road To Gobbler's Knob*, travel writer Geoff Hill describes the preparation for his trip up the Pan-American Highway in a way that rings so true for me.

"I wrote a basic list of things to do... when I got to number 78, I sat looking at the screen thinking that motorbikes are supposed to be all about freedom from sitting looking at a screen all day, but organising an adventure on one involved exactly that."

I spend long days and even longer nights building my website and carefully honing pages of 'to do' lists that are so long and thorough they daunt me to the point of procrastination. For a period of approximately five months, I do precious little paid work to enable me to concentrate on my preparations, made so monstrously time-consuming by the painfully slow restoration of the bike. 'How could someone in full time employment actually manage this?' I ask myself as I sit in front of my computer at midnight, working away on new lists of spares I might need.

Falling back on the old adage of 'one step at a time', I begin posting letters at a rate of two or three per week to potential kit sponsors. As positive responses begin to come in, I do a rough tally of the cost of all the equipment. It makes me appreciate just how expensive overland motorcycling is. When I think back to my ride through India and Nepal in 1988, Jude and I spent a pittance on kit. We only bought a couple of basic crash helmets along with two sets of ex-Indian army jackets, trousers and gloves. Haphazardly strapping our belongings onto the back of the Enfield, we naively set off with the handful of basic tools that came with the bike and not a single spare part.

How things have changed, myself included, we've all become so much more concerned about quality, image, having the right gadget et cetera. I think we're all so much more safety conscious too. Forget body armour; in '88 we didn't even have travel insurance, which would be absolutely unthinkable today.

It has to be said, however, that as the pile of motorcycle and expedition equipment grows ever larger in my spare room, my excitement keeps apace. The dream of the journey seems more of a reality, even if the completion of the bike is in stasis, as much a result of months of unfathomable procrastination as my mechanical ineptitude.

In the early part of the year I make a low budget film, my first commercial expedition into this medium. Aided by an new Apple Mac and a series of film-making lessons at my local Apple store, I set about making a documentary on the life of trials riding legend, Johnny Brittain. I'm proud of the outcome and receive much positive feedback on the finished product. Moreover, I enjoy the film-making process so much that I decide to shoot a documentary of my ride to India, roughly along the lines of *Long Way Down* and *Round*, but without the crew, large budget, support vehicles and all.

Preparations for the trip involve meeting a number of people who can give me travel advice and teach me some of the skills I might need to keep myself going. Investing in a new camera, I take the opportunity to film all the proceedings.

Top of the list is learning how to change a tyre inner tube. The very fact that after twenty-seven years of motorcycling, I've never done this only serves to illustrate just how little hands-on mechanical experience I have. Fortunately, the guys at Central Wheels, the UK's largest classic motorcycle wheel builders, don't seem to hold this against me. They rebuilt both of my wheels early on in the bike's restoration using stainless rims and spokes, a beautiful job. To my delight, they seem more than happy to spend time teaching me this rudimentary skill.

I visit their Birmingham premises one sunny Saturday afternoon. A young but experienced tyre fitter, Craig, deftly runs me through the process. He makes it seem so straightforward, which in fact it is, but just to give me a thorough grounding he's chosen an old tyre with age-hardened rubber to practice on.

"If you can master that, you'll be able to change anything," he says with certainty. Two sticky, knuckle-grazing hours later, my hands and trouser knees blackened with old rubber, I've done the job three times.

'Good enough' I think, hoping I never have to put my new abilities to the test.

Without doubt the single weakest part on my bike is the magneto. Used heavily in the aviation industry because it's a self-contained ignition system requiring no battery, magnetos also provided the sparks for most motorcycles built before the mid-1950s. However, they are prone to overheating which causes the insulating material, usually shellac, to melt. Ergo, no spark. I've had mine completely restored, hoping that modern insulating materials and a rewound coil will see me through. Just to play it safe, I go for a lesson in magneto maintenance from Britain's 'Mag-Man', Tony Cooper of TC Motorcycles, Halesowen.

In his garden sit a series of small workshops where he restores and assembles all kinds of vintage ignition systems. In one such room, surrounded by shelves of small plastic buckets containing goodness knows how many tiny olden-days electrical gizmos, Tony runs through the routine for swapping out a failed magneto armature. This includes how to 'shim' a new one so that it runs true. I studiously take notes and film the procedure, praying that I'll never have to attempt the job for real.

I had toyed with carrying a complete spare unit, but they seem to be made from an alien metal from the planet Zog that weighs over five kilos.

"Its mass will destroy anything you put in your panniers with it. It might even bend the boxes out of shape," Tony warns.

He hands me a spare armature, complete with bearings and spacer ring, which only weighs a quarter of the complete unit in its magnetised body. I'm grateful for his help and he pats me on the back as I leave.

"Don't worry about it. I'm certain you'll be giving me the spares back unused in a couple of month's time," he says.

I begin my quest for hands-on motorcycle travel experience with Richard Miller of Bournemouth. Richard is also a big Royal Enfield fan and has undertaken two massive journeys on them, from India to the UK in the late 1990s on an Indian Bullet and from Bournemouth to Cape Town and most of the way back in 2007, this time on an older British machine. We meet up at a campsite the evening before a major bike show. With barbecued veggie-burgers sizzling in the background, I grill Richard on his experiences.

"You'll need to carry far more water than you imagine," he begins. "I had a rear tyre puncture crossing the Iranian desert. It took me about an hour to change and I guess I drank three litres of water in that short time. Oh yes, and try to have some kind of temporary shelter you can rig up to keep the sun off you whilst doing it" he warns.

I'm keen to learn about modifications he made to his bikes to toughen them up.

"The rear subframe struggles to cope with the weight of luggage. Mine broke twice going through Africa, but there again, I was travelling two-up with my partner, Sascha, and carrying camping and cooking equipment too."

It's a concern I'm all too familiar with, even through I'm travelling solo.

"I think you'll need a good sump guard as well, you never know what kind of rocky roads you'll end up on," he explains.

That's one I think I've already got covered until Richard goes on to describe his version.

"I made one that wraps right round the bottom of the engine and comes up each side, protecting the oil pump housing and the lower portion of the primary cover."

That, figuratively speaking, makes my guard look like Speedo trunks as opposed to a diver's wetsuit. Hmmm.

He continues, "I also recommend you carry all the consumables you think you could possibly need. I've several times been caught out buying locally produced fakes of branded spark plugs, points and even chains that have given up the ghost just weeks later."

But not all of Richard's tips carry foreboding.

"You'll have a ball, meet so many interesting people, and no doubt, like me, find there are always good people out there who offer help when you most need it."

Jonny Krause, an Englishman living in Scotland who rode to India in 2007 to raise sponsorship for the charity JBF, is the other bearer of good counsel. I stumbled across Jonny's travel blog whilst he was midway through his ride and got in touch with him at the time, wishing him well.

He travels to me meet me on the bike he took on his overland marathon. It's a 1983 Yamaha XS850, a huge brute of a machine. After shaking hands I ask if I can sit on it. Heaven's above, without any luggage it weighs far more than my old Enfield ever will when fully laden. If Jonny can ride this to India, I think, there's hope for me yet!

I've sent him a long list of subjects I'd like to discuss, amongst them being 'what did you carry that you wished you'd left at home?'

"Nothing," is his reply. "Even though I didn't use most of my spares, I'm still glad I had them all with me. Two things I did find handy tho', were a pair of riding sunglasses and a solar battery charger for my camera and mobile phone."

I've already got the first covered as my Halcyon MK49 goggles have been fitted with tinted, UV protectant lenses. The solar battery charger sounds a good idea and I add it to my list.

Jonny also had a puncture, this time out in the mountainous wilds of Pakistan.

"But a group of local guys in a jeep came along at just the right time and were a great help, refusing to leave until they saw me safely ride off." It's an encouraging tale.

Jonny goes on to ask me what kind of pump I'll be taking in case of a puncture. I naturally tell him it's a 1950's style hand pump to match the bike. Without comment, he goes to his Yamaha's panniers and finds a modern, miniature foot pump.

"Take this," he says. "you might need it. Using a hand pump is a no-go in that heat."

Next I ask about how much water he carried.

"I'm a tea addict and took a multi-fuel stove thinking I'd stop by the roadside and make myself frequent cuppas. But I never used it as I found tea shops and cafes so readily available, and for me, that was a great way to meet people."

It's not only useful for me to hear about Jonny's journey, I also get a chance to learn more about JBF, one of the two charities I plan to visit and raise awareness for via my website.

Jonny tells me that several years ago, whilst visiting Delhi as a tourist, he came across a dog with a broken leg that had obviously been hit by a car. Carrying the dog around for hours, he found there were hardly any facilities able to give veterinary care to stray animals. When he did eventually find one such organisation, he decided its work was so valuable, yet so understaffed and underfunded, that he spent the rest of his time in India working voluntarily for them.

As that organisation became more established, Jonny started a new charity, JBF, to assist the many hapless injured cows that wander the streets of Delhi. Then, after more visits to India, he expanded the charity's scope by setting up a small community school to assist the street children that live in and around one of Delhi's worst slums, Viklang Basti.

"The slum inhabitants are from all parts of India and come to Delhi to escape drought, famine or disease," explains Jonny. "Unfortunately, as these people are illiterate, innumerate and lacking extended family support, they're right at the bottom of the social structure. Those who have what we would call work collect rags, bottles, paper and the like to sell on as material for re-cycling. Those without this work beg for their daily income. The children of Viklang Basti lead the same lives as the adults, so we created the Informal School project to try and break the cycle of poverty and give these children the chance of joining mainstream Delhi life"

It's inspiring stuff and I feel really keen to do what I can to help.

Carrying a monstrous pile of spares seems essential to the success of the ride, as I won't have time to wait for replacement parts to be mailed to me. Furthermore, my experience to date has been that a good number of parts for the newer Indian-made machines cannot be easily retro-fitted to the older British bikes. As the list of spares grows ever longer, filling three A4 sheets of paper, the question of how to carry it all becomes increasingly worrying.

To my delight I find a pair of unused genuine 1960's vintage steel pannier boxes for sale on eBay. Due to the way they're listed, no one else bids and I pick them up for a song. Perfect, I think... until it comes to fitting them.

Aha... pannier frames are required. I rummage around in the dusty recesses of my garage, triumphantly emerging with a tatty but very solid pair that came as surplus parts with an old AJS I'd ridden in New Zealand. Only, how do I make them fit a Royal Enfield... especially one still sitting half-finished in my first floor flat? I call in the help of the village 'Jack of all trades', who should theoretically be a safe bet as he's a retired car mechanic and a biker to boot.

"Yes, I can weld them up, no problem," he says, holding the pannier frames in his hands and sagely nodding.

A week passes, then another and still no word of the frames. I harass and chase him, but two weeks grow into a month and still there's no noticeable activity. Eventually, all but dragging him to my flat, he sets about sawing, hammering and welding some steel brackets into shape.

"Your bike belongs in a museum, not on the road," he says in a grudging tone as he struggles to make them fit. When he leaves a couple of hours later, I know that his shoddy work just won't be up to the job; it's too flimsy and doesn't fit precisely enough to take the load.

Into the breech steps Derek Thom with an altogether different approach. I had only met Derek and his lovely wife, Liz, a few weeks earlier during a motorcycle autojumble held at Netley Marsh in the south of England. He'd been very friendly towards me and, when I told him about my forthcoming trip, offered to help if he could. A couple of weeks later I delivered indicators and a mudguard-mounted rear carrier to him. Sure enough, he did a marvellous job of customising them using precisely finished stainless steel components, and all within a couple of days too.

"Derek, I'm really struggling with the rear panniers," I tell him on the 'phone just seven weeks prior to departure, "heeeelp!".

Within hours he's on my doorstep, tools in hand and ready to start work... an absolute star.

With panniers solidly affixed, I'm jump-started into action and everything else on the bike begins to take shape very quickly. I get my electrics working, despite a couple of setbacks with short circuits and poor earths. I discretely fit a pair of small horns under the headlamp, again on stainless 'Thom-special' brackets. Andy comes up trumps with a specially modified trials-type sump guard, smartly turned down allen bolts for the top of my rocker covers, a modified timing cover to take an oil pressure feed and some adroit adaptations to my saddle to ensure it bolts securely to the frame. Everything that needs painting goes off to Essex-based Maldon Shotblasting and Power Coating, who apply a coat of extra-tough Dupont paint to all surfaces, promising me the finish is tough enough for a battleship, not just an old Brit bike. They're returned in double-quick time too, which really helps keep the project's newly found momentum going.

At last it's done. I stand back and admire it, feeling exceedingly proud of my first fully restored motorcycle. I've been a bit of a perfectionist about it, demanding only the best of everything be used, from a raft of stainless steel fixings to the highest quality internal components. Even the exhaust downpipe was custom made to a pattern from an original one that Andy has.

It gleams in front of me, its paintwork a rich, deep lustre and its alloy and chrome twinkling in the summer sun that shines through my bedroom window. I realise it's not going to look anything like this in a few weeks time and only hope my letting go of an almost obsessive dedication to its perfect appearance isn't too painful an experience.

Thursday 10th July is crunch time for me and the Enfield. My planned departure date is just six weeks away and the day has finally arrived to move my motorcycle from its cosy, carpeted 'workshop' out into the real world, namely my garage. I strip everything heavy and protruding off it and manoeuvre it towards my front door. In the evening I collar my genial neighbour, Jamie, who (fortuitously) works out regularly at a local gym.

"Sure I'll give you a hand," he says merrily, not yet aware of what sort of object I'm actually asking him to manhandle down a flight of stairs.

The look on his face when he sees the motorcycle is priceless, but good to his word, he valiantly grabs hold of the rear and together we hump the dead weight round the tight corners of doorways and balcony and, step by step, down the stairwell.

"Crikey," he says breathlessly when the front wheel actually reaches terra firma. "Never thought we'd make it."

I have to confess that I had my doubts too and am mightily relieved to push it around the back of the building and into my garage.

My next challenge is getting the bike on the road, and not being one to put pressure on myself, I have arranged the first step, its MOT, in five days time! Bolting everything back on is a straightforward enough task, but getting the bike running for the first time is another matter altogether. Compression is high and after an hour of kicking, my right leg is just about numb. I try bump-starting too, but that just locks the rear wheel up and creates a black patch of rubber on the driveway where the tyre has rubbed on the concrete.

Just as I'm about to give in, and without doing anything different, the engine suddenly catches and my Bullet bursts into life. Deep joy! As chance would have it, Andy Berry shows up five minutes later and, with a little fettling, we manage to establish a fairly even rhythm.

'Phew', I think, not realising what still lies ahead.

The next morning I take the bike to the MOT testing station, a Kawasaki dealership half a mile away, all down hill. I get there without any difficulties and the bike passes with flying colours, although the tester does worryingly add, with a toothy grin,

"If you're mad enough to ride it, I'm mad enough to pass it."

The trouble begins whist riding uphill home. It simply won't pull, straining to respond when I open the throttle.

"It's probably the taper needle height in your carb," says Andy on the telephone in response to my pleas for help. "It sounds like it's running too rich and you'll have to raise the needle jet to lean out the mixture."

This is certainly a learning curve. Up until now, I've done nothing more complicated than change throttle cables on carburettors.

Day after exasperating day is spent in trying to improve performance. The procedure becomes ingrained in my consciousness: remove tank, saddle, air filter box and carburettor, reposition the needle jet, replace the whole lot before testing for any improvement. Repeat ad infinitum. Each set of changes takes at least an hour, eating into my time so badly that I get behind with many of my other preparations, including the crucial thousand mile running-in of the engine I had hoped to do before departure.

Still running rich, I at least get the bike working well enough for the next important step, registering it for the road. This procedure, which involves taking the bike to a DVLA office to be inspected by an expert, should be a formality as I have all the required paperwork to authenticate it as a genuine classic. All goes well until the examiner asks,

"How did you get here?"

"Just on local roads," I reply. "I'm keeping my speed under forty whilst running it in and didn't want to chance the motorway whilst going so slowly."

He looks at me with a mixture of dismay and amusement.

"I actually meant where's your van or trailer," he explains. "You're not supposed to ride it on the road until I've examined it and you've been issued with an age-related registration number, which will take at least another week."

Holy Moley! He leaves after issuing me with an application reference number. Apprehensively, I climb back on the bike and set off for home. I get about half a kilometre when the engine slows, surges, slows again then cuts out. I've run out of petrol. Calling myself a noodle-brain (or words to that effect) and thinking I'm going to have to become far more organised if I want to get out of the UK let alone ride all the way to India, I commence pushing.

Appearing like a mirage in the distance is a BMW motorcycle dealership. I sweatily push my bike around the back to the workshops where I ask a mechanic for directions to the nearest petrol station and also if it's okay to leave my bike with him whilst I go to get some. The sales manager joins us and they hold a quick confab,

"There's a filling station another half a mile along that road," begins the mechanic, pointing up a steep hill. "I'll get you some fuel from that crashed bike over there which should help get you going."

Whilst he goes about draining some petrol from the sad wreckage, the manager questions me about my machine. He thinks I'm pulling his leg when I tell him of my imminent departure for the subcontinent.

"You've got to be kidding," he says. "What you need is one of our new GS Adventurers, as ridden by Ewan and Charley ..."

The mechanic jokingly winks at me as he tops up my tank with petrol. With sincere thanks and a wave, I set off for more fuel and home.

There's surprisingly little paperwork to do in the final preparatory stages before departure, but what there is proves exceedingly time-consuming.

I usually travel on my New Zealand passport, but come a cropper when I start applying for visas.

"How are you in the UK without a stamp in your passport?" I'm asked by an Indian consular official in Birmingham.

I explain I have dual citizenship, to which I'm told,

"If you want to use your New Zealand passport, your visa application can take up to a month. A visa in your British passport can be processed in three days."

I opt for the simpler, quicker option.

The Pakistan visa is a doddle, processed in one day at the friendly Manchester Consul. When I return late in the afternoon to collect my now-stamped passport, I experience a slice of Pakistani hospitality that's embarrassing but quite touching. A long queue of men, at least thirty deep, stand patiently waiting their turn to collect passports and other documents. As the only Westerner, I'm taken in hand by a couple of men at the tail of the line who frog-march me right to the front. I try to protest, explaining I'm very happy to wait my turn, but more men, this time at the head of the queue, join in. One says,

"No, you are our guest. Please..." pushing me gently forward towards the consular staff member so I can be served first.

The Iranian visa is the trickiest. I've done some research online and getting a visa does appear a rather hit and miss affair. Indeed, Richard Miller told me that he and Sascha were refused an Iranian visa in the build up to their trip to Cape Town. Furthermore, the protracted wait while their application was considered delayed their departure by a month, which for me is a scary thought.

I decide to get some expert assistance and find a helpful travel agency online, Tehran-based Iranianvisa.com. For a very reasonable fee, the company secure pre-approval for my visa from the relevant government department. I then catch a coach to the Iranian embassy in London with my passport, approval code and a selection of photo-booth images. In the waiting room I meet a couple of tourists who have waited over three weeks for their visas. Mine is processed the same day, within just two hours in fact. One pleasant moment occurs when a member of the embassy staff ambles around the visa section waiting room offering delicious cake to all visitors, which is certainly a first for me. I sit for five hours on the coach back to Manchester, feeling that the biggest bureaucratic hurdle has now been overcome

The other essential document for the journey is a Carnet de Passages en Douane. In effect a passport for my bike, a carnet is often required for access to many of the world's poorer nations which tend to have high import taxes on foreign vehicles. In my case, this means a financial guarantee is held on deposit in the UK which is refunded once my carnet shows I have left each of Iran, Pakistan and India with the motorcycle still in my possession. As if I'd sell it! The process is made surprisingly easy by the RAC, who handle all carnets issued in the UK. It arrives within two weeks of making my submission, a service that surely gets top marks.

The frustrations with my richly running carb continue and I find I'm constantly cleaning a black, sooty spark plug, I check on the phone with Andy and Hitchcocks, who originally supplied the unit. Both offer more suggestions, but after several additional strip downs, things are no better and the words of comfort accurately repeated by both parties, "Better to be running rich and cool than lean and hot," don't help me sleep any easier.

I share my concerns with Derek, who once again hops onto his motorcycle and rides over, old spare carburettor at the ready. We remove my Monobloc carburettor, which I've now become quite adept at, and put his in its place. Setting off on a test ride, I'm amazed by the result, the bike runs beautifully and the spark plug isn't fouled.

"Now let's see what's wrong with yours," he says, rubbing his hands together in anticipation. He takes it apart and finds the finest of hairs in the pilot jet housing, no doubt the culprit. Together with a more free-flowing air filter, one of a handful generously sent to me by Richard Miller, we reassemble everything and go for another short run. The result is an immediate transformation in performance. Fantastic.

"Now don't go doing anything else to it," says Derek with mock severity. "Just make sure you get all the way to India and back safely," he adds.

It's now less than two weeks to 'D-day'. To clock up some much needed hours on the engine, I ride a hundred and seventy miles over the course of the weekend, mostly in heavy rain and high winds... typical British summer. The bike never misses a beat and it's an excellent test of my new Altberg boots and Jafoma rainsuit too, both of which pass with flying colours. Best of all, my carburettor problems are now a distant memory. I have a perfectly coloured spark plug and the bike starts first kick, whether hot or cold. For the first time in several weeks, I actually believe that I'll be able to set off on time.

I make an evening visit to Andy Berry's house in Preston, some fifty miles north of where I live. We do some much needed fettling, including changing the oil in my front forks, fitting an oil pressure gauge and checking the engine timing. He hands me a well thought through gift; three ten-inch long studs of varying thicknesses that he's threaded at each end.

"If any of the studs on the bike break, you can replace it with one of these sawn down to the correct length," he says.

People and businesses really seem to like the notion of me riding such an old machine on the journey. Several, like Iwis Chains and Penrite Oils, go to great lengths to offer assistance. One chap, Barry Vincent of Vac-Bag, the company that produce vacuum-sealed bags to protect motorcycles from the elements throughout winter, provides me with a brand new Cromwell helmet, one of the products he sells at bike shows. Barbour sponsor me with one of their classic *International* wax cotton jackets, Forcefield with some ultra-light and flexible body armour and Britool send me an assortment of the most beautifully crafted tools I've ever laid my hands on.

The 'going the extra mile to help attitude' is typified by Pete of Lincolnshire-based Carrot Cycles. Again I come across the company at a bike show. When I tell them about my plans and the difficulty I've been having getting spare cables to suit my bike, they immediately offer to help with a set of sponsored brake, clutch, and throttle cables. Leaving the bike unrideable in my garage, I send them my only working set just two weeks before departure, giving them precious little time to make copies and return them all to me. As the cable ends and fixings are quite different from those they've previously made, they get a day behind schedule. Pete 'phones the following morning.

"I'm still working on them now, but should have them finished this afternoon. Give me your home address and I'll personally bring them over."

Later that evening, making a two hundred mile round trip on a new Triumph, Pete delivers the spare cables and my masters.

"Just glad to help," he says, cup of tea in hand. "I think it's great you're riding an old British bike all that way and we're just pleased to be a small part of making it happen."

Such support is priceless.

Early in the final week I ride to Shipley, West Yorkshire, where Specialised Covers make a made-to-measure cover that fits over my bike, including flyscreen and panniers, like a Saville Row suit. I then ride cross-country under the shadow of an ominously cloudy Pendle Hill. Thankfully unaccosted by witches, which the hill was renowned for in Medieval times, I reach Andy Berry's in the late evening. He immediately sets off on my bike for a quick test run, which it passes, and then I receive some much-needed basic maintenance lessons. There are even more potential problems than I'd imagined and I make another long list of his helpful recommendations... arrgh!

With just two days to go, it's time to begin saying au revoir to my nearest and dearest. It starts with my parents, Martha and Iain. They've been wonderfully supportive all of my life, always encouraging me to follow my dreams and unwaveringly backing me in whatever way they can. My dad, who hitched around Lake Victoria in Africa as a young Scottish soldier on leave from doing his National Service, has a love of travel that I've no doubt inherited. He's pretty laid back about the dangers of riding my motorcycle eight thousand plus miles, or at least gives a good impression of it. Not so my mum, who, like mums the world over, is visibly anxious and teary as we say goodbye. Seeing her so upset makes me feel awful, but with little time left and so much to do, I put my feelings on the back-burner and press on.

I make a succession of brief phone calls in the evening to friends. The last of these is to Hilda in New Zealand. We're now the best of friends and I can no longer contain the build up of emotions behind the rather insouciant facade I've put on in my previous calls. I earnestly tell her that in the event of anything fatal happening to me, I want her to know that she's been a major and inspirational part of my life. This conversation makes me take a much more circumspect view of my journey. Unlike all my previous travel adventures, the distance-induced fatigue, road conditions and generally dreadful driving standards I will encounter make this trip especially dangerous. I'm a father too, and I know I'm avoiding facing what will be the most difficult farewell, when tomorrow I will see my partner, Jane, and our son, Jacques, for the last time.

I groggily rise at six on the penultimate day, with fresh lists that seem almost as long as my originals of months ago. By ten I've managed to cross a lot of things off, but the number of items that still need attention, especially things that will allow my non Overland To India life to tick over in my absence, is daunting.

I head out to do some shopping, having left to the very last moment a number of essential purchases such as malaria tablets and sunblock. My plan to pick up three bags of camp food, the kind you simply add boiling water to, at my local outdoors store have to be abandoned. They only have a choice of meatballs or beef spaghetti in stock and I'm a vegetarian. Cursing myself for leaving that particular purchase to the eleventh hour, I head off for another essential; foreign exchange.

I'm normally far more organised than this, with preparations such as these usually carried out weeks before a trip. Not for the first time I curse that hair in the carburettor. It's 1 pm before I even begin to pack all the spares I've amassed into plastic boxes, wrapping the more delicate pieces in bubble wrap and slotting the rest in tightly, hoping they won't rattle too much.

The same goes for the remainder of my kit, although I have to smile at how little clothing I'm taking. With the huge amount of film equipment, travel books, emergency camping gear et al I'm carrying, space for a change of clothes is reduced to one pair of trousers, one shirt, one t-shirt, a couple of boxers shorts and two pairs of socks. Admiring this minimalist pile from a distance, I have an ooo-err moment and rush to the kitchen to fill up a small bottle of clothes washing liquid... I'll certainly be needing it!

I carry everything down to the garage and load the pannier boxes with the spares, which mercifully all fit in, but abandon the rest on the garage floor and head off to Jane's to play with Jacques for a couple of hours.

Our farewells are just as hard to make as I'd feared. Jane and I have a difficult relationship, having failed to make a success of living together and embodying very different temperaments and priorities. But she has, whenever she's been able to, given me her heartfelt care and support.

One of the biggest problems with me going away for great chunks of time is that Jacques becomes distressed, and the knock on effect has a major impact on Jane. I've allowed just six weeks for the ride to India, with another week in reserve in case of any problems, precisely with this in mind. I'd love to take longer, but know the price for this will be paid by Jacques and by proxy, Jane.

Saying goodbye is painful. Jacques is upset in a rather withdrawn way, not fully yet aware of how long six or so weeks actually is. Jane is concerned for Jacques and for me too.

"He needs his father," she says a couple of times, meaning 'make sure you stay alive and get back in one piece'.

We have what Jacques calls a family hug, all three of us with arms wrapped tight in a circle and I tell them again and again that I love them. Eventually, feeling wretched, I leave.

There's still so much to do, mostly paperwork, cheques to be written, my flat made safe. I'm also concerned about the weight in my panniers. Andy had warned that the rear mudguard could be too close to the tyre once the bike is fully loaded, advising I raise the rear shock-absorbers a notch to lift it higher. I can now see he was right. With the special Hagon tool in hand, I quickly make the off-side adjustment but can't get the tool to lock in place on the drive side. A neighbour, returning from a late night out, walks past my open garage door at just the right moment, enabling me to temporarily remove the pannier box which he holds whilst I raise the suspension height. Job done.

It's past midnight and I really need to get some sleep. Tomorrow, as they say, is the big day.

Day 1 Manchester to Oxford, UK
181 miles

I've already lived through this morning so many times in my dreams that there's a sense of unreality about it when I awake. It was my hope to be on the road by 8.30 am at the latest, but this seems a remote possibility, even though I jump out of bed just after dawn bristling with nervous energy.

It takes until nine to complete all the last minute chores and get myself down to the garage. In my mind, I'd planned a couple of fully-laden test rides, including one on a bumpy local farm track, so that I could perfect evenly distributing the load and practice handling it. Back to the real world... today is my first opportunity to even see if all my luggage can fit onto the bike. It does, just, thanks to a combination of Andy Strapz and Rok Straps that not only secure the larger items to my rear carrier, but also two smaller bags onto the front crash bars.

Teetering with the unaccustomed dead weight, I wheel the bike backwards out of the garage and park it in the lee of the apartment block. I set up my camera and tripod then film myself starting the bike. Feeling a complete prat, I ride off for all of thirty metres, make a wobbly U-turn, then return to switch off the camera. I don't get it quite right the first couple of attempts and attract the attention of a few neighbours looking out of their windows, doubtless wondering, "what's he up to now...?"

With filming duties complete, I check the odometer. It reads 606 miles. I hide the bike back in the garage and head upstairs for a final check before I lock everything up. Ten minutes later I'm back at my bike and this time it's for real. Neither Jane nor I wanted any big tearful waving off ceremony and as it's a Friday morning, everyone else I know is at work. I start the bike, climb on board and with rather false nonchalance, depart for India.

As I power up the steep slope of my driveway, the bike's front end feels worryingly light, the consequence of so much weight on the back. I make my first of many mental notes on the journey to try to move more weight into the tank bag and onto the front crashbars.

There are so many things on my mind: what I might have forgotten; will the bike handle okay; how's Jacques this morning; will I be rudely late for the meetings I've arranged today...? The first couple of hours of the journey consequently pass without my active engagement, even dealing with the buffeting headwind and the brief shower that catches me around

Stoke On Trent without really noticing.

By the time I turn off the M42 and approach Chadwick End, the home of Hitchcocks Motorcycles, the sun is shining, the wind has blown itself out, and I find myself in an ebullient mood. As well as producing most of the performance parts in my engine, Hitchcocks are the world's largest supplier of Royal Enfield spares and a good deal of the general items I've used in the restoration have originated from here.

Owner Allan Hitchcock is away on a family holiday, but his team are all keen to see the bike. Temporarily abandoning the telephones that so often ring hot, two of the company's stalwarts, Graeme Holt and Richard Ross, stop to drink a cup of coffee with me and share in my excitement about the journey. At the last minute I remember I've sent through an order for some additional spare parts. I can almost imagine my motorcycle groaning at the thought of more weight, but this last handful of items is light and can be squeezed into a corner of my already bulging rack bag.

Next on the agenda is a visit to UK Royal Enfield distributors, Watsonian Squire. Their headquarters is tucked away on a rural industrial estate at the outskirts of the small Cotswold village of Blockey, some thirty miles south west of Hitchcocks. For the first time I get the chance to ride fully laden on some twisty country roads. The bike feels reassuringly solid when I lean round bends, and braking is good enough... just. What is more than adequate, however, is the motor, which pulls like an express train in response to even the most delicate of throttle twists.

I ride into the Blockley trading estate just under an hour later. It's a fascinating place, a WWII prisoner of war camp that still sports a number of original Nissen huts. As I make my way around the tiny lanes that link the many small businesses that trade here, there's an almost tangible air of times past, a perfect place for the venerable Royal Enfield company to trade from.

The team at Royal Enfield are waiting and full of good spirits.

"You're behind schedule already," jests Technical Director, Mike Raahauge. "Do you want me to call the factory in India and warn them you'll be an hour late there too?"

The lighthearted repartee doesn't stop there.

"You've got a puncture," jokes spares manager Rob Jones and "Who's paying the bill for our forecourt to be cleaned of your oil leak?" asks Sales Director, Ben Matthews.

I have a great deal of respect for the company, who, over the last decade, have transformed both the reputation and sales of Royal Enfields in the UK. Under the former importers, the Indian-made motorcycles were perceived as having questionable reliability, inconsistent support and dubious quality standards. Through the consistent hard work of building up a rock solid dealer network, liaising with the factory to improve build quality and developing an in-house range of cafe racers and trials style variants of the standard Bullet, sales in the UK have grown to the point where they outsell established quality brands such as Moto Guzzi. Strategically targeted marketing that emphasises the classic heritage of the motorcycles and their thrifty fuel efficiency has resulted in many thousands of people in the UK now aspiring to own an Indian-made Bullet.

It's around 4 pm when I finally leave, with the cheerful banter of the Watsonian staff a perfect antidote to any remaining first day nerves. My final destination of the day, Oxford, lies around fifty miles south east along some of England's finest country roads. Following my satellite navigation's instructions, which are transmitted along wiring I've secured to my bike's frame into a MP3 headphone in my left ear, I pass through a succession of pretty Gloucestershire villages and small towns. Starting with the idyllic Chipping Norton, resplendent with numerous picture-postcard thatched cottages, I progress to the classic high street of Moreton In Marsh before finally sweeping through the curiously named Stow-on-the-Wold.

Along the way, my mind starts to unfold the words,

"I must keep myself safe for Jacques. I must survive this for Jacques." I don't know where this mantra comes from, but it is to stay with me for the rest of the journey.

Managing to avoid Oxford's busy centre in all its Friday rush hour glory, I pull up outside the city's Youth Hostel just before 6 PM. It's a member of Hostelling International (HI) a non-profit organisation composed of more than ninety different Youth Hostel Associations that represent over four thousand Youth Hostels. From humble beginnings in 1912, when the first hostel was opened at Altena Castle in Germany by Richard Schirrmann, the organisation has grown rapidly, spreading its network of accommodation worldwide and is now represented in over eighty countries

There's something rather special, in my opinion, about the philosophy of Youth Hostelling, the aims of which are:

"To promote the education of all young people of all nations, but especially young people of limited means, by encouraging in them a greater knowledge, love and care of the countryside and an appreciation of the cultural values of towns and cities in all parts of the world, and as ancillary thereto, to provide hostels or other accommodation in which there shall be no distinctions of race, nationality, colour, religion, sex, class or political opinions and thereby to develop a better understanding of their fellow men, both at home and abroad."

Long may it continue.

I park up in the restaurant courtyard, unload, and make my bike secure for the night. I've fitted a modern Acumen motorcycle alarm, craftily hidden away in the timing-side toolbox. It's as much an anachronism as the sat nav unit that adorns the handlebars, but when I press the key fob and am rewarded with a reassuring loud electronic bleep, I know I'll sleep more soundly tonight because of it.

Youth Hostels have come along way since my childhood, where my memories are of austere, poorly insulated Lake District houses where you were forced to do more dishwashing than at home. The Oxford establishment is a perfect example of the advancements made. For just £15 including breakfast, I get a bed in a modern, well carpeted four-bed room. All the fittings are finished in quality wooden laminate, including the capacious lockers where I store all my gear. I still have to make my own bed in true Youth Hostel fashion, but the sealed bed linen and continental quilt I unwrap look like they've just been bought from Habitat or Ikea. The modern shared bathroom, unlike the facilities of yesteryear that resembled a sunday footballer's shower room, is for the sole use of the four inhabitants of my dorm and there's even a separate toilet as well. I know for certain that on my travels I'll end up paying much more money for far less comfort.

I have dinner in the open, feeling rather foolish as I film myself eating, then move into the large reception area where there are a number of internet terminals. Looking around after I've updated my blog, I can't help noticing the number of backpackers who now carry laptops, taking full advantage of the hostel's free Wi-Fi connection. Just like the splendid kit us motorcyclists now carry, your average backpacker has moved up-market too.

One of my roommates is readying himself for sleep when I enter my quarters with the same intention. We shake hands, asking the usual travellers' questions; where are you from and where are you going? It transpires he's an Aussie on a working holiday in the UK, but not having much luck with finding the 'working' bit. He asks me where I'm going next.

"Oh.. err.. India," I answer as I climb into my bed, falling asleep like the proverbial log.

Day 2 Oxford to Folkestone, UK
148 miles

Breakfast is a lively, communal affair. The hostel restaurant opens at 7.30 am. By 8.00 am there are at least fifty people sitting around the shared, long wooden tables tucking into cereal, bacon and eggs and cups of coffee. I observe my fellow travellers. Along the table a chirpy young black American woman is discussing the merits of staying in Oxford for one more night so that she and her female companion, who is undeniably French, can go clubbing. An Australian couple in their early twenties study a map of Scotland and across from me a middle-aged woman seated on her own is fully absorbed by a Lonely Planet guide to Britain. The buzz of being amongst them is infectious and for the very first time it sinks in that my journey is actually under way.

It takes four trips to convey all my belongings from second floor bedroom to bike. I realise I should turn the bike around so it's facing the exit before I load it up, but this involves the cooperation of two groups of diners who are eating their breakfast at outdoor tables which are in my turning circle. The table most disrupted is occupied by a Dutch family of four. Fortunately, the father and son are fascinated by my old bike and they not only clear space for the manoeuvre but help push me around.

Loading the bike doesn't go well. My rainsuit, which I intend to strap onto my front crashbars, keeps twisting around and threatens to settle on the exhaust pipe. I fix my bright red Ortlieb tail bag into place, then strap tripod, camera bag, aluminium water bottle and D-lock onto it. I remember that my satellite navigation mount is still inside the bag and have to unload everything to retrieve it. Next I fumble with my tank bag. The considerable weight of luggage on the back of the bike means the front wheel lifts off the ground. This causes the handlebars to swing backwards and forwards knocking my hand each time I try to zip up the tank bag mount. I make a mental note to load it first in the future.

By now I feel pretty incompetent and imagine that everyone is watching my useless performance. Fortunately, when it really counts, things go well. The bike starts first kick and settles into a steady (and in the confines of the courtyard somewhat raucous) beat. Nevertheless, it has taken more than an hour to get ready. Hopefully practice will reduce this.

I ride through the centre of Oxford without really experiencing any of its charms. Soon I join the M40 which is, in my opinion, one of the more enjoyable motorways in Britain. In particular, there are three large climbs and descents which give commanding views of the surrounding countryside. It's a route into London I've followed often, though never before on a warm summer morning astride a motorcycle. There's little traffic at this time on a Saturday and I have a thoroughly pleasurable ride as my bike reassuringly pulls up the biggest of the hills in top gear.

I've arranged to meet an old friend, Trevor Reeves, at London's Ace Cafe. It's a mere two minute diversion off the main road into central London. I'm about thirty minutes late, but Trevor is just relieved I've made it. He gives me a huge bear hug as soon as I park up.

I've known Trevor virtually since I moved to the UK in 1999. Over the years he's been a business partner, a customer, a confidant and at times a real lifeline. We've spent numerous alcohol-soaked evenings together endeavouring to understand one of life's greatest mysteries ... women. (With little success I might add.) We've also hatched many a fanciful money-making plan and given birth to countless dreams of adventure, several of which involve riding off into the sunset on motorcycles. That said, we've never actually ridden our bikes together. Today is to be a first as Trevor plans to lead me through central London and then accompany me to the south coast.

"Great to see you Gordy. Do you want a coffee mate?" he asks.

Trevor, like many friends, calls me Gordy. It's a term of endearment I particularly like and hearing it today infuses me with bonhomie.

He makes his way to buy the drinks, leaving me in the company of a cheerful couple, Michelle and John. They astound me by saying that they visited my website, read the blog, which mentioned my plan to visit the Ace Cafe today, made an educated guess about my arrival time, then set off to meet me. They excitedly tell me John plans to do a trip similar to mine in roughly six weeks time. He wants to do it on a Royal Enfield too, and hopes to go looking round dealerships to buy a bike later in the day.

"John's still working in Spain and won't be based back in the UK again for a few weeks, so I'm doing all the organising and planning so he can go on his adventure," Michelle says with real enthusiasm and sincerity. Lucky man, I think.

She has a notebook and pen and between them they ask quickfire questions about visas, my route, my spare parts list and secondhand Royal Enfield dealers. At first I feel a bit daunted; it's only the second day of my journey and I'm being consulted like some overland motorcycling guru, which I'm certainly not. However the questions are all about my planning experiences and make me realise just how much work has gone into the preparations. They're smashing people. Bright and friendly, they depart on their bike-hunting expedition with smiles and wishes of mutual good luck.

Trevor and I soak up the atmosphere of the Ace Cafe, or should I say, The Ace, as I frequently hear it referred to.

It was first opened in 1938 as a transport cafe catering for truckers. Thanks to its location on London's North Circular Road and its 24-hour opening hours, it soon attracted plenty of motorcycling customers. Damaged by bombing in World War II, the cafe was rebuilt with its present-day guise in 1949. In its heyday, the 1950s and early 1960s, the advent of rock and roll, 'ton-up boys' and a booming British motorcycle industry saw the cafe flourish.

All of that changed in the late 1960s. Rock N' Roll had been overtaken by other forms of music and youth culture, motor cars became cheaper and British bike manufacturing was in steep decline. The Ace closed in 1969.

The return of the cafe is an inspiring story of vision and determination by present-day owner Mark Wilsmore. In 1994, Mark organised the first 'Ace Cafe Reunion' to celebrate the twenty fifth anniversary of the cafe's closure. An estimated twelve thousand people attended. Buoyed by the overwhelming response, Mark made it an annual event and by 1997 attendance had grown to well over twenty five thousand people. It was always Mark's ambition to reopen the cafe, a dream that inched its way towards reality when he was able to finally acquire the cafe site, form the Ace Cafe Club and from December 1997 open parts of the old building to the public on weekends and bank holidays. Once planning permission was gained, the cafe received a complete refit and finally opened it's doors full time in September 2001.

I've only been to the cafe once before. That was in 2002 when a Royal Enfield gathering took place on its forecourt. Today, the mixture of people and bikes is much more eclectic. I see two heavily customised Harleys which sport far more chrome than paint. There are several new Triumphs lined up alongside a pair of 70's Bonnies. A Triton cafe-racer sits on its own, its bulbous alloy tank gleaming in the sunlight. Nearby is a modern Guzzi cruiser and there are even a couple of sporty-looking modern 125 cc learner bikes. Leather clad bikers mix with more conservative Cordura-wearing middle-aged motorcyclists. Milling around in equal numbers are people who have come by car. They're easily identified by their shorts, t-shirts and sandals They give the place a holiday atmosphere as today is one of the few genuinely hot, sunny days after a miserable summer in the UK.

All too soon it's time to set off. Trevor has planned a route and it's quite relaxing following him.... at first that is. He manages to miss a turn off a roundabout which would lead us along wide roads through White City, Earls Court and Knightsbridge and instead we end up on the tight, congested streets near Paddington station. Worse still is Oxford street, packed with red double-decker buses and thousands of shoppers ducking in and out of traffic as they head for Selfridges and John Lewis.

Things go from bad to worse. We get separated by a red traffic light. Trevor pulls in to the roadside to wait for me. I'm feeling pretty hot so in a leisurely fashion unclip the tube on my Camelbak hydration pack, open the waterflow toggle, insert the rubber mouthpiece into my mouth and start to drink. I should know better; this is London and nothing can be done at a leisurely pace. It seems that traffic signals here change at twice the speed they do anywhere else in the UK. They must be on a twenty second cycle for no sooner have I taken my first glug of water than they are back to green and with split-second timing the black cab driver behind me impatiently honks his horn.

I let the mouthpiece fall from my mouth and set off. Trevor is far more acclimatised to the pace of London driving and is already rolling as I turn right to follow him. I immediately become aware of a damp sensation emanating from my crotch and spreading down my legs. It's most disconcerting. I look down and see water syphoning out of my abandoned drinking tube and gushing straight down onto my trousers. Poor Trevor has to wait again whilst I stop and sort myself out.

"Had an accident, mate?" he says looking at the wet patch with a huge smirk.

"No," I reply. "just using all available resources to keep myself cool."

"Of course," he laughs.

The twenty mile trek across the capital takes nearly two hours. It's stop, start, swerve and curse all the way. It's my first experience of riding this bike through packed city streets and I don't do it well. I over rev, slip my clutch far too often and generally drive with little finesse. I'm not sure who gets most hot and bothered; me or the bike. When we eventually clear the city limits and join the relatively quiet M20, I reflect on journey lesson number one; avoid large cities.

Trevor sits on my tail the rest of the way. We pull up on the outskirts of Folkestone to say our farewells.

"Blimey Gordon," he says. "Your exhaust is deafening. I had to pull back as it was actually hurting my ears."

I know I should be concerned about the bike producing an anti-social sound, but perversely I feel quiet pleased. After all, don't all bikers want their machines to sound big and powerful. Moreover, the thudding sound made by a classic single cylinder engine is one of the most endearing British motorcycle characteristics.

Trevor agrees, “Yeh, it’s too loud but it sounds brilliant.”

He rides off with a wave and it feels strange to be left riding on my own once again.

I lived in Folkestone for nearly three years in the early 1980s. Its an unusual place, a mixture of worn out kiss-me-quick British seaside daytripper resort and restored grand Victorian splendour combined with Channel Tunnel prosperity and unemployed poverty reflected in unoccupied shops and some fairly dodgy housing estates. For all that, it holds a special place in my heart.

I especially like the Leas Cliff, a cliff-top walk over a mile long, The Leas begins in the town centre and follows the coast east towards the quaint shoreline village of Sandgate, which these days seems to have more antique shops than houses. It was *the* place to be seen in Victorian times, and indeed still sports a charming reminder of those glory years in the form of one of Britain's last remaining water-powered funiculars. One of my favourite features is the Leas Cliff Hall. Outwardly this looks nothing more than a small pyramid-shaped cafe perched on the cliff tops. Its small outer appearance belies its true size. Underground, built into the actual cliff face, is a cavernous concert hall. Over the last three decades, many notable musicians have played here, often in preparation for a more major British tour. It's a real gem of a place for a town this size.

I plan to stay the night with old friends, Tony and Jan Henry. Tony and I shared a flat in central Folkestone for nearly two years. We had both just turned twenty and were still unsure of what paths we would follow in our newfound adulthood. We have less common ground these days, but the relationship built in those intense formative years has given our friendship a deep, solid foundation. Jan became Tony's girlfriend whilst we flatted together. She’s one of the loveliest women I know, always encouraging and supportive. She's also a brilliant cook. Give me a pen and paper and I could probably list every meal she's cooked for me over the last twenty odd years, each one is so memorable. I park up outside their house with great anticipation!

There’s a note on the front door. ’Gordon, we’re in the back garden. Come across the field’. I return to my bike and ride three hundred metres down the road until I spy an open gate leading to a field of golden wheat stubble. It presents the first opportunity for me to test the bike off road. I set off in first gear and do my best Johnny Brittain trials riding impression, standing high on the footpegs, as I follow the edge of the field around.

Convoluted as it is, this is the only access to their back garden. I reach the top corner of a long hedge then turn right. There are four adjoining cottages of which my friend's is the second along. Each has the most enormous garden, somewhere in the region of half a football pitch in size. I finally come to a halt. Over the hedge I see Tony, Jan and another long-standing friend, Karen, drinking tea around a dark wooden table. Their faces all burst into big smiles.

It's great to see Karen. We first met when she lived in the flat above Tony and myself. We lost contact for several years but managed to reconnect via the internet. She has a bouncy, cheerful personality and I think everyone she meets just adores her, although being the gentle, unassuming person she is she would probably refute that. Karen is a qualified nurse, but works as a senior manager in a vast East London hospital. After years living in the capital, she bought a beautiful restored old house in Whitstable, the Kent seaside town where she was born. The drawback is that Karen commutes for up to twenty two hours per week, setting off at 5.30 am to avoid the worst of London's traffic. She's rarely home before 8 pm. It's a gruelling regime. She would love to be able to work closer to home, but there are precious few opportunities at Karen's level in Kent hospitals and there's a big mortgage to be paid on her house.

Seeing her is a sharp reminder of just how lucky I feel not be caught up in the rat race and to have the chance to undertake this journey to India. Indeed, over the last few weeks I've received a handful of emails from motorcyclists who, on reading about my plans online, wrote how much they would love to be able to make such a journey themselves. However, commitments to their wife, mortgage, job, children etc tend to preclude this. How do we choose between or balance our intrinsic nature or dreams and our responsibilities? It's a tricky dilemma and one which I'm not exempt from. In order to travel as much as I have, at the age of forty four, I do not own my own home. I also have to admit that by far and above the biggest downside to my frequent long absences is that I have left a pretty unsatisfactory situation for Jane and Jacques. I guess that freedom often comes at a price.

Jan soon leaves to work her wonders in the kitchen. I unload the bike then discuss with Tony where to leave it overnight.

"There's a problem," he tells me. "Our neighbours hold an annual all-night party in their garden... sod's law, it's tonight. They expect a dozen or so cars to drive across the field and park up pretty near to where your bike's sitting right now."

It is a problem; the last thing I need is for some late night reveller to knock the bike over. Tony and I walk into the field and scratch our heads whilst we assess the options. I certainly don't feel comfortable leaving the bike standing alone by the roadside all night. Maybe I'm being over-protective but it seems too big a risk to take so early in my ride. The best I can come up with is riding the bike to the very top of the field, several hundred metres away, and parking it under some trees. Tony wanders off. When he returns it's with a far better solution.

"It'll be safest in the garden. I'm going to cut a hole in the hedge then we can wheel your bike through it."

It's an enormously generous offer because to me this seems a rather drastic measure. I also mention my concern about the prospect of negotiating the hedge on my own at 6 am tomorrow.

"You don't think I'd let you leave without waving you off," says Tony. "I'll help you get it out in the morning." What a star.

Tony attacks his new project with glee. He locates a tool in his shed then runs a long extension lead across the garden to the site of the proposed 'entrance'. The tool is a wicked combination of chainsaw and electric pruning sheers. In no time he assembles a large pile of gnarled trunk and thorny branches. Unfortunately, he unearths a ditch on the field side of the hedge but Tony is unperturbed and asks me to follow him. Earlier in the year he demolished a large outhouse and had it replaced with a beautifully built sleepout cum entertainment room, quirkily called Badger's Mount. There's still a pile of timber left over from the demolition, including a solid wooden door. Together we carry it across the garden and place it over the problem area. I test its strength by bouncing up and down on it a couple of times. It doesn't move an inch.

Kicking the bike into life, I approach the gaping hole with caution. It's been cut to exactly the right size. Tony guides me through, first waving his hand to the right then signalling me to ride straight on. Much to my relief I'm through and parked up in a jiff.

Our timing is perfect. Within minutes Jan arrives carrying another memorable creation and a couple of bottles of wine to boot. We talk about many subjects and reminisce on times past but the conversation inevitably comes back to my bike, route and safety.

After we've said our goodnights I head for bed. It's around midnight and just as the party next door gets into full swing. I had been looking forward to testing out the bed in Badger's Mount, but it's pretty close to the booming sound system, so instead I bed down in the other summerhouse, humorously called Badger's End. Despite the thudding rhythm of dance music that drifts across the garden and my excitement about the next stage of the journey, I fall immediately into a deep sleep.

Day 3 Folkestone to Mainz, Germany
392 miles

As good as his word, Tony meets me at the crack of dawn over coffee in his kitchen. Together, we steer the bike back through the gap in the hedge and load it up much more efficiently than I did on my own yesterday. I'm ready to leave. I get another huge hug then set off across the field. I pause when I reach the gate and look back over my shoulder to give Tony one final wave. In the early morning light I see his tall frame silhouetted against the pale sky and think to myself, "My friend is wondering if he'll ever see his friend again." It's a rather eerie sensation. To dispel it I set off with a roar.

I've never travelled on Eurotunnel, the car and truck train which crosses underwater from Britain to France, so I'm excited by the prospect. I get caught in a heavy shower as I approach the train loading area. There's no shelter and I have to wait my turn. I have no choice but to huddle down and sit it out. I'm the last vehicle to board and to my surprise, as the only motorcyclist on the train, have a compartment to myself. Unlike on ferries, people stay with their vehicles for the duration of the crossing.

The carriage's grey steel walls are so cold and utilitarian that it feels like being imprisoned in some kind of alien spacecraft. The train gently eases forward and through a small window I see my view of the damp English morning change into the dark wall of the tunnel. It's a good job I'm not claustrophobic! I've parked my bike diagonally across the carriage on its sidestand. Holding it steady through the tunnel I use the time to think through the day ahead. Without doubt, at approximately three hundred and ninety miles it will be the longest days ride I have ever made.

I think back to my previous longest ride. In July 1984 I made a seven hundred mile round trip in two days to see a Bob Dylan concert. That was on a fast Japanese bike with a fairing and I was able to comfortably cruise on the motorways at 85 MPH. I sold that bike soon after and have ridden much slower and, I must confess, less reliable British bikes ever since. Today's challenge is made even more difficult because I'll be riding on the right hand side of the road, a feat I have only ever done once before.

The train journey lasts for just thirty minutes, which is good as it prevents me getting too anxious. I disembark and reset my watch an hour forward. It's now 9.30 am and I estimate I have ten and a half hours of daylight to reach my next stop, Mainz in Germany. I've pre-programmed the ride into my satellite navigation. It shows my arrival time as 3.30 pm but that doesn't take any account of fuel and rest stops, nor my lowly eighty kilometres per hour cruising speed. It's raining lightly so I unpack my rainsuit and head off, taking great care not to swing out onto the left lane.

My route is all Autoroute and Autobahn. The first hour goes well and apart from a short stop for fuel the bike powers steadily on, resolutely absorbing the miles. I spot a road sign on which is written 'België'. Already my second country and still no passport controls. It represents the European Union at its best.

A beat up car and trailer overtakes me, a motorcycle strapped on the back. It pulls in to the hard shoulder ahead with all indicators flashing and a waving arm pushed out of the driver's window. I come to a halt as soon as I can. A somewhat wild-looking man leaps out of the car and comes bounding over. He's dressed in torn, faded denims, has unkempt long hair that is spiky on top and a wizened grey beard. He wears a huge gypsy earring in one ear and two large colourful parrot feathers in his hair. His looks resemble the Rolling Stone's Keith Richards but that's where the likeness ends. Before I can speak he grabs hold of my hand and pumps it up and down.

"Fantastic bike, man," he all but shouts. I think my shoulder is about to be yanked out of its socket by his over enthusiastic handshake. He may look a bit rough and ready but he's enormously friendly. He introduces himself as John Jensen, a Dane who lives in the Netherlands. In great detail he tells me all about his bike which has a 1930's 500 cc Norton engine in a '60s featherbed frame. He's owned it for many years and hopes one day to race it.

After asking me about the age of my bike comes the inevitable question:

"Where are you going?"

There's no point in lying, but I feel slightly self-conscious about my answer. "India," I reply.

I half expect a look of disbelief or perhaps a response along the lines of 'No... where are you really heading for?' but instead I get a great thump on my back and more frenetic hand shakes. He runs back to his car, grabs pen and paper, then gives me his email address.

A siren wails behind us. A police car, noticing we have parked up on a motorway hard shoulder to have a friendly chat, has pulled up next to John's vehicle.

"Keep in touch, man. Ride easy," he shouts as he runs back to tackle the police. I give a jaunty wave then set off. A couple of minutes later he overtakes me again, car horn blaring. If all encounters on my journey are so positive, I muse, I should have a brilliant time... providing of course that my right hand and shoulder are able to take the strain.

The French autoroute had been all but deserted; maybe the French like to sleep late on Sunday mornings. Not so the Belgians. The highway becomes very busy once I pass the turn off to Rotterdam. I bypass Brussels and soon cross into my third country of the day, the Netherlands. Here the cars are faster and my energy lower. I stop around 2 pm as my eyes are getting heavy. An espresso soon fixes that. Before I leave, I put in my earplugs as the fast traffic noise has become quite wearing. Back on the bike, the combination of caffeine and quietness makes me go faster and faster and I have to keep throttling back to my optimal speed of 80 KMPH. Maybe that's why the Dutch drive so quickly... strong coffee!

I soon flash past another border into Germany. If I thought the Dutch drove fast, the Germans easily supersede them, seeming all too keen to emulate Michael Schumacher. On the autobahn they zoom and zing past me at breakneck speed. My Bullet keeps happily plodding along, whether that be on the flat or the steepest gradient. I like the people-friendly German roads. There are peaceful rest stops with picnic areas every few kilometres and the routes seem to have been carefully laid well clear of major cities. The scenery becomes interesting for the first time. I ride over huge bridges that span wide valleys. Nestled in the valley sides are charming sub-Alpine villages, usually with the ubiquitous prominent church and steeple in the centre.

I pull in for fuel for the second time today. Whilst paying for the petrol I buy a soft white cheese and date sandwich. It's unusual but very tasty. I spot an air machine near the services exit. It's calibrated in BAR, a scale I'm totally unfamiliar with. When I take my miniature pressure gauge out of my jacket pocket it's a relief to find it gives readings in both PSI and BAR. Ideally the rear tyre needs 2.5 Bar (35 PSI) and the front 2.1 Bar (31 PSI). I've learned something new. My rear tyre doesn't need any air but the front requires a quick squirt.

After I replace the air hose, I push my bike off its centrestand. Disaster. I've foolishly taken no account of the camber of the road and am standing on the wrong side of the bike. It immediately topples away from me and crashes to the ground. I'm absolutely gutted. It's only the third day of my journey and I've already dropped my motorcycle... in the most stupid of circumstances too. A man comes rushing over and helps heave the bike upright. I put it on the sidestand, thank him, then make an inspection of the damage. There's none, except a couple of tiny marks on both front and rear off-side crashbars. They've done their job brilliantly. The engine fires first kick and I happily rejoin the autobahn.

I still have seventy kilometres to travel when I notice the ammeter needle is pointing to the negative side of the dial. The battery has stopped charging. Daylight is fading but my headlight appears to have a strong beam so I press on and reach Mainz just before nightfall. It´s 8.30 pm, exactly eleven hours since I disembarked the Eurotunnel train. I feel surprisingly awake and fresh. Must be that Dutch coffee.

I stay with Margot, an inspiring German lady I travelled with in Ecuador and Peru 18 months ago. We actually met on a rickety old train rattling its way through the Andes en route to the Cotopaxi volcano. We immediately hit it off and were soon discussing details of our future travel plans. I told Margot there was an excellent short train journey near to Ibarra in northern Ecuador, and that I planned to go there in two days time. To my complete surprise she showed up at 7.30 am on the Ibarra railway platform two days later! Whilst we were still happily exchanging greetings, a railway worker approached and informed us that the train wouldn't run that day as there were too few passengers. To be precise, there were only two... Margot and myself. Sensing our disappointment, he confided that we could hire the train all to ourselves for a mere $50 per day, which is exactly what we did.

From there we travelled south together, including a magnificent journey on the train to Nariz del Diablo, the Ecuadorian mountain known as The Devil's Nose. On this train, passengers ride on the roof. To this day, Margot remains the only septuagenarian woman I know who's game enough to not only go backpacking on her own, but to ride on the roofs of South America trains.

After safely parking up in her garage and a quick catch-up, I head for the bathroom. I need to freshen up before dinner but I also have a more pressing problem to attend to. Somewhat cowed, I leave the bathroom fifteen minutes later and make a confession.

"Margot, I've got an earplug stuck in my ear and can't get it out. I think I've pushed it in too far."

She immediately offers to help, but like me has absolutely no luck using her fingers. What follows is almost farcical. She gets numerous implements from her makeup bag, trying each one with no success. By now my ear is throbbing and very tender. Dinner is temporarily suspended whilst we both look around for a better 'fishing' device. I resort to the ultimate tool, my Leatherman. It's a stainless steel multi-tool that I carry virtually everywhere. As well as various screwdriver heads, a file and a can opener, it sports a very strong pair of pointed pliers. Even in Margot's hands they look highly menacing, but I simply have to get the blasted thing out. I'm rigid with terror as she inserts their pointed nose deep into my ear. Seen from the outside, I'm certain our exploits would make an alarming sight.

"Aha,'" Margot exclaims as she finally manages to grab the earplug in the pincers and mercifully extract it.

"I feel we just got to know each other a lot more intimately, Margot" I joke.

It's an encounter we laugh about again and again both over dinner and for the remainder of the evening.

Day 4 Mainz to Hahnbach, Germany
220 miles

Margot's an early riser. By 7.30 am we're sitting down to what she assures me is a typically German breakfast. It's enormous: orange juice; cereal; yoghurt; rye bread; a selection of local cheeses; eggs; espresso. I'm so full that it's hard to get motivated to move from my seat. However, I have so little time here and Margot is keen to make the most of every single minute of it. She's planned a whirlwind tour of Mainz.

It's a small city of just over two hundred thousand people located at the confluence of the Main and Rhine rivers. Margot gives me a quick resumé of her home town as we drive in her car towards the centre.

"There's been a city here for over two thousand years," she begins. "It was founded and maintained as a Roman military stronghold until it was sacked by Atilla The Hun. Centuries later, it became an important strategic location in Charlemagne's Holy Roman Empire. We have one of the very earliest German cathedrals; it was built around 975 AD."

The fascinating history lesson continues.

"In the late Eighteenth Century the city formed the breakaway Republic of Mainz, until it was occupied by Prussian troops that is. Then Napoleon Bonepart's army took control, making Mainz the capital of their German annex. But it wasn't long before we were restored to the German Confederation. The French administered Mainz again, this time under the terms of the Treaty of Versailles settlement after the First World War, but that ended in 1930. Then the centre was virtually flattened in World War Two. I think about eighty percent of the old buildings were destroyed."

Margot goes on to tell me that she remembers the war well. "I can remember hiding in air raid shelters as a little girl. It was terrifying," she recalls.

By now we have parked, taken to our feet and are soon in the old town. Wide, roomy squares and courtyard-like places are surrounded by picture-postcard "gemuetlich" half-timbered houses.

"They've all been restored using the original city plans," says Margot. preempting my question about the destruction caused by Allied bombing in WWII.

"It's taken decades and cost an absolute fortune," she concludes.

The result is delightful. Amongst the bourgeois houses are row upon row of boutiques, cafes and underground wine bars, many hidden behind enchanting Rococo façades. We wander through the airy central cathedral, then Margot leads me to a real gem, the Baroque

Augustinerkirche church. Its walls and arched ceiling are absolutely dripping with gold leaf. Next we amble to the banks of the Rhine. It seems enormously wide.

"You'll ride over that bridge when you leave later," says Margot, pointing downstream. As we walk back to her car, she points to the street signs, some of which have their names written in red.

"That dates from Medieval times," she explains. "Most of the houses were built of wood and fire was a real problem. All the red street names lead towards the Rhine. In the case of fire everyone would know which way to run to get water."

Saving the best until last, Margot drives me to the spectacular St. Stephen's church. It looks fairly innocuous from the outside but once we open the doors I see the most beautiful stained glass windows imaginable. Framed by towering stone arches, the windows' images are mostly made from numerous shades of luminous blue glass. I am completely awed. Seeing my face, Margot smiles and explains.

"They depict scenes from the Old Testament and were done in the 1970's and 80's by the Russian Jewish artist, Marc Chagall, who was a close friend of the church priest." They are truly incredible.

"Tourists come from all over the world to see them," continues Margot. "Mainz is only a thirty minute train ride from Frankfurt airport and many come for a half day stopover en route to another destination."

After a hearty lunch, I load up and get ready to leave. I could happily spend a couple more days in Margot's bright and energetic company and Mainz is so charming that it would be a joy to pass hours relaxing in its many street cafes. But the road is calling me. I want to get close to the Czech border today and I'm full of the anticipation of riding my bike again. I promise Margot I'll return soon, most likely by picking up a ticket with one of the many budget airline cheapies that fly to Frankfurt.

"It's a deal," she says.

I'm immediately on the lookout for the Rhine bridge Margot showed me earlier but it's so wide that I don't realise I'm actually crossing it until I spot a slice of riverbank close to terra firma on the far side. My Bullet's engine sounds particularly good today; it's mechanically quiet but with a meaty, booming exhaust note. German motorists seem to like it too and I receive many toots, waves and thumbs up as I ride on the autobahn.

I'm concerned about my charging system and try to conserve battery power by running without my pilot light and switching off the satellite navigation except when approaching major intersections. This, however, is not my only worry. My original Smiths chronometric speedometer, which cost an arm and a leg to have restored, is on the blink. It first appears to be stuck at 50 MPH. Then it fluidly winds itself back to zero. After a few minutes I look down and see it's showing 120 MPH! I judge my speed still to be 50 by the feel of the engine and the tone of the exhaust. Fortunately, the odometer and trip meter still accurately tickover the miles that I ride. I can cope without knowing my speed, but I'd be lost without being able to track the distance I've covered, both in terms of gauging when to refuel and calculating my daily mileage.

My worries increase when I stop for petrol. The pump attendant walks over to me. Instead of asking which grade of fuel I require, he points to the ground under my bike. I've only been parked up for a minute but already a pool of oil the size of a small plate has formed. I shrug and try to look unperturbed, but I know it's a problem. After paying for my fuel I check the engine oil level. It's definitely sinking low on the dipstick and I decide it's wise to top up. At this point I realise I've not packed a funnel. I'm rather clumsy and waste some of my precious reserve of Penrite oil by spilling it down the side of the gearbox. I make mental note number one on my virtual checklist for future overland trips: Take a small funnel.

Margot has suggested an area in Bavaria near to Amberg that she believes has several small villages with pensions where I can spend the night. I first follow autobahns south towards Wurzburg, then in the middle of rush-hour around Nurnberg. Traffic thins as I head east towards the Czech border and start to climb into the mountains. I exit about twenty kilometres short of Amberg and head for the first village on the hunt for accommodation. Almost immediately I spy a small inn. I park and enter its dark, rustic interior. The landlord approaches me and we try to converse, but he knows as much English as I know German... none. I press both my hands together as in prayer, put them on my right shoulder, rest my head on them and make a snoring sound. We both burst out laughing at the same time, but it doesn't do any good; he signals with his hands that there are no vacant rooms left.

I restart my bike and ride through the village. Two buxom, weather-beaten elderly women talk with a third woman over her garden fence. They are all attired in white blouses, dark skirts with colourful aprons and matching headscarves. I pull up and repeat my sleeping performance. They issue me with a stream of instructions in German that make absolutely no sense. My nonplussed expression alerts them to my incomprehension and they wave down the road, giving me the impression that I have to ride on to the next village.

I do... and the next, but there's still no sign of a bed. At the end of the third village a roadsign informs me the next place is another 12 KM. I judge I have now fruitlessly ridden twenty miles west, which is diametrically opposed to the Czech border. Light is fading and I'm beginning to worry about finding a room before dark. I decide to retrace my tracks and head towards Amberg. The roads is beautifully sealed and almost devoid of traffic as I roar back through the villages I've already inspected, and continue east.

The sun set some time ago and I'm forced to put on my headlight, which emits a weak-looking glow. At a road junction I flick on my indicators. There's no response. The battery is all but flat. It's also virtually impossible to ride in the twilight with my tinted goggles, so I lift them to my helmet crown and brave insects hitting my spectacles. I waste time looking around another small town without success, then come to a much quainter village, Hahnbach. It's my last hope before dark and a night of enforced bivouacking in a field. I stop on the main street and ask a passing pedestrian if there is a pension.

"Of course," he replies in heavily accented English. "Just three buildings along. If you turn right here, then take the first road left, you will see its beer garden where you can put your bike."

With great relief I follow his instructions. I park up under the inquisitive gaze of a group of locals swigging from tall steins of frothy beer, then enter the pension. I'm greeted by the proprietor, Herr Ritter, who confirms he has a single room for thirty Euros. He steps out from behind the bar to show me the room. I do a double-take at his attire; he's wearing leather lederhose knee breachers. He follows my gaze then looks back into my eyes. Thankfully he has a good sense of humour.

"This is Bavaria," he says with a grin.

After agreeing to the room, I lead him outside to my bike. He had initially said it would be safe parked in the beer garden, it being a small, quiet village. However, once he sees the age and gleaming condition of the bike he quickly changes his mind.

"Just give me a few minutes," he says "I'll move my car out of its garage. We can lock your bike in there, then we can be sure it will be left untouched."

It's great news as its safety is just about as important to me as my own. I take dinner in the bar, a vegetarian lasagne they manage to muster, then swill it down with a stein of my own. Herr Ritter is hosting a party of his old school mates, a monthly gathering I'm told. They become rowdy and boisterous, progressing from beer to schnapps in the time it takes me to eat my meal. I'm invited to knock back a glass of the clear spirit with them, but I have no head for strong alcohol and decline. I can hear their shouts and laughter as I climb the stairs to my room, but tonight, as I'm sure will be the case on many more nights to come, I'm too tired to care. By 9.30 pm I'm out for the count.

Day 5 Hahnbach to Cesky Krumlov, Czech Republic 181 miles

Today's first job is to wheel my motorcycle out of Herr Ritter's garage. Worried about the oil leak, I'd made an immediate mental note of the wipeable gloss floor tiles the previous evening, but nevertheless, speedily wipe up the overnight seepage with newspaper before it's spotted. The morning is already quite hot by the time I come to pack my belongings onto the Enfield. People must find me a bit curious as I roll it into a sunny patch in the beer garden, set up my video camera and tripod, and film myself loading up from three angles. It takes nearly an hour.

I then do my newly-evolved safety checks. I've developed a loose system whereby every nut and bolt gets tested on a three day rotation. This involves hunkering down with a handful of spanners and shuffling my way around the chassis, testing the tightness of all the major fasteners. I next try to tackle the charging problem. I check the wiring to the dynamo. It seems fine. I open the rightside toolbox and check the electronic regulator. All four wires appear to be properly connected. I follow two black earth wires to the frame. They look good as well. My brain does a mental shrug and I get ready to depart, hoping more ideas will come to me as I ride today.

Looking at my map, I see the autobahn I followed yesterday afternoon continues in a straight line across the border into the Czech Republic. The road through Hahnbach runs parallel to it for another twenty kilometres, at which point I can join the motorway. I ride through an archway that forms part of some ancient defensive wall around the village and head east. The road meanders up and down some magnificent rolling hills. I inwardly sigh; this is joyful motorcycling and I feel somewhat deflated when the time comes for me to rejoin the autobahn.

Riding on for another half an hour, I pass at speed through what appears to be an abandoned set of toll booths. It takes a few kilometres before I realise that it was the old border crossing post, defunct since the Czech Republic joined the EU. It's amazing to think what a transformation this has made; only a couple of decades earlier this country formed part of the east/west cold war divide, the Iron Curtain. Now everyone can cruise across the frontier at 100 KMPH without even needing to carry a passport. Who could have ever imagined it.

The motorway takes a north easterly tack, heading ultimately for Prague. I turn off just short of Plzen, or Pilsner in English, the birthplace of Pilsner beer and home to the country's largest brewery, Pilsner Urquell.

I'm tempted to stay here! Showing a certain restraint, I turn right and head south east down route E49 towards southern Bohemia.

Czech roads soon reveal themselves to be quite different from the routes I followed this morning through Bavaria. They are straight for miles on end, twist and turn through a small town or village, then resume their arrow straight course once again on the other side. The many slow trucks heading in both directions have a tail of frustrated cars behind them, but I'm easily able to overtake, managing to duck into safety before the next string of north bound vehicles pass. The towns and villages I travel through are quite eerie. They seem deserted, except for the occasional mother and child or elderly pedestrian that hugs the inside of the pavement. The houses look strange too. A few are gaily painted in cheerful pastel colours, but by far the majority are clad in crumbling grey concrete. They certainly don't give out an air of prosperity. To the contrary, they appear much more like the utilitarian housing of the Soviet era.

To my left I see a small village with a slender red tiled church which stands out quite exquisitely against the fields of sun-baked corn encompassing it. Time for some filming, I think. Stopping my bike, I unload the video camera, fit a wide angle lens then attach it to its tank top mount. It feels a bit loose in my hand. I try to tighten the securing wingnut but it cannot turn any further. It still doesn't feel terribly secure so I gently move it from side to side. To my horror the mounting peg sheers in half. It signals the end of filming from the bike, at least for now. It's a real blow.

After resignedly packing everything away, I continue on my way southwards. There's a choice of two places to spend the night, both of which I visited some years ago with Hilda, České Budějovice and Český Krumlov. The former is a small city, with a delightful old town centered around a vast cobbled square, It's also famous for producing the original Budweiser beer. The latter option is smaller but more touristy and somewhat twee. It's a walled medieval town complete with fairytale thirteenth century castle that's nestled in a U-bend of the fast-flowing Vltava river, which inspired Smetana's musical piece of the same name. I keep an open mind about which I will choose until I get to the outskirts of České Budějovice. It's 4 pm and traffic is building up quite heavily. I decide to keep rolling and head for the second option of Český Krumlov

Half an hour later I drive round the outskirts of the town until I spot an in-road that crosses a bridge and clearly leads towards the towering castle. I take it. A signpost shows that cars are forbidden but there's no indication that the ban extends to motorcycles. Staying in first gear, I carefully inch my way along narrow and rather slippery cobbled streets. Following a downward sloping lane I emerge into the small town square. The surrounding ring of restored Renaissance buildings have mostly been converted into cafes and bars and the gothic town hall looks as though it belongs on the front of a postcard.

The noise of my Enfield echoes like thunder and everyone turns to look as I pass. I'm keeping an eye open for a pension with parking, but the majority seem to be without any. I cross a small stone bridge with ancient looking ramparts which strides another bend in the river on the southern side of town. Ahead is a pension next to a large arched-shaped gate.

The engine's getting quite hot and I struggle to find neutral. I'm feeling tired and begin to get frustrated with myself. There's an enormous backfire as I stall the bike and a plume of black smoke billows out from the air filter box. I sharply kick out the sidestand, jump off, run round the bike and frantically remove the filter element. It's smouldering. Phew, I think, there's a fine mist of oil on the outside of my engine and I just wouldn't know how to start putting out a fire. Both the bike and I have had enough for one day, so it's good news that there's an attic garret available in the pension as well as space in a locked yard for my bike.

I've committed to write a daily website blog and the number of people following it has been really pleasing. I last updated it in Mainz and that day alone the website had more than four hundred visitors. I wander the streets of Český Krumlov in search of an internet cafe, but both I see are already closed. This is a great surprise as the number of old buildings converted to hotels, eateries, wine bars and souvenir shops by far outnumber those that remain as regular shops and residences. The town looks like a living medieval museum and is obviously a tourist haven, which makes the lack of functioning internet facilities seem very strange. All is explained when I reach the tourist information centre.

"It's the end of a very busy season," says the lady at the help desk. "Most businesses are rushed off their feet throughout summer, but visitor numbers drop off in the autumn and most places close before six in the evening."

It's a bit of a blow for my blog but it means I have the town virtually to myself, which I like a lot. I wander down to the riverbank and sit on a narrow strip of grass. The sound of the water burbling over an old, partially disintegrated weir is rejuvenating. After a while I meander through slender back alleyways. Here there sit several houses that haven't yet received the seemingly obligatory tourist makeover. They have flaky rendering and the wood that surrounds their window frames looks dry and faded. I hope they manage to stay that way, as they add a certain realistic charm to the place.

After a while I find myself in front of the Church of St. Vitus, a marvellous gothic structure that dominates the northern side of the town. From there it's only a minute's walk back into Nam Svornosti, the town square, and a particularly scrumptious pizza, which I eat seated outside one of the many open-air restaurants.

Before going to bed I tell myself I must spend more time in the morning looking for the cause of my oil leak and having another go at resolving my charging issue. It weighs on my mind because I've so far only travelled eleven hundred miles. There are still around seven thousand miles to go!

Day 6 Cesky Krumlov to Hustopece, Czech Republic 163 miles

After a quick breakfast I devote more than an hour to the charging system. I try to be methodical in my approach, but it's not my strongpoint. My problem-solving strategies rely more on intuition than a systematic, orderly approach. Not for the first time I think 'what on earth am I doing undertaking such a journey on an old bike when I don't even understand its basic operating systems?' But what the heck, I'm determined to keep going.

I unpack spares and tools from my pannier boxes, cut up some short strips of wire and rig up a temporary connection to my backup regulator, which is one of the old fashioned Lucas types. Starting the engine I keenly watch the ammeter. It's to no avail... the needle stays firmly on the neutral line. My next angle of attack is the dynamo itself. According to my well-thumbed 1950's maintenance bible, *Pitman's Book of the Royal Enfield*, the brushes and commutator, whatever that is, may need cleaning from time to time. I remove the outer cover and rub a piece of petrol soaked rag onto a brass ring which, judging from the diagram in the book, must be the commutator. It turns completely black. Aha! I spend the next twenty minutes leaning over my bike with the rag wrapped around the blade of my largest screwdriver. I gently press this onto the commutator whilst slowly turning the engine over with my right foot. When the rag no longer turns black I fasten everything up and start the engine. The ammeter needle resolutely remains stationary. Damn!

The oil problem is equally frustrating. I use a handful of napkins, swiped from the breakfast table, to remove much of the oil covering the crankcases and surrounding components. Lying on the ground I peer underneath the engine but can see no obvious point where the oil is escaping. I begin to suspect it's blowing back through the oil filler cap, a theory which is to erroneously occupy my thoughts for the following week. Somewhat disheartened, I strap everything onto the bike and depart.

I need to head due east most of today, aiming for the northern border of Slovakia. My map shows a main road that leads to a lengthy motorway, but my satellite navigation produces an alternative which appears to be both shorter and more interesting. I put my trust in the electronics... after all, I reason, it's too expensive a piece of kit not to make full use of it.

It turns out to be an excellent decision. I again pass fields of corn, this time lined with heavily laden apple trees. In the middle of the fields lie tiny picturesque villages mainly centered around old churches crowned with imposing angular steeples. The road I take, the E151, proves to be one of those routes that motorcyclists thrive on. Sweeping bends, steep inclines, even a couple of hairpin turns. My spirits soon soar and I find myself happily singing to myself. Thankfully no one can hear me above the din of the Royal Enfield; my abilities as a singer rank even lower than my skills as a mechanic, which I assure you is a scary thought.

I stop for lunch at an outdoor cafe that has large shady umbrellas over wooden picnic tables. Nearby, four Czech touring cyclists, two men and two women, are having an animated discussion around a map. They're fully kitted out in fluoro riding shirts, cycling pumps and clingy jet black shorts that make their legs look powerfully muscular. They come over to ask directions. I can offer little help apart from showing them where we are and the route I have just taken. Nevertheless, as fellow two-wheeled travellers on this sublime strip of tarmac there's an instant feeling of comradeship between us. With cheerful waves, they energetically set off, leaving me to try to order lunch.

It's not easy; there's absolutely nothing vegetarian on the menu. The waitress, a Prague University student working here in her summer vacation, speaks excellent English.

"I'm sorry, I don't think there are many Czech vegetarians. Everything we have has meat in it," she explains.

It's a bit of a blow; I expect my eating options to shrink as I travel further east (until I reach the veggie gastronomic delights of India, that is), but this is far sooner than I expected. I resort to my tried and tested fallback.

"Can you make an omelette?" I ask.

She departs to check with the cook and returns a minute later with a wide smile and a thumbs up.

Back on the road, I begin to look for a car or bike shop. My latest charging system rescue plan is to buy a battery charger that I can hopefully use in my hotel room each night. Over the next couple of hours I try two motorcycle shops but neither has such a thing for sale. Third time lucky, I stop at a Jawa dealership run by a tall, pale, dungaree-clad Czech called Michal. He can't speak any English but soon grasps my predicament. Disappearing into a workshop at the rear of his showroom, he returns carrying an old Russian-made charger. I pull out my wallet but he flatly refuses any payment for it. He simply grins and repeats:

"Gratis, gratis".

It's an unbelievably generous gesture.

My good luck continues. About an hour later I find myself riding through a hilly forest inhaling the rich aroma of pine trees that have been superheated by the sun. I look towards my speedometer; it's reading 45 MPH. I accelerate and it instantly responds. I brake and immediately it adjusts to my slower speed. Why it's suddenly started working again I've no idea, but it's excellent news. I then notice my satellite navigation has come to life all by itself. I look further and see the ammeter needle is hard to the right meaning the battery is furiously charging. Great joy; here's to a clean commutator! I realise it can stop again at any minute and I'm sure Michal´s kind gift will be called upon at some point, but for now I´m a very happy man.

One of my biggest concerns has always been the toughness of the bike's pannier frames. In the last few weeks before my departure, Derek did a great job replacing their brackets, but in fairness, he had little time and was working from a badly bodged starting point. Until now they have been untested, but all that changes once I turn onto the E114. It's so patched up and bumpy that I spend upwards of an hour standing upright on the footrests at less than 30 KMPH. I stop several times to check they haven't buckled or twisted under the strain. Thankfully all is well.

I call it a day fifty kilometres shy of the Slovakia border in the town of Hustopece. It's a place I know nothing about, indeed I ended up here purely because its name appeared in the boldest writing on a roadsign. The first place I try for accommodation turns out to be a noisy, smoky pub full of truckers seemingly well on the way to being drunk. I ride around the town centre and notice an accommodation sign pointing up a hill. Following its direction I wind up at a large, bare-concrete building. It looks austere and rather unwelcoming but I walk around to the side for a closer look.

The wall of the entrance is freshly rendered and gaily painted a sunny lemon colour. In a small terracotta courtyard are dining tables and a friendly looking man. His name is Jan and he can speak more than passable English. He unlocks a couple of doors and leads me to the accommodation wing. The rooms are modern and very comfortable, a far cry from the building's outward image. At first Jan says my bike can stay in the courtyard, but once I've wheeled it in he quickly warms to it.

"Wow, what a beautiful old-timer motorcycle," he enthuses as he lovingly caresses the headlamp. "You can bring that inside the main building tonight, then you can sleep without worrying about it," he adds. Nothing is too much trouble for my host. I tell him about my oil leak and within a couple of minutes he has covered a section of his floor with bubblewrap. I push the bike in, throw the cover over it to smother any petrol fumes, and head for a shower.

After dinner I spend a pleasant hour talking further with Jan. His is an interesting story and one no doubt shared by many others in the new Europe. He was raised under the Soviet regime and forced to study Russian at school. Privately, he learnt German and English by listening to the radio. The fall of communism and the opening of European borders presented him with new opportunities.

"I work in an office in Austria," he tells me. "I commute for just over an hour each way every day, which isn't too bad, and get paid far more than is possible for me here. It's allowed me to build this place, which my wife runs. It's still early days and the outside needs finishing, but this is the only wine growing region in the Czech Republic. We hope one day that tourism will grow to the point where we are busy enough for the pension to support us both."

I like his optimism and admire his positive outlook. He's very hospitable too. When I ask where to head for an internet cafe, he tells me there isn't one in Hustopece.

"Come into my house," he says, "you can use my computer for as long as you need."

His house is built along one side of the pension's courtyard. I follow him inside and he leaves me to work away on my blog. It's so relaxing sitting in the homely atmosphere, surrounded by potted plants and simple brocade wall hangings. Jan's eight year old son ducks in and out of the room, playing his own version of peekaboo with me as I type. It's a poignant reminder of little Jacques, who right now will probably be playing in his home before going to bed.

Jane has sent me an email telling me that Jacques is missing me terribly and that at times she is struggling on her own without a break. I so much want to share the joys of my trip with her, but in the strained circumstances it's not easy. Before heading to my own bed, I send a short email which simply says I'm safe and missing them both very much.

Day 7 Hustopece to Szarvas, Hungary
301 miles

Slovakia was integrated with the Czech Republic as Czechoslovakia for most of the 20th Century. The 1989 overthrow of communism, known as The Velvet Revolution, paved the way for a peaceful dissolution of the Czecho-Slovak Federative (as it was known for a short period} and the declaration of sovereignty by the Slovak parliament in 1993.

Between the two countries, the Czech Republic gets the majority of tourists, with the jewels of Prague and southern Bohemia as the obvious drawcards. However, I've read there is some beautiful countryside to be seen in Slovakia, including the Tatra mountains, and a population that has retained its folk traditions and is welcoming to visitors.

I experience déjà vu at the Czech Slovak frontier. Just like two days ago, I once more pass through a deserted border control post on the motorway without having to stop. Overhead roadsigns tell me there are just eighty five kilometres to run to the centre of the capital, Bratislava. It's still early morning and I feel that I'm really getting into the groove of riding my bike. It's running beautifully, except for the worrying oil leak. I seem to be acclimatising to longer periods between breaks in the saddle too. Time flies. In less than an hour I find myself looking sideways at areas of heavy industry which form the outskirts of Bratsilava. They're unappealing to the eye, and as I don't want to get sucked into heavy city traffic I keep trucking on.

It's a beautiful morning, the motorway is relatively quiet and I'm feeling strong and buoyant. In my mind I have a vision of turning off the motorway and taking a more minor route towards the Hungarian border, fancifully stopping in some secluded village. Amongst old wooden houses, I'll break for a feast served by some smiling local in folksy clothing. Reality bites when I cast my eye over my speedometer. The tripmeter reads 217 miles, indicating that I'm close to running out of fuel and that becomes the priority.

Much to my relief, I see signs for a service station within a few kilometers. I take the slip road and pull up next to some petrol pumps. Until now, nearly all the garages I've visited have been self service, but at this one there's an attendant and he insists on filling my tank personally. Once complete, I enter the adjoining shop to pay. The price comes up in Florins. I scratch my head, thinking, 'I thought that was Hungarian currency.' Somewhat baffled, I pay for the fuel and my daily energising Snickers bar using a debit card, then head for the door.

A young hitchhiker stands admiringly next to my bike.

"Can I have my photo taken with your old-timer motorcycle?" he asks, handing me his mobile phone.

I happily oblige then question him about Slovak currency.

"Slovakia?" he replies, "yeh, it's called Koruna I think."

It starts to dawn on me that I've made a bit of a boob, but I ask for confirmation, just in case.

"Er, which country am I in?"

"Hungary, of course," answers the hitcher.

We laugh together when I confide that I've blasted through Slovakia without stopping, without even speaking with a solitary Slovak, and have been completely oblivious to my entrance into Hungary.

"The border's at least forty kilometres north," he tells me with a guffaw.

I outwardly laugh but inside I'm deeply disappointed not to have had any experiences at all in Slovakia. I toy with the idea of turning around, but it just doesn't add up in terms of my overall journey, so I decide to continue on through Hungary, promising myself to make sure I stay at least one night in this country.

I haven't fully made up my mind which route to take, but will certainly bypass the capital, Budapest. I spent nearly a week there in 1987 when it was still part of the Soviet Bloc. At the time I was a hitchhiker too, wending my way across Europe from Istanbul in Turkey to Algeciras in Spain and ultimately Morocco. I remember it as an alluring city, well actually two cities, predominantly residential Buda and commercially developed Pest, which also houses the magnificent parliament buildings. The two are divided by the broad, shimmering waters of the mighty Danube, and I have fond memories of many happy hours wandering along its crowded banks, soaking up the atmosphere. However, it's a large city and on this journey that means it is destined to be passed over.

I stop near the beginning of the city ringroad to weigh up my options. There are three clear choices of border crossing points from Hungary into Romania. None of these offer any clear advantage over the other except that I've received five emails from Hungarian Royal Enfield owners asking if they can meet up for a ride or offering accommodation for me en route. One of these comes from Csaba, who lives in Bekescaba, a small city close to the crossing point into central Romania. I think it would be great to meet up with a Hungarian Bullet owner if time allows, so decide to head in that direction.

The motorway that circumvents Budapest is heaving with trucks of many shapes, sizes and, judging by the oval stickers on their tails, nationalities. For the first time I see TR labels, signifying Turkish trucks, which makes me feel that I'm really getting somewhere on my journey. Congestion forces everything to slow right down. Giant Turkish, Serbian, Romanian and Hungarian articulated lorries continuously shift lanes, jostling to move forward a few feet further. It's tough going as they emit hot, noxious fumes and their continuous jockeying for position makes it nigh on impossible for me to slip between them. Heading in the opposite direction I see the first obviously overland motorcyclists since my departure. Their giant BMWs are heavily laden and we exchange big waves as we cross paths. I spend quite some time wondering where they have been and where they might be going...

Eventually leaving the motorway in the late afternoon, I trek cross country on the E44, heading due east towards the Romanian border. As the sun gets lower in the sky its orange glow casts elongated shadows of me and my Enfield which playfully race down the road ahead. It's so often the small things in life that give the greatest pleasure! There's no way I will reach Bekescaba before dark, so I begin to keep my eye open for accommodation. I pass through several sleepy spa towns popular with Hungarian tourists... a fact that is reflected by high hotel prices. In the small town of Szarvas, one very basic hotel charges 90 Euros. When I politely decline, the clerk suggests I sleep in a field!

"It's not a problem in Hungary" he adds.

It's not until I find a reasonably priced room and view myself in a full length mirror that I see another side to his suggestion. I'm black with the oil blow-back from the engine. I look like a weathered scarecrow!

I have a couple of hours before bed to explore Szarvas. It's a quiet place, built on the banks of a slow-moving, deep green river. Twinkling lanterns adorn the main bridge into the centre, and a large monument, set in a small midstream island, is highlighted by tastefully placed spotlights. This leads to a wide central boulevard that is lined with large, manicured trees, behind which sit restored and subtly lit 19th century municipal buildings and churches. The town council have obviously put a lot of effort into making this an attractive, pleasant place for residents and visitors alike.

Right in the centre of the town, opposite prosperous looking shops and an internet cafe, is a sharp reminder of the country's not-so-distant communist past. A depressingly stark concrete apartment block of obvious Soviet design occupies this central position. It looks so incongruous juxtaposed with the rest of the town's elegant fineness that I can't help wondering why the town planners could possibly have allowed such a monstrosity smack bang in the middle of so charming a high street.

My hotel has a bustling restaurant and bar just a short walk from the banks of the river. Its menu, sadly, has nothing suitable on offer. Down a central side street I see a sign for a pizza restaurant. Perfect, I think. Every pizza place offers a basic tomato and cheese margherita. Today's lunch was a paltry cheese pastry and chocolate doughnut so I enter the eatery almost salivating with anticipation. Inside, it resembles a sports bar more than a restaurant. Two wall-mounted televisions show a Champions League football match and several tables are occupied by groups of beer-swilling men who shout loudly at the screens. A Hungarian team, Győr, are playing and by the sounds of things are not doing terribly well.

To my delight there's a pukka vegetarian pizza listed on the chalkboard menu. Without question I order a large one and settle down to drink a glass of cold juice in anticipation of its arrival. Today's lesson is to ask exactly what the veggie component of a vegetarian pizza is. When mine shows up five minutes later it proves to be frozen peas scattered on a doughy base smeared with tomato paste and processed cheese. Yum!

Before I turn in for the night I walk round the back of the hotel to check on my beloved bike. Tonight it rests in a cage at the back of the bar alongside crates of beer. Every night I pat it on the tank and thank it for carrying me safely this far. The cage is locked, so I poke my hand through a gap at the bottom and touch its wheel.

"Thanks, my friend," I say.

Its a good job no one can see or hear me.

Day 8 Szarvas to Truckstop west of Sibiu, Romania 198 miles

Video-making is the first order of the day. I park up on Szarvas's main street and begin by filming the grander municipal buildings and modern shops, then move onto the ugly block of flats. Two of the shops remarkably sport a British fashion theme in their windows. In one, slender trans-gender mannequins clad in trendy urban clothes pose around a backdrop of Big Ben and the Houses of Parliament. Another store, flatteringly named 'London', has a window totally plastered with Union Jack flags. It's a strange sight.

Back at my bike I begin to pack the camera away. A voice hollers out,

"Gordon? is that Gordon? It is; I don't believe it!"

I look around in amazement at the sound of my name. A smartly dressed man bounds across the road from his car and begins to vigorously shake my hand. It's Csaba, the man from Bekescaba who contacted me by email with the offer of a bed for the night. Neither of us can believe he has spotted me here, some fifty kilometres west of Bekescaba. He explains that he is returning to his office after an early meeting at a nearby town and noticed my Enfield whilst waiting at traffic lights.

It transpires that Czaba's brother, Ferenc, owns a one-year-old 350 cc Bullet. There's another serendipitous connection too; Csaba tells me his wife is a teacher at a school that is twinned with a school in Redditch, the place where my motorcycle was built all those years ago. After more backslapping and another "I can't believe it" Czaba heads off to contact his brother and arrange a meeting later in the morning.

Less than an hour's ride east, I spot a gleaming black Bullet sitting by the side of a roundabout. Two men, easily identifiable as Csaba and Ferenc, stand next to it waving their arms like windmills. Ferenc hops on his Bullet and offers to guide me to the Romanian border post twenty kilometres away, promising a brief guided tour of Bekescaba en route. We set off with Czaba following in his car snapping photographs of the two Enfields at every opportunity. It's such a joy to be riding with another bike, let alone another Royal Enfield. Ferenc stops at several traffic lights to point out places of interest and check he's not going too fast for my old and heavily laden machine. His English is limited but his pleasure and good-nature are infectious and I feel thoroughly warmed that he has actually ducked out of work to be able to share part of my journey and lead me safely to the next country.

We part at the border. Ahead, I see a checkpoint manned by men in military-looking uniforms. Although Romania became a fully fledged member of the EU in January 2007, my research has prepared me for frustrating long delays, time-eating bureaucracy and all manner of petty charges at the crossing. How wrong could I be? The official takes a quick look at my passport, asks me if I have documents for the bike, which he declines to inspect, then waves me through. Is that it, I wonder as I look around anticipating that I'll be hauled back for innocently riding past more formal checks? I ride as slowly as possible, looking from right to left at the handful of buildings, but no one emerges and signals me to stop. Ahead is a petrol station with a money exchange booth. I buy some local currency, oddly called Leu, fill up my tank, and happily set off again.

It's immediately apparent that Romania is considerably poorer than its neighbour. The roads are broken, patched and broken again. Small villages appear run down and there are many groups of unemployed young men hanging around outside their houses or playing cards at tables beside grungy-looking shops. I see no obvious signs of industry or even small-scale manufacturing. Certainly in this region, the economy seems to be mainly agrarian. Again and again I pass horse and carts hauling wood, hay and mounds of fruit along the road. This causes havoc with faster traffic and judging by the many warning signs, accidents are common.

As the day progresses, I experience see-sawing changes in conditions. A European flag on a sign signifies recent investment and an excellent, fast road ahead. A few kilometres later, typically round a blind bend, it all turns to custard. I hit troughs and ruts in the tarmac deep enough, if hit incorrectly, to throw me buckaroo-style off the bike. Some patches are so poor that I'm again forced to ride several kilometers standing up on the footpegs, unable to get out of second gear. Just as unexpectedly as before, the road suddenly merges into another stretch of delightfully smooth tarmac and I'm off at speed again. The lay of the land is fairly hilly, with much of the lightly wooded landscape so redolent of the Highlands of Scotland and just as deserted.

For the first time I'm chased through villages by mangy mutts. I'm glad not to be free-camping here as there are often packs of three or four wild dogs ranging the edges of remote forests.

Highlight of the day is lunch. I gorge myself on freshly picked watermelon eaten at a roadside stand seemingly in the middle of nowhere. Three generations of a family are present. The grandmother looks very peasant-like in floral skirt and plain headscarf. She carries a small scythe which she uses to harvest the fruit, trundling it over to the stand in a battered old wooden wheelbarrow. The young-looking mother and cheerful father, who is busy loading a sack of apples onto a beat-up scooter, are dressed in cheap track suits. Their bored fifteen year old son sits astride a mountain bike. He wears an earring and doesn't give the impression he wants to follow in the family business! They all make me feel so welcome, despite our only common language being hand signs. The succulent flesh of the watermelon's deep red interior is absolutely divine and I unashamedly eat with its juice dribbling down my chin.

Moving on, I negotiate my way through the grimy city of Sebes then come to a halt behind a motionless line of vehicles. Several static minutes later a long stream of traffic approaches from the opposite direction. It takes just thirty seconds to pass before another silent five minute wait. By now most of the motorists have stopped their engines and several have climbed out of their cars to look up the road. I do what just about every other motorcyclist would... pull out into the left lane and slowly make my way forwards.

I go for about half a kilometre before I'm forced to squeeze into the row of stationary traffic to allow the next batch of approaching vehicles through. This is repeated again and again as I ride past the queue, which I estimate to be somewhere in the stress-inducing region of ten kilometres. It's necessary to ride carefully as there are so many people wearily wandering on the road; I reckon they must have been waiting here for hours. Finally I get to the front of the line by a red traffic light. Another short stream of vehicles comes through then the light blessedly turns to green. I roar ahead and make my way through a pretty innocuous-looking two hundred metre stretch of roadworks administered by a group of uptight and harassed police. There's not a workman in sight and my heart goes out to the thousands of people trapped both behind me and in the monumental queue I now see waiting on the other side of the obstruction.

The bike's charging system is on the blink again, causing me to worry about how much time there is before dark and how long my lights will last. By tonight I'd hoped to reach Brasov, home of Count Dracula's famed castle in Transylvania, but have to dismiss that as being well out of range. Sibiu, the cultural heart of the region, is my fall back. However, as light fades on a highway pounded by an endless stream of trucks and coaches, I give up on that too. I pull in at a roadside motel mostly used by long-distance truckers and overnight coach travellers.

The mustached night-manager, who is dressed in black trousers, bold blue and white striped shirt and a black waistcoat, comically reminds me of René from the WWII sitcom *Allo, Allo*!. It's hard for me to take him seriously as I have to constantly restrain myself from talking to him in pigeon-English with a silly French accent. He thinks my motorcycle will attract more attention than his cafe if I park it out the front. and hastily agrees to it being securely stored in his kitchen service area next to sacks of potatoes and onions. It's an arrangement that suits me fine.

I go to sleep with my battery mercifully charging on the bedside table, thanks to Michal.

Day 9 Truckstop west of Sibiu to Giurgiu, Romania 262 miles

'René' and last night's restaurant staff are still on duty when I take breakfast. They've been going for at least ten hours and look utterly spent; visibly wilting as they serve me toast and coffee. Both my battery and I, however, are fully recharged.

The weather is against me even as I liberate my Enfield from the vegetable store. It rains incessantly for the first three or four hours and the roads are treacherous. My route follows a long winding valley through the tail end of the Carpathian mountains. I've read that this vast range is home to Europe's biggest concentration of brown bears, wolves, chamois and lynxes. Diesel spills glisten on the glassy tarmac and I'm forced to edge my way round the numerous bends in order to stay safe. This so completely absorbs my attention that I have no time to look sideways into the forested hills for wildlife, which in any case is probably sheltering from the vile weather as any sensible creature should. By lunchtime, when the sun finally breaks through the dense, black clouds, my bike and myself are both absolutely filthy.

For the second day running a roadside fruit stand provides me with lunch. Today's delight is an assortment of black and green plums and tangy red apples. The stall proprietor, dressed like a Romany gypsy, looks as old as the hills. Her face is craggy and worn and her white hair, under a faded headscarf, wild and straggly. When I remove my helmet and goggles she realises that I'm a foreigner and her face cracks into a wide, beaming smile. I eat my fill of fruit then tie another bulging bag onto the top of the panniers for later.

My motorcycle is still running delightfully well, but in the afternoon I notice that the oil leak is quite a bit worse. Up until now I've joked with myself that I'm leaving a trail to follow home and that I'm saving myself the trouble of changing the oil as my frequent top-ups create a constant state of change. However, the volume escaping has definitely increased and I start to seriously worry. The viscous black puddle I leave behind me every time I stop is also becoming an embarrassment. Numerous people, especially at garage forecourts, point it out and I have no means of answering their sincere concern except by shrugging. I try to console myself by recounting what I've heard Bullet owners in India say;

"My Bullet doesn't leak oil... it's simply marking out it's territory!" but even this provides little solace.

By now I've seen countless peasants driving horse or donkey drawn carts on Romania's highways. Late in the day, whilst giving one such outfit my usual wide berth, I notice something rather bemusing that makes me slow down and stop some way further along the road. I look back and stare... the empty cart is hauled by a bedraggled old horse and is followed by a sad-looking donkey on a rope. However, there's no human in sight. The horse is plodding steadily along, unmanned, and how far it's been going I simply cannot guess. I wonder if I'm not giving the horse due credit; it appears to know exactly where it's heading. I ride on, an amused smile on my face.

Reaching the Romanian border town of Giurgiu around 6.30 pm, there's still at least an hour of daylight left but I have doubts about crossing into Bulgaria tonight. My guidebook says that there can often be delays here, sometimes caused by bureaucratic nonsenses such as charging travellers for their vehicles to be disinfected. I approach the control posts but turn back at the last minute, deciding to stay the night on the Romanian side and to face any frontier challenges early tomorrow.

It seems that Saturday night is peak party time at Giurgiu's hotels. The first two I try are both fully booked, citing large birthday parties as the reason. The third hotel has a room and a safe place in a courtyard for my motorcycle. The only drawback is they are hosting an enormous wedding reception. Guests begin to arrive just as I start to unpack my bike.... hundreds of them. I spot a coach unloading even more as I stagger through a crowded entrance clutching all my bags. Already, several men have had their photos taken next to my Enfield. I become quite stressed as the bike is caked in a tacky layer of silt, grime and sprayed engine oil. They are all dressed in their best clothes and seem totally oblivious to the hazard of leaning against it. I cover up as quickly as possible, hoping to return later when the party is in full swing to remove the battery for another charge.

The hotel restaurant has been taken over by wedding caterers so I wander the central streets in search of a decent meal. Restaurants seem to be in short supply and when I stop to ask a man for assistance he points me back towards the hotels I had initially tried for a room. Just as my energy is flagging and my spirits sinking I come to a halt outside, you guessed it, another pizza joint. Musing that my face will end up circular if I continue to eat pizza with such regularity, I enter.

"Hey, welcome. Come on in," bellows a wiry middle-aged woman with a strong New York accent. She bustles with energy around my table, giving me a quick-fire synopsis of her life to date.

"I managed to escape to The States in the late 1980s during the final years of Ceauşescu's rule," she begins, referring to Romania's former communist dictator. "He was a megalomaniac! Life was awful here in those times. There were often food shortages and power blackouts. He borrowed so much money from the West which he invested real badly."

She continues," I set up a small pizza restaurant in New York, boy did I love living there. But I missed my family and things had been getting so much better here that three years ago I moved back."

Things certainly look up when I tell her I'm vegetarian.

"You've come to the right place. I grow virtually all the vegetables for our pizzas myself. How about a large pizza with home-grown tomatoes, capsicum, onion, mushroom and black olives?" she asks.

It sounds perfect. My host goes on to offer me a beer on the house. I look over towards the basic but perfectly functional bar. There are two choices, both of Scandinavian origin; Tuborg and Skol. The latter brings a childhood memory rushing back to me. My mind conjures up a picture of my father, head thrown back, drinking from a can of Skol one sultry summer's evening whilst on a family caravan holiday. Until today, some thirty odd years later, I don't believe I've ever seen the brand again. I go for the Skol, first toasting my host and then, when I'm on my own, quietly toasting my father.

The enormous pizza lives up to its billing and I wander back to my hotel full almost to bursting point. Outside the hotel, the young-looking bride and groom are positioned by the doors where they greet a short line of glamorously-attired late arrivals. Inside, celebrations are in full swing. The unusual music, to my ear a form of traditional folk music played in a Euro-pop fashion, blasts out at rock concert decibel levels. Peering around the open door of the main function room, I see row upon row of people seated around long lace-covered tables. Just about everyone appears to be in deep conversation, heads pressed closely to their neighbour's ear. How they can hear anything above the din of the band is beyond me.

I attend to more mundane but still important tasks. Firstly, I retrieve the battery from my bike so that it can receive another life-giving charge. Then I endeavour to cut a makeshift oil gasket from the back page of my AA Europe map book. In the morning I plan to fit it to the neck of the crankcase oil tank, which I still believe to be the cause of my problems.

"This'll fix it," I tell myself with all the conviction I can muster.

Day 10 Giurgiu to Kazanlac, Bulgaria
143 miles

Things have moved on considerably since my Bulgarian guide book was written in late 2007. I approach the border checkpoint with a fair amount of trepidation; just how much of my Sunday morning will the predicted red tape take? Less than five minutes, it transpires.

I'm greeted by two brawny guards resplendent in almost ceremonial myrtle green uniforms. They ask for my passport, which I hand over without comment. After a quick flick through its pages they turn their attention to my bike.

"How old?" asks the officer closest to me.

"55 years old, " I reply. "1953."

They admiringly walk around the loaded Enfield, talking amongst themselves in Bulgarian. My passport is handed back accompanied with smiles.

"Have a good visit to Bulgaria" I'm told as they turn their attention to a car that has pulled up behind me. I pass under a large white stone archway and am officially in the country, with no sign of Customs and the anticipated disinfection fees.

I immediately warm to Bulgaria. It seems so much cleaner, brighter and more vigorous than when I was last here twenty one years ago. The roads are far better than the ones I've just left behind in Romania and the almost emerald green, rolling countryside is lovely.

Alas, I can´t enjoy the ride. Straight after breakfast I fitted my improvised seal to the oil tank filler cap. I stop after a few miles to check on its success but find the leak to be just as bad, if not slightly worse, than yesterday. I ride for another hour or so but am dangerously distracted, obsessively craning my neck to monitor the now grave seepage.

I stop at a fuel station and set about making more comprehensive repairs. The first task is to clean up the crankcases, a job that's made much easier by the assistance of a pump attendant who's taken pity on me. He runs backwards and forwards to his small office, bringing me sheets of tissue paper and a soapy sponge. Next I fill up the oil tank, using the last of the Penrite 20/50 I'd brought from England. On my mental notepad I impress the words 'buy more oil at first opportunity'. Finally, I set about fully sealing the filler cap. Cutting a long strip of rubber from my spare rim tape I fix it around the filler cap with a combination of gasket goo and a jubilee clip. Since I've stripped off my biking gear and have all my tools out of the pannier boxes I decide to give the dynamo commutator another clean for good measure!

The moment I set off I'm rewarded with a fully functioning charging system, but around the base of the Magdyno the flow of escaping oil continues unabated. Several exasperating miles later I pull off highway E85 and park up at the stunning municipality of Veliko Tarnovo. The town is located in the sharp S-bend of a deep gorge and is overlooked by the towering Tsarevets fortress. Being Sunday lunchtime, the pavements are packed with young couples walking hand-in-hand, groups of laughing students and tourists.

Two such tourists, who are quite obviously English, come to a halt beside my bike. I'm lying in the gutter peering under the exhaust trying to reassess my oil problem.

"A long time since I've seen one of these," the white-bearded man says. I'm not sure if he's talking to his female companion or me. I studiously concentrate on the bottom of my crankcases. He repeats his comment and I deduce that I must be the intended recipient of his remark.

When you take on the ownership of a classic motorcycle, I believe you inherit an obligation to talk with passers-by about both the bike and their motorcycling memories. It's an even more frequent occurrence for Royal Enfield owners because their continued manufacture in India is an additional talking point. Sometimes these meetings and conversations arise when you're in a hurry, or perhaps when you're not feeling particularly chatty, but there's an unwritten law amongst classic bike riders that you must still talk enthusiastically about your bike and listen, if only briefly, to their tales of motorcycles past.

Today I simply do not have the resources to do it. There's a small oil slick on the tarmac next to me, I'm sweating under the midday sun that beats down from directly overhead, and my hands are covered in piping hot oil. Moreover, I'm seriously concerned that the leak could jeopardise my whole expedition. I ignore the second comment, pretending to be oblivious to it; I'm far too worried to cheerfully enter into a motorcycling memory-lane conversation.

After a while I realise the couple have walked on. At the very best they might presume I don't speak English but it's far more likely that they think I'm rather rude. I quietly scold myself for being so ill-mannered. It then occurs to me that the man may have had mechanical knowledge that could aid my plight had I just taken a few minutes to converse with him. I feel even more despondent and decide I need to have a good meal and try to clear my mind of its tribulations.

I draw up next to a thriving outdoor restaurant. My timing is impeccable as a roadside table empties just as I climb off my bike. The food is great and I really start to enjoy the relaxed feel of Veliko Tarnovo. It would be worth staying the night here just so that I could visit the magnificent citadel. There's been a fortress on the site since the fifth century and the current structure, which was built in the twelfth century, was the location of the royal palace during the Second Bulgarian Empire. However, tinkering with the 'great oil escape' means that I've covered precious few miles today and I grudgingly convince myself that I must ride on.

The road south takes me over the first mountain of my journey, which appears completely out of the blue. The straight. open road starts to gently climb. I round one bend which is rapidly followed by another and another. Large leafy trees crowd in on the road and obliterate the sun. The frequency and tightness of the bends increases until I find myself roaring round a string of sharp hairpins. My Bullet may be slowly losing its very life-blood, but it gloriously powers up the ever-steepening incline. Best of all is the exhaust note, which rebounds off the inner craggy mountainside with a deep, strident snort. Half way up, I switch on my satellite navigation and select altitude mode. It's fascinating to monitor my ascent, which finally slows and stabilises at twelve hundred metres.

The descent is just as captivating, with sneak previews of the golden plains below through the layer of trees that ring the cliff edge. At the bottom I realise that I've become so fully absorbed with the ride that I have, at least temporarily, forgotten my woes.

Continuing on, I arrive at Kazanlac, a town situated in the enchantingly named Valley of Roses. Judging by the baked and bare countryside, I reckon I must be here at the wrong time of year to see the blooms. I head, as usual, for the centre and find the stark concrete Grand Hotel, a former Balkantourist establishment. Parking is a concern as there is no secure area for guests' vehicles, but the concierge instructs me to park up next to the large plate glass windows of the hotel foyer, assuring me the night staff will keep a close watch on my machine.

The hotel rooms are strange, a mixture of bare utilitarian design overlaid with recently upgraded fittings. The bathroom is particularly odd, with its toilet all but stranded in the middle of the floor so that you have to walk behind it to get to the sink. For all that, I like it, especially my small private balcony which gives an uninterrupted view of the popular town square.

The best news is that Kazanlac has an internet cafe with cheap phone booths... the first for 5 days. In desperation I dial Andy Berry´s number, joyfully catching him at home. He is, rightly, very proud of his workmanship and horrified to hear that one of his engines is so profusely leaking oil.

"Make sure you don´t photograph it covered in oil!" he says, only half jokingly.

We work through the problem, which Andy feels must be caused by a build up of crankcase pressure forcing oil out of the hidden seal between the timing pinion and the magneto. He makes some suggestions, top of the list being to shorten the duck-bill type end of the crankcase breather pipe.

Under the curious gaze of the hotel night staff, I remove the rubber pipe and take it to my room. Before bed it receives a small surgical procedure.

Day 11 Kazanlac to Edirne, Turkey
130 miles

The day starts badly. My shaver has vibrated apart and I spend fifteen frustrating minutes failing miserably to put it back together. I look in the mirror and ask my reflection;

"How can you possibly keep a fifty-five year old motorcycle running another six thousand miles when you can´t even piece together a poxy Tesco razor?" I have to laugh.

The hotel's vast dining room, large enough to accommodate a banquet, is empty. The solitary waitress sits at a nearby table, awaiting my signals for service for her only customer. I put the shortened oil breather pipe on the table while I eat breakfast. Looking at it from several angles, I wonder if such a seemingly simple solution can possibly resolve all of my problems.

Before departing, I fit it back on the bike, remove the make-do rubber seal from the filler cap and carefully scrape the remnants of gasket sealant from around it. As I set off I sing to myself,

"Things can only get better!"

Sadly, that's not the case this morning as I'm again slowed by numerous enforced checks on the state of the blasted oil leak. The shortened bill on the breather seems to have worked until I start going fast, when oil flows out again and I´m back to square one. I fill up with petrol at the quirkily-named town of Styara Zagora. A quick check of my oil dipstick tells me that the level in the tank is getting dangerously low. The garage has a plethora of choices of oil, but none are 20/50. I dare not mix in anything thinner, so resort to opening the five litre reserve of Penrite straight 50 I'm also carrying with me. It's gut-wrenching to do this as I've hauled this cherished liquid for two thousand miles, saving it for the extreme heat I will experience crossing Iran and Pakistan, where I am assured its higher viscosity will be much more able to protect my engine.

To make myself feel better I tuck into a tasty muesli bar, one of a prized horde I've been saving for moments of low energy or as now, low spirits. It dawns on me to try fitting my spare breather pipe, after all, I think, there's nothing to lose. I rummage in my panniers and locate it amongst a container of electrical components. It looks identical to the one I cut up last night, but I fit it anyway. I say farewell to another obliging garage attendant who has allowed me to sully his forecourt with a black slick and, as an afterthought, ask him how long it will take me to reach Turkey.

"At least 3 hours," he replies, "maybe more. The road is not good."

It's hard to believe as the road thus far has been perfect and a look at my map suggests it should take half that time to cover the distance to the border.

Again my attention is diverted downwards as I ride. Hey presto, the oil leak is reduced to nothing more than a light weep on fast runs. It's unbelievable. Phew! That's actually a really big 'phew'. My relief is both an emotional and physical experience. I try without luck to locate suitable oil at three more garages, but it seems a far less pressing problem now that the flow has been been stemmed. Andy will be thrilled.

I ride past an enormous lake where several people sit fishing on the idyllic sandy banks. The beautiful scene is marred by a monstrously large, ugly cement works that has been plonked on the western shore. Once past this giant blot, I corner a bend at speed and suddenly have to haul on my brakes. There's an almost straight line in the road that marks the end of a smooth surface and the beginning of a broken, old strip of asphalt. Without doubt, it's the worst road of my journey to date. It's so poor that I ride for long stretches standing on the footpegs in first gear. Trucks using the route weave from side to side to avoid the worst patches and this forces me to absorb some big bumps down ruts and sunken manhole covers in order to keep out of their way.

I remember that I'm supposed to be making a film of my adventure, however instead, I've been so preoccupied with my oil leak that it has been completely overlooked. I stop and set the video camera up on a tripod by the roadside. I sit astride the bike and ride in the direction I came from, turning to film myself riding towards the camera along the awfully patched highway. Once there, I turn the camera around and film myself heading into the distance. When some moments later I return to the camera, I realise I've not pushed the record button on, so, with slightly gritted teeth, have to repeat the procedure again.

Just as I finish 'take 2' a large truck, travelling at such speed that it appears to be almost gliding above the ruts in the road, sweeps past my camera and blows it over. I rush back and gather it up. Fortunately it's fallen backwards into some bushes and is undamaged, but I reflect on how different it so easily could have been. Furthermore, I realise that I've just spent thirty energy-sapping minutes in the hottest time of the day producing what can only amount to fifteen seconds of footage once edited into the film. I now know why Messrs. McGregor and Boorman needed a cameraman riding with them. Even a riding companion would make the whole process so much more viable. Ah well.

Just when I think the bad stretch of road is finished I have to endure two kilometers of bone shaking cobbled road. I dismount and carefully check that all the nuts and bolts are still present, which they are. Great stuff that Loctite.

It gets hotter as I approach Turkey. Stopping by the side of a field, I stretch my legs and wipe my brow. As the engine is ticking over the awareness of a strange repetitive squeaking sound creeps into my consciousness. I whip off my helmet and anxiously listen to the engine. That seems OK so I rush to the front and rear of the bike with my right ear pressed against metal. The sound remains, but I can´t quite place it. I kill the engine but the squeaking continues. Relief slowly fills me as I realise it's from crickets chirping loudly in the adjoining field. I really need to learn how to relax!

It takes almost two long hours to clear Turkish Immigration and Customs. It´s not especially busy and not even particularly bureaucratic. It is simply badly organised, with officials sending me round in confused circles for a collection of stamps and forms. Even the bank adjoining the immigration building seems to operate a similarly ineffectual system.

"We convert your US Dollars into Euros at this rate, then from Euros to Turkish Lira at that rate" I'm told when I ask their exchange rates.

"Can't you just change Dollars for Lira?" I ask

"No, it's not possible," is their reply.

Eventually I'm sent to a remote portakabin to have my passport ratified by a policeman. It's the final check. I ride off, delighted to finally be in Turkey. Checking my mileometer, I note that I've travelled exactly 2,300 miles since my departure. It marks quite a milestone in the journey as Turkey represents the end of my dash across Europe and the start of a much more challenging leg of the ride.

I call it a day eighteen kilometres later in Edirne. a large town dominated by the very attractive, mammoth Selimiye Camii mosque. I have no idea where to stay, but follow my nose and come across the Hotel Tuna (inadvertent pun). My bike just fits in its narrow garden and there´s a superb restaurant across the way serving delicious Turkish vegetarian food. As I sit down, an almighty boom echoes across the town, followed immediately by the call to prayer, Adhan, which resounds from several mosque minarets simultaneously.

"It's the first day of Ramadan" the waiter tells me. "That's Iftar, the signal that the sun has set and we are able to break our fast."

A month of daytime fasting lies ahead for muslims and I´m sure at times for me too. Oh boy!

I wander the city streets until all the shops and cafés close. There's an almost carnival atmosphere, a result, no doubt, of the end of the day's fast. In the nick of time I enter a sweet shop and buy some baklava, the sweet, syrupy Turkish pastry made from layers of filo, chopped nuts and honey. It's divine. I simply can't wait until I reach my hotel room, so eat it as I walk through the quietening streets, my fingers sticky with syrup.

Around the corner from my hotel I suddenly remember I haven't bought a bottle of water to see me through the night. Two men sit talking on stone steps outside a general store. The door is partially open, although the shop lights have been switched off for the night.

"Can I buy water, please?" I ask the older of the two men.

He signals the other to go inside and fetch me some. When he returns with a litre bottle I lean over to the older man with payment.

"No, you need a drink. No problem." he adamantly replies, waving me away with a shake of his hand.

It's a simple but powerful message of hospitality and kindness that I'm to learn is so much a part of the tradition and culture of this region.

Day 12 Edirne to Izmit, Turkey
219 miles

I spent six weeks backpacking around Turkey in the late 1980s. Day-to-day details of the journey are now quite hazy in my mind, but I retain the overall impression of a beautiful, exotic country and friendly, helpful people. I decide to take the morning off and rekindle some of those memories by further exploring Edirne.

It's a fascinating mixture of modern, cosmopolitan Turkey together with its ancient past. Edrine was originally founded by the Roman emperor, Hadrian, and was initially named Adrianopolis after him. For a short period in the fourteenth century the city became the capital of the Ottoman empire and after WWI it was seized for a short period by the Greek army.

Walking its meandering streets this morning is like wandering through a living, open air museum. There are crumbling old city walls, ancient houses, mosques and even a Greek church. I stop for coffee, made in the traditional Turkish fashion with a concentrated layer of black grounds settled at the bottom of the cup. It's served with a dusty pink slice of Turkish Delight on the saucer. Mmmmm. Next I stroll through the colourful indoor bazaar where many of the traders are in the process of moving displays of their wares onto the sidewalk. The vividly coloured shops selling dried fruits, cheeses and selections of appetizing nibbles are my favourite. The dates, which I indulgently buy, are heavenly.

I love the way everyday modern words have been incorporated into the language. Fotokopy and taksi are really easy to comprehend but I struggle to grasp the significance of calling a minibus company Lipigloss. Maybe it's a generational thing.

Lunch is surprisingly easy to find. I try the same place as last night and am without hesitation served a delicious meze of potato, aubergine, yoghurt and tangy tomato beans along with chunky slices of warm, fragrant fresh bread. Relishing the moment, I sit by the window watching people going about their business. Many of their faces are surprisingly European in appearance and the majority wear clothes that make them indistinguishable from people walking the streets of any European or North American town or city, which is quite unexpected.

I could easily sit here all day, but I calculate I'm already a day behind the loose schedule I have in my mind, so around 12.30 I load up my motorcycle and make my way out of the city onto the toll road to Istanbul which lies approximately two hundred kilometres to the south east.

I pull off the motorway at a modern service station. My fuel tank is all but empty and it takes nearly thirteen litres of Super Benzine to fill it. I get quite a shock when I come to pay; the petrol costs approximately £1.65 per litre! Wholesale oil prices have rocketed in the last twelve months and in the UK people loudly complain about paying £1.25 per litre, a good deal of which is duty charged by the government. Like many, I've assumed that fuel prices are cheaper on continental Europe, which is simply not true. Apart from France, where the price per litre was 2p cheaper than the UK, every other country has been more expensive. £1.65, however, is a new high and quite a blow to my budget as I have over eleven hundred miles of Turkey to cross.

On the plus side, the shop stocks that most elusive of entities... 20/50 oil. I buy a litre and go to check my engine's oil level. I remove the filler cap, which secures to a short neck on the crankcases with a bayonet mount, and check the dipstick. The oil level is fine. I refit the cap and fasten it tightly to the neck. I pause; something doesn't feel quite right. I release the cap then secure it again, this time only part way.

Sometimes I think I must go through life in a stupefied daze, or maybe it's just that I get so focused on one thing that my brain deals with everything else in a automatic, semi-conscious way. I'm sure Jane would sassily say it's a male thing. Here is my confession: I am the sole cause of my oil leak. Standing on that garage forecourt I realise that I've been tightening my filler cap down into the air-tight locked position that's designed to be used only when the bike is being transported or stored. This has resulted in the buildup of crankcase pressure that has produced my leak. Yesterday I must have inadvertently pushed it only half way down, which is the correct position for when the engine is being used. This 'error' is what resolved my problem, not the new breather pipe. I'm torn between laughing at and berating myself... what a numpty!

A strong headwind gets up as I rejoin the motorway. It soon becomes a howler, hitting me with great gusts when it unexpectedly veers to the east and dangerously tugging at my front wheel as I ride over two bridges. It's power almost yanks me off the bike and by the time I reach the outskirts of the capital, my neck and shoulders ache acutely.

Here I hit the rush-hour traffic jam from hell. Istanbul's drivers seem to lack any level of patience, cutting and weaving in and out of every lane to gain the slightest few metres of headway. As a motorcyclist I just don´t count. Cars, trucks and buses all encroach on my lane, edging past just inches from my knees and hands.

I'm startled by the wail of a minaret that erupts suddenly into life nearby. I look around wondering what on earth the noise is, then spot the mosque over my right shoulder. About half an hour later I hear a similar noise and in my now acclimatised state, ignore it. The sound persists, indeed, almost seems to follow me. I continue to pay no heed. Peripheral movement catches my attention. I look over my left shoulder and am jolted to see a police car forcing its way past me. The officer in the passenger seat looks furious; he's waving his free hand, aggressively signalling me to move out of the way. In his other hand he holds the mouthpiece of a microphone. It finally registers that the noise I'd been deliberately ignoring had not been the call to prayers of a mosque, but was this police vehicle insisting I shift out of the middle of the lane and let it through. Somewhat sheepishly, I move over and it surges forward, the belligerent voice on its roof mounted tannoy now urging the cars ahead to move aside.

Highlight of the day is crossing the Bosporus. As I slowly drive over the enormous eight-lane bridge, with the waterfront streets and iconic mosques of Istanbul vaguely visible in the hazy distance, I'm filled with a deep sense of pride in my wonderful old motorcycle. It has carried me right across Europe and now into Asia. The sides of the bridge reverberate the hearty thump produced from its silencer which somehow makes the moment seem even more poignant.

Traffic rapidly thins on the other side and I contentedly ride for another hundred or so kilometers before settling on the small city of Izmit as today's final destination. I stumble upon a hotel with a small locked garage in the adjoining building. With another worry-free night guaranteed, I eat a hearty meal at a streetside cafe. I share my table with a smoker. At home I would find this difficult, if not impossible. Here for some reason it's fine. More so, the aromatic aroma of Turkish tobacco somehow evokes exotic connotations and adds to the atmosphere.

Day 13 Izmit to Safranbolu, Turkey
201 miles

Rather than the days all merging into one, I feel a fresh surge of excitement every morning I uncover and unlock my Bullet. My first undertaking is always a thorough check around the bike and most often a degrease for the dynamo. This morning I try a new tack once the commutator is free from grunge. Using a tube of silicone, I make a seal around the edge of the dynamo cover in the hope this will keep oil and muck well and truly out.

For once I have the joy of riding with a tail wind. As I enter the enormous Anatolia region the scenery becomes dramatic and spectacular. My concentration, however, is absorbed by a search for the illusive D-100, the major east / west highway that spans Turkey. For the first time the electronic mapping of my Garmin Zumo is well out of synch. I travel due east on a toll motorway, the O4. The sat nav shows the D-100 first running parallel then crossing the road I'm on. Standing high on the footpegs, I strain to spot it. There´s absolutely nothing in sight except fields and hills. Looking back at the display, I'm fleetingly shown as riding on the D-100 before it again vanishes and I'm left with the picture of a motorcycle crossing an empty green screen.

After eighty miles of uncertainty, I stop and unpack a map. Thankfully it shows the motorway I'm on, with the D-100 a few miles north from where I've stopped. I leave at the next exit and locate it by dead reckoning along minor roads. Almost immediately it climbs up to a high plain, around fourteen hundred meters, which provides spectacular aeroplane-window views of the low-lying area I've just passed through. I'm filled with a heartfelt sense of contentment; mulling over an email I was sent shortly before my departure. It read,

"Gordon, I'll be thinking of you when I'm stuck in the daily grind of my commute to work. Good on you for taking the risk to follow your dreams and make the most of every minute of your journey!"

I draw in a deep breath of fresh, unpolluted air, absorb the heat of the sun into my body and say another thank you to Royal Enfield, Andy Berry, and everyone else who helped prepare my bike, for getting me here.

I approach a small town and the sat nav mapping disappears yet again. I drive around looking for road signs and hit the most horrible unmarked roadworks imaginable. It's only a single cutting, roughly 50 cm wide and 25 cm deep, but it has very sharp edges. There´s a resounding bang at the front end which travels like a shockwave through my wrists and forearms. I stop and dismount. The jolt was so severe that it has driven the front mudguard upwards into the top of the crashbars, causing a sizable dent. Measuring it loosely with my hands, I estimate it's about 18 cm of travel. I spin the front wheel; it wavers slightly at one point, signifying a slight buckle. Fortunately, the forks seem undamaged and steering is unaffected when I again set off.

Today I've picked the village of Safranbolu as my stopping place. It's a good forty kilometres ride north from the D-100, but it's shown in my guidebook as a Unesco World Heritage Site and must surely be worth the diversion.

After a frustrating thirty minutes driving round Safranbolu without any sign of 'a village containing over 400 restored Ottoman houses on quaint cobbled streets', let alone a pension, I ask a shopkeeper for help. It transpires I'm in 'new' Safranbolu; 'old' Safranbolu is a further two kilometres along a twisting mountain road. Aha!

A smartly dressed policeman commandingly flags me down when I get there. He's standing in a small square and appears to have the combined roles of tourist information guide, town crier and law enforcer. I ask him to recommend a pension, which he does, issuing rapid 'turn left, second right, along the alleyway' type instructions. I repeat it all back verbatim to ensure I've got it right, then set off.

The ride along ancient, steep village lanes is almost beyond me. The cobblestones are in fact large irregularly-shaped rocks. They're highly polished and what's more, some are missing or dangerously protruding upwards at odd angles. Quite a few pedestrians compete for space too, making my slithering progress even more hazardous. Downhill I slip and slide in first gear with the brakes almost fully on. Uphill I rev hard and the whole bike jumps from side to side as it bounces over the badly misshapen surface. Both front and rear suspensions take a serious pounding, as do my hands and arms.

The recommended accommodation is unsuitable; its front door opens straight onto the lane and there's no parking within sight. The owner suggests I park back near the village square but I flatly refuse to leave my bike out in the open. I then get lost trying to navigate my way back out of the labyrinth of closed-in lanes. The end result is one very sweaty and fatigued rider, one even hotter bike and no suitable hotel. I try to ride up a steep ramp that forms a short-cut around the back of a mosque. By now the engine is spitting hot, the heat radiating off it nigh but burning my inner thighs, and it splutters to a halt. I wearily get off and let it cool for half an hour before a further attempt to navigate my way out of this maze.

I decide to ride back to 'new' Safranbolu, reasoning that there must be a large hotel with parking there if I look hard enough. Before I even manage to get into second gear I spot a beautifully restored Ottoman house with a large hotel sign swinging over its door. Better still, there's a walled garden next to it that serves as an open-air restaurant and could easily double as a resting place for my bike. Perfect. When I enter I'm shown the most entrancing room which has a dark wood panelled ceiling and floorboards, picture windows with carved wooden shutters, pretty crochet curtains and crisp white linen bedding. The bathroom is typical of bathrooms in many South East Asian countries; it's tiny, hardly bigger than a large wardrobe. The shower works on a 'soak all' principal, which means you have to use the lavatory and sink first and relocate the towel and toilet paper to the safety of the bedroom before turning on the spray. I feel like Alice In Wonderland as I shoehorn myself into this tiny chamber.

After a quick soaking I decide to check on my bike, giving it an extra pat and 'thank-you' as an apology for the hammering I've given it today. 'Old' Safranbolu redeems itself as I take a stroll through the delightful village streets. It's such a charismatic place yet strangely devoid of the flocks of tourists I presumed would be here. I eat dinner at a small café and do some serious thinking.

I need a rest and my motorcycle could also do with a full service. This seems a perfect place to take a day off and give the bike the attention it deserves. That decided, I consider the state of my film. I've been on the road for almost two weeks and have shot no more than three hours of footage. The broken camera mount in the Czech Republic was a major setback as it thwarted my plans to film whilst riding. Furthermore, it prevented me from unobtrusively capturing my everyday encounters with people en route. I now realise that I've also underestimated just how many hours a day I will spend in the saddle and how much of the remaining free time will be taken up by motorcycle maintenance. Consequently, I'm simply not recording enough essential filler shots, showing scenes, places of interest, the faces of people on the streets etc..

Before my departure, lots of people referred to the *Long Way Round / Down* DVDs and asked me, tongue-in-cheek, if I was taking two support vehicles, a couple of cameramen, a producer, director, doctor, security guard and the proverbial kitchen sink with me. I laughed along, after all, from the outside it does appear over the top. But I can now see a completely different side to the equation. Without that kind of support, riders Ewan and Charley would never have been able to make a professional documentary about their journey, especially as it was filmed over such a short period of time. Judging by my experiences, I would need, at the very least, twice as long to do justice to my journey.

I need to be honest with myself; in the time frame I have it will be impossible to make a film that I can be proud of and I can see no way of changing the circumstances. I head for bed feeling a strange mixture of genuine disappointment and the release of an onerous pressure which I had not, until this point, been conscious of.

Day 14 Safranbolu, Turkey
0 miles

It feels strange to awaken in my 'doll's house' room knowing I'll not be riding today. Breakfast is served in the garden where my motorcycle has securely spent the night. As well as the usual staples of white goats cheese, bread, olives and jam, I encounter a new delight; chocolate nut spread, of which I eat considerably more than my share.

First order of the day is to service my Royal Enfield: spark plug, tappets, points, grease nipples and levers all get some much needed attention. I also check and tighten every nut on the bike, including further damping down the steering head. This has been a bit of a concern since departure as the weight of luggage at the rear of the bike causes the front end to wobble under severe braking or if ridden slowly with just one hand on the bars. Andy and myself had torqued it down as far as possible to counter this, but two weeks of hard riding have created some free play and it easily winds down a full turn further.

I check the oil. Still no leak (yippee), but it needs changing. Reasoning that a bona fide workshop will be able to properly dispose of my old oil, I head off to new Safranbolu and find the *Dogan* bike repair shop. This dark, single room establishment is situated in a long line of car workshops and spare parts dealerships downhill from the main shopping area. The owner, Faruk, and a couple of his friends come out to see what kind of machine can possibly be making such a loud noise. Faruk speaks no English, but by a series of gestures I ask if I can use his premises and borrow a drip tray to do my oil change. He welcomes me and the Bullet inside and provides me with all I need to do the work.

By the time I've removed three drain plugs, the oil feed plug and the oil filter, a crowd of watchers and would-be helpers has assembled in the workshop. One man tells me in faltering English that he has a 1948 3T Triumph and a C11 BSA, both of which he has restored himself. He's enthralled by my Bullet and constantly moves around the bike taking photographs from every conceivable angle. A party atmosphere develops, with people coming in off the street to have a look, take photos and ask questions, then eventually move on when it becomes obvious that the new 'mechanic' works at a pace even a snail would consider pedestrian.

Faruk is obviously a quiet and gentle man yet seems to be completely unfazed by the circus that is developing in his premises. He makes sure I'm okay and have everything I need, then calmly gets on with an engine rebuild. Over an hour later I declare 'job done'. Faruk absolutely refuses any payment for the use of his facilities. He explains, via the Triumph owner, that it is his duty and privilege to help me.

My next mission is to get the bike cleaned. I'm directed to the adjacent workshop, which as luck would have it is a one-stop car cleaning business equipped with high pressure jet-wash equipment. The proprietor is sleepy and somewhat lackadaisical. He quickly declares the bike finished, but large areas, especially around the engine and underneath the panniers, still look cruddy. Faruk pokes his head around the corner, notes the poor workmanship of his neighbour, and instructs him in no uncertain terms to do it all again!

Once accomplished, Faruk helps me wheel the bike into another neighbouring workshop. I can't work out what kind of business is carried out here, but he indicates it's run by his friend. They produce some polish and together give the bike a far better clean than the man I've already paid. They take great pride in restoring the lustre of paint and chrome and even remove the black plastic that has melted from one of my bag straps onto the exhaust downpipe. I struggle to think of a way to repay Faruk for his generous help. He won't accept any money and this being Ramadan I can't thank him with food or a drink. I say farewell, still racking my brains for a suitable solution.

I decide to take the opportunity to fill up with fuel at a nearby station. Unfortunately, my motorcycle doesn't want to play ball. Water from the jet spray has penetrated its electrics which causes the engine to run quite lumpily. I freewheel downhill onto the petrol station forecourt, top up the tank, then sit in the afternoon sun sorting out the problem. Spark plug, points and HT pick up all require a thorough dry. The attendant, who watches me work with interest, disappears then returns with a bottle of ice cold Coke. It's a gift, a kind gesture that once again flabbergasts me. I simply cannot imagine a forecourt attendant in the UK or even New Zealand for that matter, treating a stranger in such a way. It seems to please him just as much as me when my bike fires up and settles back into its usual regular rhythm.

I return to my hotel, grab my camera then motor back to Faruk's garage at speed. He's delighted by my offer to take his photo with my old Enfield then send him a copy on my return to the UK. When I say my farewells this time I feel far more comfortable about the time and trouble he has given to assist me.

All this takes seven hours! I can't believe that it´s 4 pm before I have lunch. I find a small cafe that serves menemen, an exquisite Turkish concoction made from eggs, tomatoes and green peppers and eaten with freshly baked bread, then I slowly amble round the hot, fairy-tale streets of Safranbolu. It´s a beautiful place where time appears to have stood still for the last couple of centuries. Most houses, whether grand merchant's dwellings with whitewashed stucco walls or simpler artisan's homes, are superbly well preserved. Lit by the amber light of the setting sun, the cobblestone alleyways take on a iridescent glow and the empty small plaza, ringed by the walls of the old mosque, fruit and vegetable stalls and a couple of tourist gift shops, has a hushed, almost ghostly ambience.

I buy some sun-dried prunes, a veritable taste sensation that I chomp my way through as I walk uphill to the surrounding fields. Once clear of houses, I sit and survey the village from on high. The air is beginning to cool to a very pleasant temperature and various coloured butterflies flutter around my feet. Bliss!

The evening call to prayers rings out from the central mosque, followed seconds later by a boom that bounces around the hillsides like a clap of thunder. Another day of fasting ends for the local population. I make my way back to the centre where the streets are now completely deserted as most people appear to stay in their homes to eat. However, one prosperous café seems to have the monopoly on feeding local men. I look through a window and see that all the tables are full to overflowing with diners tucking into long-awaited meals. I go in search of a meal myself, self-indulgently choosing mememen again, with a glass of cherry juice as an aperitif and an equally heavenly glass of peach juice as a dessert.

On the way back to my hotel I pass the busy café that I had earlier seen. It's still packed out, but now the tables have been cleared of plates and the occupants are all deeply engrossed in various games of cards and backgammon. Going inside for a cup of tea, which is served black inside a small, slender glass, I sit and soak up the convivial atmosphere. There's an almost tangible buzz of bonhomie and revelry around the tables as participants in the numerous games become happily animated about their luck, whether good or bad.

Later, drifting into to sleep, I dream of all the delicious treats I have eaten today, with chocolate smothered toast the last image I remember.

Day 15 Safranbolu to Amasya, Turkey 249 miles

At breakfast I set about making last night's dream come true. Eight slices of toast topped with scrumptious chocolate butter later, I prepare the bike for departure. It's my best start to date as all of my routine checks were made during yesterday's mammoth maintenance session. I roar out of Safranbolu just before 8.30 am and head back towards the main highway.

A delightful thrill grips me when I open the throttle on the first steep hill and accelerate powerfully up it. Over the last few days I've had to manually retard the ignition to avoid pinking on steep hills. Today, that irritating knocking sound has vanished. I don't know whether it's the result of the hard-to-find 97 octane benzine I bought yesterday or the adjustments I made to the tappets and points, but it sure feels good to be riding a motorcycle that's running so superbly well.

Once I rejoin the D-100, I check my Sat Nav's altimeter. It reads sixteen hundred metres. The plains I traverse are spectacularly bare, burnt to a dry sand colour by the heat of summer, and punctuated with isolated dark green trees that make a stark yet beautiful contrast.

I ride mile after mile across the Anatolian high plateau. My mind wanders, latching onto the Clint Eastwood movie title, *High Plains Drifter*, as it's the only phrase I know that's linked to the landscape I'm passing through. I start to whistle Ennio Morricone's theme-tune for *The Good, The Bad and The Ugly* as I don't know the melody for *High Plains Drifter*. Dry lips and the wind in my face make my whistling... challenged. But it gets worse. I'm enjoying today so much that I burst into song. In terms of my street credibility I would have liked things to be different, but what embarrassingly emerges from my mouth is the title-track to the movie *Flashdance*. Why my brain has stored this piece of 80's sentimental synth pop (or should that be pap) I can neither explain or excuse, but sing it I do, at the top of my voice...

"What a feeling, bein's believin'".

Woeful!

After a while the road begins to follow a twisting river. Both banks are covered in lush verdant vegetation that to my eye appears artificially landscaped. It takes me a while to realise I'm flying past hundreds of acres of rice paddies, which is not at all what I expected in this baked area of Turkey. I slow to a stop to take it all in. I now see the zig-zag lines of irrigation ditches that feed off the shimmering pale blue waters of the river. It's an amazing spectacle.

After clocking up one hundred and thirty miles, I stop for lunch at a large petrol station which has a restaurant attached. I sit on a shady verandah and eat cheese, bread, tomatoes and olives... yet again. The latter come served on a separate plate and must number at least fifty. They're plump, salty and totally irresistible. The two young waiters are enthralled by my presence. They first sit at the next table, then, when they can contain their curiosity no more, move in opposite me.

"What country?" one asks.

He must be around sixteen, with jet-black hair and an innocent face that hasn't yet seen a razor blade. I answer, then immediately point back at them and repeat their question with a smile. It tickles them that I should ask, and they reply, "Turkey" in giggling tones.

I arrive at my overnight stop, Amasya, in record time; it's just 3.30 pm. Amasya is the former capital of a Pontic kingdom and is dramatically situated in a deep ravine overlooked by barren craggy hills with several regal tombs hewn into their sides. The lazily moving river Yesilirmak splits the town in half. Its northern embankment is lined by picture-postcard Ottoman houses whilst the southern side contains a more modern town centre. Riding along both banks in search of a bed, I cross backwards and forwards over three narrow bridges. Accommodation is plentiful, but I settle on a secluded converted Ottoman house that has a leafy courtyard in which I can leave the Bullet. It's a wonderful place, featuring a fully restored open air kitchen with a log-fired stove and cast-iron and copper cooking implements hanging on white rendered walls.

My small room is on three levels with scattered Turkish carpets and saddlebags on the wooden floors. I decide it looks like the inside of an old fashioned gypsy caravan and feel bad about spreading my dirty biking gear around. The bathroom presents me with an even tougher problem. The last few pensions I have stayed in have had dark coloured towels. Not today; these are lily white. I avidly wash my face and hands three times before attempting to dry them, but it's to no avail, I still leave great black smudges on the towel.

Thanks to my early start there's time aplenty to wander the streets. I spy a bakery where a crowd of men has gathered, patiently waiting for fresh bread to take home for the end of their fast. The bread is baked in an open-ended oven which the baker's assistant feeds with huge chunks of timber. The loaves are long, flat and even from the street smell delectable. A couple of customers and the baker simultaneously beckon me to enter. I do. The bread is kneaded then butter and sesame seeds sprinkled on the top. A third assistant sits beside a table with a notepad and pen, which he hands to me so that I can add my name to a list. I order a carton of peach juice and wait my turn in the queue.

There must be at least fifteen men waiting with me and although none can speak English, they mostly smile and make me feel very welcome. A batch of loaves emerges from the oven and I'm handed one wrapped in paper by a fellow customer. It´s at least eighteen inches long and blistering hot to the touch. I go the counter to pay for it only to be told that both it and my drink have already been paid for by another patron.

The baker points to a man who is making ready to leave the shop. He comes over, shakes my hand and simply says "welcome". I look into his eyes and am met with nothing more than uncomplicated friendliness and sincerity. I leave after him, once again in complete awe of the hospitality and generosity that I find here.

I carry it back to my pension and sit outside at a small table covered in a checked red tablecloth beside my still cooling Bullet. The young pension manager, Ahmed, notices me picking at the huge plain loaf. He momentarily vanishes, returning with some tangy yoghurt to dip the bread into. I lounge around afterwards, utterly content after such a wonderful day. The shadows are already long and I soon hear the now familiar blast that signifies Iftar. Ahmed has been busy preparing a table for his dinner and he now beckons me to sit with him. I do, assuming he would just like some company. As I sit down I notice he has prepared a place for me opposite him. He proceeds to share his meal, pouring mushroom soup from a pan into my bowl then his own. I watch with fascination as he glugs down a whole glass of water in one swig, his first in over fifteen hours, then waits for me to begin eating first.

I offer my apologies as I pass on the main course, which has meat in it, and share a couple of bananas with more yoghurt for desert. While Ahmed puffs on his first cigarette of the day, we communicate using a well-thumbed English / Turkish dictionary that he produces. We then look at photographs of his family and listen to his favourite Turkish pop songs which are all stored on his mobile phone.

Before bed I reflect on how I treat strangers and how I have so much to learn from the open, genuinely kindhearted people I have met on this journey.

Day 16 Amasya to Erzincan, Turkey
228 miles

Buying contaminated petrol has been a concern since I entered Turkey. To date I've had no problems, but I brought an in-line fuel filter with me as a precaution. This morning, I decide, is an opportune moment to fit it. The pension's manager, cleaner and two other guests all gather round to watch. Once done, I pack for departure, somewhat concerned about the decibel levels my engine will reach in this small courtyard.

The Bullet doesn`t start first kick and the engine feels sluggish when I turn it over. Indeed, after a few attempts I climb off and put it on the centre stand. Things like this always happen when there`s a crowd watching! It loudly starts first kick on the centre stand, so noisily that the cleaner jumps back in fright. I realise that the SAE 50 oil I switched to in Safranbolu is quite a bit thicker than 20/50. When cold, it restricts the momentum I can generate whist kickstarting from the saddle. That`s one I won't forget for future mornings.

The first couple of hours of riding are a joy and I find myself grinning from ear to ear. The scenery reminds me so much of New Zealand. The main road, yes still the D-100, is very similar to State Highway 1, which I've driven many times from Wellington to Auckland. There`s not a cloud in the sky and traffic is minimal, in fact, I'm quite alone for five to ten minutes at a time.

Out of the blue a policeman steps into the road and flags me down. Two smartly-attired officers sit next to a small folding table, a thick ledger in front of them. It`s a police checkpoint and they ask to view my papers. I've seen several of these over the last couple of days but until now have somehow managed to avoid them. Thankfully, formalities are over in a couple of minutes. The police are intrigued by my Camelbak hydration pack, which is, as usual, strapped to my back.

"Parachute?" one asks. I show him how it really works and then we all share the joke when I pretend to pull the drinking tube like a ripcord.

"Are you hungry?" asks the constable who initially stopped me. "We have plenty of apples if you would like some," he continues.

The Amasya region is famed for its apples and I've seen evidence of the vast scale of production at many roadside stalls. However, without exception the apples are sold in bright red 20 KG sacks, and strong as my Enfield is...

I tell the policeman that I do very much like apples, so he beckons me to follow him into the police station garden. It`s beautifully kept, indeed, one of the officers is mowing the lawn as I walk around. He makes quite a strange sight, pushing an ancient hand mower backwards and forwards whilst wearing sharply pressed navy trousers, highly polished black shoes and a crisply ironed sky-blue shirt complete with sergeant stripes and epaulettes. I'm led past a border of neatly planted flowers towards a couple of apple trees. Both are so heavily laden with fruit that their branches visibly sag under the weight.

"Please, fill your pockets," says the policeman, which I do, gratefully thanking him.

Back on the main road I try one; it`s crisp and fresh tasting. All three officers shake my hand before they proceed to hail the next vehicle to stop for inspection.

In the early afternoon the road changes dramatically. Gone is the smooth, wide single lane highway I've enjoyed so much. In its place are relentless miles of roadworks with hideous ridges, swells and ripples in the tarmac. Time and again I`m lulled into a false sense of security by an easily rideable stretch. I build up speed only to hit a bad patch concealed by the shadow of a poplar tree or somehow invisible amongst the patchwork of repairs that have previously been made to the road. I hear the springs in the rear shock absorbers creak as they compress and can feel the weight of my luggage bouncing behind me. I decide to write a letter of thanks on my return to Hagon, the manufacturer of my shock absorbers. It`s amazing they can take so much punishment.

Towards the end of the ride I notice that I`ve been climbing for some time. I check the elevation on my sat nav. 1900, 2000, 2100, 2200, and finally 2250 metres at the summit. The Enfield has climbed ninety percent of it in top gear, which pleases me enormously. The air is noticeably chillier which reminds me that Ted Simon, in his iconic book, *Jupiter`s Travels*, was caught out by snow on a mountain pass shortly after entering Turkey from Iran. I hazard a guess that this could be the place he wrote about.

Shortly afterwards, I descend to the heat of the plains and enter the small but thriving city of Erzincan. A modern hotel is situated right in the middle of the main through road which makes the decision for me to continue no further today. The hotelier stores my bike in the hallway of a neighbouring apartment block that is currently uninhabited. He's a font of knowledge on the city's history, filling me in on its past before I'm even shown to my room.

"Erzincan is famous for its earthquakes," he begins, painting a scary picture of death and destruction that's not necessarily conducive to a good night's sleep.

"There have been many big ones, but 1939 was the worst, with nearly forty thousand citizens killed," he continues.

Then he tells me about the local economy, a healthy combination of heavy industry, particularly sugar refining, and horticulture.

"You must try the locally produced grapes," he enthuses. "They are delicious and now is the best time of year for them."

I promise to follow up on his recommendation. Wandering the streets, I receive many smiles and nods from people. Erzincan doesn't feel like a place that tourists come to. There are no monuments, places of historic interest or spectacular views, but it`s clean, bustling and friendly. What's more, true to the hotelier's promise, the black grapes I buy from a pavement stall are about as good as they come.

I eat at a self-service restaurant popular with young office workers. They all get their meals then sit patiently waiting for the signal that the sun has set and they can begin to eat. Out of respect I do the same with my meal. As the loud boom reverberates around the city streets it`s fascinating to watch about forty people all reach for a glass and gulp down their first drink of water in unison. The temperature has been well in the high thirties today and I admire their dedication to abstain from drinking in such heat... I`ve drunk four litres whilst riding and am still thirsty.

Ambling back to my hotel, I see an older building with a small domed roof. Next to a recessed wooden door is a plaque which reads Hamam. It's a Turkish bathhouse, just what I need after today's long, hot ride. The first room I enter is a general waiting area with a row of small locked changing compartments along one side. I'm silently handed two towels and a thin cotton sarong by the attendant, who points me towards an empty changing room.

Emerging a few minutes later wearing nothing but the sarong around my middle, I'm led through a doorway into the business-end of the establishment. It's a steamy, classically domed room with aged plaster walls. Marble benches are situated along two of the walls, with three stone fonts filled by dripping brass taps at their ends. In the middle is a large marble slab where an overweight older man is having the living daylights beaten out of him by a strapping young masseur.

I sit for a while and watch the painful proceedings, then make my way through a doorway into the next room. It's much hotter in here and I break into an instant sweat. Two other men recline on marble benches and a third washes himself down in cool water that he ladles from a font. I follow his lead. The water feels icy in comparison to the room temperature, but it's deliciously cooling. I dip into it frequently over the next half an hour whilst waiting for my turn on the slab.

The masseur comes to get me. I lie down on the acutely uncomfortable marble. Beginning by stretching each of my arms in turn, he then goes on to remove at least three layers of skin with a coarse glove he wears on his right hand. He sagely points to my arm which I see is covered in hundreds of tiny rolls of black dead skin. The rest of my body gets the same thorough rasping before a bizarre soapy wash. Nothing could have prepared me for this procedure. A large pillowcase is soaked then rubbed into a solution of lavender-scented soap. The masseur proceeds to hit me all over with it, creating giant airy puffs of bubbles which get into my eyes and up my nose. He follows this by using his hands to knead my muscles whist simultaneously rubbing the soap into my already stinging skin.

After a thorough soaking with cold water, I'm treated to the kind of pummeling I'd witnessed earlier. With the fleshy inside of his fists, my assailant beats my back and leg muscles then karate chops my neck and shoulders. Moving happily on, he strongly pulls my hands, legs and arms to what feels like their breaking point and yanks each finger and toe until it clicks. I manage not to call out in pain, but it's touch and go.

He laughs when I weakly stand up, giving me one final slap on the back in a rough 'no hard feelings' kind of way. I leave feeling incredibly clean and refreshed but rather wobbly at the knees.

Day 17 Erzincan to Dogubayazit, Turkey
301 miles

Today gets off to a great start. I ride along a narrow valley which follows a fast-flowing river that twists this way and that with the contours of the surrounding hills. Catching a movement out of the corner of my eye, I notice a train running parallel to me on the opposite bank. Our paths seem to be merging, then it races across an iron bridge just ahead of me. I can see that it's a long-distance overnight service as sleeping compartments and a dining carriage make up about half of its length. Predominately painted a rich cream colour, it's topped with a rounded royal blue roof and has subtle red and blue pinstriping along its sides. Softly illuminated by the early morning light that highlights it against the golden rocks of the valley sides, it makes a handsome sight.

The train is now ahead of me but on my side of the river. Inch by inch I gradually overhaul it. I can just read the boards positioned by each carriage door, ERZURUM EXPRESS, and I guess it must be the overnight train from Istanbul. Until this trip by motorcycle, my most memorable journeys have been made on overnight and intercontinental trains. There's something magical about the atmosphere of anticipation at railway stations, the rat-a-tat-tat of steel wheels on railtracks, pleasant company around a dining carriage table and the gentle rocking rhythm that infuses a deep slumber in a couchet car.

Filled with these romantic and reminiscent thoughts, I eventually draw up alongside the locomotive. The driver has one elbow casually placed outside of his open window and he's obviously aware of me and my steady progress up the length of the train. Just as I wave to him he sounds his horn and simultaneously waves to me. I toot my horn back and shout out 'yeeha!', over-the-moon about the synchronicity of our encounter. Within a minute my road crosses a another bridge and we part company.

Much of the day`s ride is at altitudes between fifteen hundred and two thousand metres. The countryside becomes wilder and more barren the further east I travel. As foretold by Jonny Krause, I run into roadworks like none I have ever seen before. When the Turkish transport authority decide to upgrade a road, they certainly do it on a grand scale. One set of roadworks involves opposing traffic sharing the same narrow space for more than five kilometres. The top has been scraped off the old road and rocks and potholes are everywhere. Trucks coming towards me throw up huge clouds of dust and send a shower of small stones clattering in every direction. It's impossible to get out of first gear and I have to weave from side to side to avoid the worst patches. I stop after a while, remove the air filter element from its housing and tip a fine layer of dust, sand and even granules of stone into my hand.

Passing many tiny villages, I note that the style of housing has definitely changed. Gone are the apartment blocks and modern concrete dwellings I've seen right across Turkey. These villages have ramshackle stone cottages, most with a mud brick outbuilding shaped like a tall termite mound. I`m not sure what these are but guess they must be some form of rudimentary food storage facility. The architecture of mosques has changed too. In western and central Turkey, many were built in a modern style with stainless steel minarets at their side that made me think of the Saturn 5 space rocket. Here, they are much simpler affairs, often little more than a small concrete minaret attached to the side of a slightly bigger but nonetheless regular looking dwelling.

The people look different too. Their skin colour is much darker and they're certainly more vocal as I pass. I'm called to and waved at by most of the folk that notice me. The children are especially expressive, often running to the roadside, hollering and waving at my approach. In the fields I see the most gorgeous donkeys with their babies, mountains of loose hay waiting to be collected and herds of cattle which ragamuffin-like boys shepherd with the aid of huge white farm dogs.

Roughly fifty kilometres from Dogubayazit, I round a bend and behold a spine tingling site. Snowcapped Mount Ararat lies directly ahead. It has an almost ethereal quality seen from this distance with a faint heat haze concealing the lower slopes and its fairy-tale white peak glowing in the late afternoon sunlight. I`m under pressure to reach Dogubayazit before dark, but cannot resist stopping to take a photograph.

Looking for a suitable place, I crest the summit of a hill and brake hard to pull into a dirt track that leads towards a large farmhouse. Just as I come to a standstill, rapid movement to my left catches my attention. Two enormous hounds, one a savage-looking white sheepdog and the other a fierce Alsatian, are cornering a bend in the track like greyhounds after a hare. It might be fascinating to watch the muscles ripple down their backs as they scorch over the ground in the most fluid of movements, but I am obviously today's hare and judging by their large bared teeth, I reckon I need to get the hell out of here.

I accelerate away just in the nick of time, following their vain attempts to catch me in the bike's mirrors. They eventually come to a halt, howling at me with obvious disappointment. Seeing another photogenic spot a few kilometres further on, I stop, set my camera to self-timer mode on the top of a pile of sand, rocks and stones that's at least three metres high, and dash back to the Bullet to get into shot. My first attempt is a disaster when I tumble head over heels down the slope and just reach the bike, cursing and covered in dust, as the shutter clicks. My second, more cautious attempt is happily successful.

I can't stop thinking about my motorcycle in the most glowing, almost loving terms. Andy has built a peach of an engine and I'm delighted by how it performs. It just goes on and on, no matter how hot if gets or how many hours a day it's ridden. It pulls smartly up hills despite my heavy bags yet is flexible when crawling around busy city streets as I look for a hotel.

I'm feeling pretty elated by the time I finally pull up in the rear car park of the Hotel Grand Derya in Dogubayazit. Today was a huge ride with just over ten hours in the saddle. My hands ache and my neck is stiff, but I'm now within fifteen miles of the frontier with Iran and will cross tomorrow morning. It`s a country that I`m deeply excited about seeing and experiencing, but I can't help feeling that I've only, naturally I suppose, scratched the surface of Turkey with its magnificent scenery and wonderful people.

The Grand Derya is a throwback to much more prosperous times. It has a large foyer with numerous sofas, lounge chairs and coffee tables and the reception desk is long enough to accommodate four staff working side by side. Sadly, business doesn't look that good. The carpet is threadbare and the lone man behind the counter, the duty manager, tells me that I'm the only foreign guest tonight. I'm somewhat surprised given the close proximity of Mt. Ararat, the supposed resting place of Noah's biblical ark. After filling in the registration form, I ask for directions to a restaurant where I can get vegetarian food.

"Please come back in forty-five minutes," he replies. "It's Ramadan and I'm just about to eat my meal; but afterwards I will escort you to a suitable restaurant."

I shower and begin to sort through my belongings. There's a knock at the door. It's the duty manager, with yet another gift of food.

"I thought you would like this," he says, offering me a plate of vegetables and a cheese pastry slice. How he's managed to procure them at such short notice is a puzzle, but they are gratefully received. Five minutes later there's a quieter knock at my door. A boy of about ten smiles up at me, holding a fruit slice and cream on a plate for me to take.

He runs away laughing when I take possession of the treat and thank him.

I spend my final night in Turkey drinking tea on the main shopping street. An area of three blocks has been recently pedestrianised, with numerous wooden benches placed beside small raised flowerbeds. All of the surrounding shops remain open but they don't seem to be doing any trade as the street has been adopted as a giant open-air communal café. A dozen waiters walk up and down the paving delivering glasses of tea to groups of men who sit talking, playing cards or smoking cigarettes. Three old men chatting quietly amongst themselves huddle closer together and, using hand gestures, invite me to sit and share their bench. The hubbub is energising as I watch hundreds of people walking up and down, greeting friends and sparking up new conversations.

"Welcome to Kurdistan," says a stranger, sticking his hand out for me to shake.

I grasp the proffered hand and thank him. He smiles and continues on his way. His salutation reminds me that Dogubayazit is part of the often troubled region of western Iran, northern Iraq and Eastern Turkey inhabited by Kurdish people who have long demanded self-rule. The armed conflict of the 1990's may now have passed, but the desire for autonomy by the Kurds apparently remains strong. The chattering buzz gradually recedes as people begin to make their way home and I head for an internet cafe to try to catch up on my blog, which is embarrassingly behind schedule.

Day 18 Dogubayazit to Maku, Iran
44 miles

Mt. Ararat looks completely different this morning. The sun rising behind it creates a surreal effect as its slopes appear dark and foreboding against the glow that spreads around its edges. It's so eye-catching that I constantly have to remind myself to pay attention to the road ahead.

Leaving Turkey proves to be more difficult than entering Iran. I spend over an hour taking my passport and motorcycle documents to a succession of officials in various offices and booths to get their approval. This means leaving my bike and equipment unattended for long periods of time. At the start of my journey this would have made me very nervous but now I feel quite comfortable with it. It's surprising just how quickly one adapts to new situations. Eventually the gates to Turkey close behind me and those into Iran open ahead.

It takes just one stamp in my passport at a quiet immigration counter and ten minutes for two customs officials to process my carnet, before I am free to enter Iran. There's a bank in the immigration hall so I take the opportunity to change money. I hand over US $150 and I receive in return 1,452,000 rials in 10,000 rial notes. The bills are all used and about the size of British £20 notes. They make a considerable wad, almost four inches thick. For a moment I'm tempted to wave it around like comedian Harry Enfield, calling out "Loadsamoney" in my best mock Cockney accent, but think better of it. My pockets cannot accommodate such a solid wedge of paper so in the end I stuff it all into a backpack on the bike. 'Where am I going to keep it all?' I wonder, just glad I didn't change more.

I'm confused about what to expect of Iran. Certainly, if the stereotypes portrayed by the western media were typical, I would be at risk of being mobbed by gangs of fanatics shouting anti-American slogans and the like from the moment I enter the country. Consequently, over the last six months I've spent more time researching the place and what I am likely to find here than I have any other country on my route. Without exception, all the reports I have read about travelling in Iran, both online and in travel books, concur that that Iranian people are exceedingly hospitable and consider it their duty to look after visitors to their country.

It's difficult to see the truth amongst all the contradictions and complexities of Iran's international image. Is it secretly developing the bomb? Or, is its nuclear energy programme, which has been inspected by scientists from the International Atomic Energy Agency on numerous occasions and adheres to the terms of the Nuclear Non-Proliferation Treaty, peaceful? Is it a serious threat to the existence of Israel, considering the incumbent president, Mahmoud Ahmadinejad, is reported to have declared "The occupying regime in Palestine should vanish from the page of time"? Or, is it tolerant of other religions, like the Christian (250,000) and Jewish (estimated 25,000 - 35,000) minorities who live in Iran and have guaranteed seats in the Majlis, the Iranian parliament? I'm also bewildered by the position of women in Iran. They can work, drive, own property, study at university (currently two-thirds of all university entrants are women), vote and become a member of parliament. Yet showing too much make-up or too little veil can result in arrest and even flogging.

Axis of Evil? For me it's more a case of axis of confusion. I decide my best policy is, as always, to take people as I find them and to refrain from judging things I cannot fully understand.

With my head full of these baffling thoughts, I ride across the Customs compound, hand over my 'cleared to go' chit at the gatehouse, and steadily make my way forward. In Iran, the clocks are one and a half hours ahead of Turkey. I decide only to ride a short distance and spend some time acquainting myself with this new country. I pass quickly through the border settlement and onto the first major town, Maku. The main street spans several kilometres along the bottom of a deep and narrow gorge. The rock formations on both sides tower high above the buildings and the dark clouds of an electrical storm coming from the west add to the enclosed feeling.

I struggle to find a hotel. After fifteen minutes driving fruitlessly around, I stop and ask a photocopy shopkeeper for directions. Within a minute a crowd of five men have gathered round me, debating my options in quickfire Farsi. A taxi stops to see what's so interesting. One of my helpers goes over to talk with him, tells him the name of Maku's best, and probably only, hotel and instructs him to lead me to it.

I follow the taxi for nearly ten minutes, during which time he picks up a fare. He comes to a sudden halt and points to my accommodation, The Tourist Inn. He gives me a thumbs up accompanied by a cheerful grin then speedily zooms off with his passenger before I have the chance to ask him what I owe for his time.

I enjoy walking the streets of Maku. Because of Ramadan, very few shops and certainly no cafes or restaurants are open. I buy fresh bread, goats cheese, tomatoes, peaches and pears, which I eat out of sight on my hotel balcony. It's probable I'll have to do self catering for lunch whilst crossing Iran. I haven't the stamina to ride all day on an empty stomach and at present, it appears that it will be more difficult to get food in the daytime here than it was in Turkey.

The day doesn't end well. The town's only internet cafe has a connection speed so painfully slow that I lose my blog entry twice then get caught out in a flash thunderstorm whilst running back to my hotel. Once the storm has cleared, I decide to do some work on the bike. As the roads have become progressively dustier and sandier I determine it's time to change the chain.

I've brought a Iwis Megalife chain specifically for these conditions. As it can run almost dry, it won't pick up as much destructive sand. I remove the old chain, which still has plenty of life in it, and thread through the Megalife. Blindly feeding it out of a plastic bag, it seems to go on and on. The starting link comes through the bottom of the drive sprocket yet I still have more than a metre remaining in the bag. With an audible groan I realise what I've done. The chain came on a five metre roll. Before setting off I cut a length of ninety four links specially for the journey. Undoubtably those links are still sitting on the kitchen table in my flat and I've brought the balance of the five metres with me. A small crowd of guests and hotel staff have gathered around to watch me work. They must think me totally mad as I replace the original chain. I determine to keep my eyes open tomorrow for a motorcycle shop that has a chain splitter.

Another tourist, wearing a sky blue Oasis t-shirt, enters the hotel restaurant where I sit and wait for my evening meal of omelette and chips. I wave for him to come and join me. He tells me his name is Dave, he's from Milton Keynes in the UK, and got his 28-day tourist visa for Iran whilst backpacking in Turkey. He's just as fascinated and excited about being in the country as I am and we spend a good hour discussing places we have been or intend to go. It's not long before, as is often the case when travellers meet, we get round to discussing the state of our bowels. This is usually more of a topic of conversation for visitors to countries such as India, but Dave has suffered a bad dose of 'Bosphorus-bottom' in Turkey and is worried about what lies ahead. He's pleased when I tell him that the tap water in Iran is safe to drink, which reminds me that I must fill up my Camelbak and spare water bottle in preparation for tomorrow's ride.

We part with wishes of "Go well," and "Have a good one."

Day 19 Maku to Zanjan, Iran
359 miles

My first experience of an Iranian benzine (petrol) station is a shocker... it's bedlam. Cars, motorcycles and trucks all vie for position. There's a queue of sorts, but many drivers simply angle their vehicles around it and somehow find their way to the pumps whilst others are left waiting out on the road. There's a lot of loud discussion and one poor harried attendant running around with a fistful of cash trying to sort it all out.

I join a queue of motorcycles which moves much faster as their average purchase is just a few litres. The sale of petrol is supposed to work on a ration card basis. I don't have one of these but the attendant produces a black-market one from an inside pocket like a magician. My tank is filled... eleven litres cost an astonishing £2.90. I feel very chuffed about this boost to my funds.

Iranian cars are of great interest to me. The poor state of the economy, a history of domestic manufacturing protected by heavy import duties and more recently, international trade sanctions, means that the locally produced Paykan is king of the road. It's a copy of the 1600 cc Hillman Hunter which was launched in the UK in 1967 and continued to be produced in a series of improved versions until 1979. Full production of the Paykan commenced in Iran in 1972 and continued unchanged until 2005! The car's paint schemes contribute to the time warp. The most popular colours I see are duck-egg green, powder blue and a deep burnt orange, all highly reminiscent of the early 1970s. There are obvious parallels between the continued production of Royal Enfields in India and the Paykan, and I love seeing so many of this venerable old machine in everyday use.

The first hundred miles of my journey today are relatively quiet, with smooth straight roads, light traffic and flat, arid countryside. The only blot on a super ride is the incidence of speed bumps in and around towns and villages. These take up so much of my attention that I invent silly names to categorise them as I go along:

The vicious kicker. Usually painted yellow and black, they're 20 cm tall and approximately 30 cm wide. They give my front suspension a brutal jolt even at low speeds.

The take off ramp. These are really tall, as much as a metre, but can be more than 4 m long so there's a long climb and descent. Hit at speed my motorcycle wheels actually leave the tarmac.

Crumblies. These have deteriorated somewhat. I change my angle of approach at the last minute to get the best passage over them. Unfortunately, every other vehicle on the road is doing the same and they're generally bigger than me.

The secret sleeping policeman. The worst of all. Unmarked, I often know nothing of them until my front forks bottom out with the shock. They're mean enough to do some serious damage if hit too hard.

As I near my first major Iranian city, Tabriz, traffic really builds up. There are so many heavily laden, old trucks pumping out nasty, choking, black fumes. I smile to myself thinking that my mum, who's Scottish, would call their smoke 'stuke'. Navigation becomes increasingly difficult as my focus is completely taken up in not becoming a casualty of this automotive nightmare. No heed is paid to lane markings by my fellow road users. Red traffic lights are run and hair-raising overtaking is commonplace. With all my luggage, the Enfield feels heavy and cumbersome. I try a spell of going slowly in the inside lane but that's even more dangerous! Buses and cars come to a screeching halt to pick up some of the many people waiting at the roadside. Often doing this from the outside lane, they end up diagonally parked across my path then, without signaling, swing back out into the traffic with equal reckless abandon. The inside lane is also the starting point for the many acclimatised jay walkers who seem remarkably cool and composed... which is a long way from how I'm feeling.

I spot a motorway sign for Tehran. It's a toll road and I drive towards it without a moment's thought. I'm waved through the toll booths that mark the beginning of the highway by a young man who smiles cheerfully at me and my motorcycle. I want to avoid the capital, a megalopolis of twelve million, but it lies in a south easterly direction so is good enough for now. For almost two hours I have the road completely to myself. It's approximately three lanes and a hard shoulder wide, but there are no lane markings. It feels like racing in a continuous sprint on an airport runway and I frequently have to throttle back as I lose concentration and pick up too much speed.

The scenery changes. As the motorway climbs, the rocky hills take on a red tinge with occasional outcrops of sage coloured stone. Some of the patterns in the rock are strangely symmetrical and quite beautiful. I see several villages made entirely of small adobe (sun-dried mud brick) dwellings. The only feature that differentiates them from the baked land that surrounds them is a coat of whitewash around their doors and windows. There are often flocks of long eared, black mountain sheep being herded nearby, which gives the scene a certain quality of timelessness.

A monstrous headwind gets up startlingly fast. As I come over the apex of a particularly high point in the road, it blasts into the front of my bike so strongly that I have to grit my teeth and hold onto the handlebars for dear life. The road begins to steeply descend. I'm in top gear riding at 80 KMPH, but the gale slows me rapidly to 70... 60... 50. I shift down into third and rev hard but continue being slowed down, weaving from one side of the carriageway to the other. It's terrifying; I'm riding down a steep hill being remorselessly driven backwards by the savage, howling wind.

A truck goes by in the opposite direction. It creates a vortex that sucks at the straining bike from underneath and almost flings me off it. Then, wham, the full force of the gale hits me again and I'm slowed to 30. I desperately step down into second gear and rev furiously, certain I'm going to be blown off at any second. The road sweeps left into a long cutting, taking the wind to my right then mercifully completely shielding me from it. I pull over to the side to catch my breath for fifteen minutes before daring to take on any more battles with the elements.

It's almost dark when I reach Zanjan, a small city renowned for the production of handicrafts such as silverware and hand-knotted carpets. Before departure, I padded my saddle with three layers of a yoga mat to increase my comfort, but after more than nine hours solid riding I'm very stiff. The city centre streets are congested with small cars and motorcycles, which makes tough going of finding a hotel. The first I try has no parking and the second is full. The third hotel, possibly my last chance for a room before dark, is around a kilometre from the centre and relatively expensive, but it has a locked compound where I can park securely.

It brings home to me one of the differences between overlanding by public transport and by motorcycle. I pay far more for accommodation when travelling by bike than I ever would when using public transport, simply because of the need for parking. Furthermore, I'm so exhausted by the end of a day on the road that the perceived benefit of having my own set of wheels to search for cheaper alternatives is actually a false one. The thought of spending an hour trawling round every hotel in town is too daunting. It's all part of one steep learning curve for me.

I draw a complete blank on vegetarian food tonight, giving in after a search that encompasses most city restaurants, the best of which comes up with a bland offering of rice and yoghurt. So I buy more bread, cheese, tomatoes and fruit along with a super-sweet chunk of helva, a Middle-Eastern concoction of sesame flour and honey. Eating in in my room, I fall asleep as soon as I've finished.

Day 20 Zanjan to Saveh, Iran
210 miles

I don't feel as though I've actually interacted very much with Iranians yet and set off today hoping to spend less time in the saddle and more time meeting people. My wishes are met almost immediately. There's a petrol station practically opposite my hotel, but it has no Benzine Super and I'm concerned about running on lowly 92 octane fuel. A man on a motorcycle approaches,

"Benzine Super?" he asks, pats his chest then points along a road.

I follow him, which is no easy feat as he ducks and dives amongst the rush hour traffic. Within five minutes I'm parked at another petrol station and this one has what I want. My guide shakes my hand then rides off.

An hour later, riding along the same toll motorway as yesterday, I'm flagged down by a policemen with a radar gun and camera. I know what's coming. The motorways are motorcycle no-go zones. There are signs at every on-ramp showing that bicycles, horsedrawn carts and motorbikes are not allowed. That said, I've seen a few 125 cc bikes riding along the hard shoulder, in fact sometimes against the flow of traffic! I've also been waved through every toll booth by the attendants, usually after they've asked what country I am from.

The traffic officer and I play a time-honoured game. He knows I know that I shouldn't be there, no matter how powerful my motorcycle. I feign innocence, language difficulties, surprise and finally conciliatory regret. He nods, lights a cigarette and turns back to his radar. I thank him and ride on. I'm sure he expects me to stay on the motorway, but duty has been done

As I want to bypass Tehran and head due south, I exit the toll road about a hundred and fifty kilometres short of the capital and begin to cross wide open plains. There's nothing in sight except the road, sand, scrubby plants and some distant hazy mountains. Two teenagers on a 100 cc motorcycle follow me for quite a few kilometres. I can tell they're struggling to keep up with my speed, but they hang on in, determined to keep apace. Every so often, engine revving way into the red, they pull up alongside and wave fervently at me, huge smiles splitting their faces, before dropping behind once again. It's a bit distracting as I'd hate to be indirectly responsible for them blowing up their engine, but their light-hearted company is very welcome.

The cross wind increases until it becomes a hazard. It whips up sand and blasts it against my right cheek. My right nostril quickly dries and begins to burn. The danger increases two-fold when large arctics and other assorted trucks pass in the opposite direction. They create a maelstrom of unsteady air that tosses my bike from side to side. I make a snap decision to pull off the road and see if the brutal wind will blow itself out.

I haul on my anchors and turn onto a barely distinguishable track that heads into the desert. I halt head-on to the wind, plant my feel securely to the hard sandy ground and brace myself. A minute later, having turned around, my two companions pull up by my side. They can't speak any English but with their hands and concerned expressions, check that I'm okay. I smile and point to my bags on the back, wobbling the bike at the same time to emphasise the difficulties I'm experiencing in the wind. Obviously more accustomed than me to riding in these conditions, they nevertheless stay with me for a good twenty minutes by which time the wind seems to have dropped a little, enabling me to set off again.

My escorts wave goodbye and peel off the highway after a further ten kilometres. I continue south, still leaning sideways to counteract the strong wind, until, feeling battered and quite drained, I reach the shelter of the town on Bo'un.

On the far side of town I stop to rest, sneaking a quick English muesli bar to boost my energy levels. I'm sprung. A man has quietly come up behind me and seen me eating. I apologise quickly and explain that I have a long way to ride and need sustenance.

"It's not a problem" he says in excellent English. "Just because my religion leads me to fast doesn't mean that you have to as well." He continues, "let me get you some tea".

Several minutes later he returns with a glass of refreshing black tea and introduces himself as Ali. We talk awhile and he gives me some insights into Iranian politics, which even he finds bemusing. Finishing his explanations, he says,

"Please don't judge all Persian or Iranian people by the messages or claims of the government."

He then invites me to stay and have a traditional Persian meal with his family. As I've covered relatively few miles and dinner is still more than five hours away, I sadly decline his offer. Like many people I meet in Iran, Ali gestures to me by putting his hand on his heart and wishes me well on my journey.

Some time later I arrive at the top of a large incline which gives me a huge panoramic view for many miles. Large storm clouds passing from west to east move slowly across the sky with clear lines of rain at their rear. They're right in my path, some five to ten kilometres ahead. I park my bike, sit down and watch them continue on their way. After half an hour I judge they've moved on sufficiently for me to continue. It feels great to be able to react to nature in this way. Very Zen, I mockingly say to myself, but reflect that at home I would have cursed, put on my wet-weather gear and pushed on, which makes it good to be able to respond differently here.

I arrive at the outskirts of Saveh around 5 pm. As usual, motorcyclists scoot round me on their Honda 125s. Many wave, smile or shout

"Hello. Are you from Germany / Italy / England?"

Today I try a new tactic for finding a hotel. I respond to the first who rides next to me and can clearly speak English, with

"Do you know a hotel with parking?"

He nods and beckons me to follow him. A few kilometres later we arrive at a smart hotel near the city centre. It has underground parking and an en suite room for less than £9 with breakfast. I would never have spotted it on my own. The bike rider, Mehmet, watches over my bike while I check in. He's very congenial and delighted to have been able to help, again, so typical of the Iranian people I have met today. They are inquisitive about where I am from and what my impressions are of Iran. If they speak English, they ask if I need any assistance and are genuine about their desire to help.

The hotel can also feed me. A break from bread, white cheese and tomatoes is very welcome. Scrambled egg, rice and salad never tasted so good! I do, however, need some bread for tomorrow's provisions. In the evening I wander the streets in search of a shop. When I ask for directions, a man roughly my own age leads me to a small bakery. There's a long queue of men on the street, with a much shorter line of women at the side. The shop has a glass window through which I can see dough being placed on a revolving grill that turns inside a large, wood burning oven. As the fresh bread emerges, it's handed to a man who collects money at the half-open horizontally split door. The women, all dressed in black chadors, get served first, with the men taking their turn once each of the women has left.

I imagine it's a scene repeated every day and there's certainly a real sense of community in the queue as people shake hands with new arrivals and make jokes with their friends. A couple of men speak English, patting me on the back and ushering me forward when it's my turn to be served. Everyone carries their loaves away in their hands, but I need a bag as my bread will have to be carried on my bike tomorrow. The shop has none, but a man next to me in the queue asks me to wait while he gets one from his house. He returns a couple of minutes later with a simple polythene bag for me to use.

I wander back to my hotel where I settle for a last cup of tea in the restaurant.

"Would you like a beer?" asks the waiter.

My mouth all but drops open in surprise. Alcohol? In Iran?

I ask the waiter if I can see the beer. He promptly goes and gets a can from a fridge. I examine it closely. The label reads *Behnoush Delster*. I look closer until it registers; of course, it's non-alcohol beer. I try it all the same and a very pleasant way it is to end the day too.

Day 21 Saveh to Esfahan, Iran
204 miles

Two young boys haul a rickety wooden handcart along the road on which I'm loading my bike. They stop, captivated by the sight of me and my obviously foreign motorcycle. I smile at them and they shyly wave, their faces all toothy-grins. Back inside the hotel, I ask the receptionist what they are doing with the cart.

"Today (Thursday) is the start of the weekend in Iran," he replies. "These boys and many like them go round collecting old newspapers on their day off school. They make a few rials recycling the paper and that gives them some pocket money."

The boys don't seem to be in a particular hurry to amass recyclables today and stay watching me for an entire thirty minutes while I clean my bike's points and check around its fasteners.

The concept of weekend rest doesn't seem to register with truck drivers, who are out in force. Most ponderous of them all are pre-revolution American Mack trucks. These worn out behemoths appear to chug along in first gear whatever the terrain. Their loads are invariably either steel or huge chunks of marble the size of a family car. They're a menace as many other slow trucks, that can actually get into second gear, form a traffic jam trying to overtake them. I joke to myself that, due to US sanctions, they're the only Big Macs to be seen in Iran.

The countryside continues to be barren, a sepia tone of dull grey and sand colours that makes a stark contrast to the beautifully vibrant landscapes I had travelled through in Europe and most of Turkey. The enormous blue skies, that give a sense of Walt Whitman's "vast rondure swimming in space", stretch across to the horizon, redeeming the otherwise harshly empty scene.

I arrive at the outskirts of Esfahan (also known as Isfahan) liberatingly early. Again, my motorcycle is filthy, this time more with dust and sand than the spray of oil which had previously plagued it. I find a car wash run by a very quiet and humble Afghan refugee. Apparently there are more than a million exiled Afghanis in Iran, displaced by the various wars and internal conflicts that have beset that country for the last three decades. He takes great care cleaning my bike, which includes protecting the MagDyno and points with plastic bags. His two absolutely delightful young children, both with rag-tail jet black hair, watch on, joining in eagerly with the soapy bit.

A crowd of onlookers gathers and some of them help by wiping excess water off the paintwork with cloths and blowing it off the engine and electrics with an air hose. Next comes a round of pictures taken beside the bike using their mobile phones. I laugh, thinking that my Enfield has a kind of celebrity status here thanks to its classic character and age.

The run into the city centre is fraught. My route is punctuated by a series of roadworks that close the main drag and force me to work my way grid-like along back streets. maintaing my orientation in order to regain the main road at some later point. The city has a population of over one and a half million and the suburbs are an absolute throng of activity today. However, when I finally reach the centre, heading along the main thoroughfare, Chahar Bagh Abassi St., traffic and pedestrians have thinned considerably, making it much easier for me to ride slowly around in search of a room.

I find a hotel with underground parking and set about some maintenance, planning to complete all necessary chores today in order to enjoy a full day off tomorrow. Top of the list is an oil change, but I doubt I'll find a workshop smack bang in the city centre where I can do it. I opt for the plastic bag method instead. It doesn't go very well. No matter how many bags I use, hot viscous oil oozes out onto the concrete floor. Fortunately, I choose a spot where many Paykans have previously parked and my small slick is lost amongst dark grey smudges caused by years of dripping sumps. The staff assure me it's not a problem, but I still spend more time cleaning up with newspaper than I do actually changing the oil.

Considering my options, I toy with secreting the bags of old oil into the hotel's rubbish bins, but decide against it as burying the stuff in landfill is a less than ideal method of disposal. I messily pour it into my empty spare fuel can, hoping I can soon safely deposit it at a car or motorcycle garage.

Returning to my room, I shower, and prepare myself for dinner. As my shoulders feel knotted and stiff from riding so many miles over the last three days, I decide to spend ten minutes lying on the floor doing yoga stretches. At home, I try to take a regular weekly Iyengar yoga class as I find it wonderfully relaxing and a valuable form of exercise. It was my plan to practice regularly on this trip, hoping it would keep me supple and counteract the number of hours I spend hunched up over my handlebars. In truth, until today I've been so preoccupied with the myriad of challenges on the journey that it has completely slipped my mind.

The result is immediately beneficial for my shoulders and back. However, whilst prostrate on the carpet a 'wee beastie' hops on board and proceeds to take chunks out of me. Within a quarter of an hour this amounts to nineteen red, itchy bites on my legs and groin. I take another shower just to make sure I'm completely rid of the little blighter(s).

After an adequate dinner in the hotel's 'penthouse' restaurant, I go, hopefully, in search of a café I read about many years ago. In his book, *Wrong Way Home*, travel author Peter Moore spends many days in Esfahan drinking tea and smoking flavoured tobacco from traditional hookah pipes. His favourite haunt is an ancient tea house under the arches of the beautiful two-story Si-o-se Po pedestrian bridge that is frequented mainly by retired locals. I find the bridge and the tea house, but it's deserted. There's not a single pipe smoker in sight. I visit two other tea houses, but disappointingly, both are closed.

I wander the riverbank and streets until very late. There are still many people about; dating couples, older families having late picnics in parks and beside the river, teenagers pulling wheelies on mountain bikes and elderly men and women standing on street corners talking. Even at 11 pm, strolling along dark tree-lined avenues beside the river, I feel completely safe.

Returning to my room, I switch on the television expecting to find nothing but programmes in Farsi. To my amazement I find the BBC World News. The major headline is a fire in the Channel Tunnel, which looks likely to close it in both directions for several days. Fortunately, no one is injured and I thank my lucky stars that I'm not one of the thousands of disappointed people trapped each side of the crossing.

The second news item has far more relevance to my journey. It's reported that American forces in Afghanistan have fired missiles on villages in Pakistan, killing innocent people in their endeavours to hit Taliban leaders thought to be sheltering there. The Pakistan government is said to be outraged as the missiles have been launched into their country without consultation. I just hope matters don't escalate before I arrive there in just a few days time.

Day 22 Esfahan, Iran
0 miles

Esfahan is a bewitching city famous for its Islamic architecture, with many beautiful boulevards, covered bridges, palaces, mosques, and minarets. For centuries it has been held in such high esteem by Persians that the proverb, 'Esfahān nesf-e jahān asst', (Esfahan is half of the world), became part of their culture.

In the morning, I wander deserted streets and end up in the mightily impressive Naqsh-e Jahan Square, which has recently been renamed Imam Square. It's one of the largest city squares in the world and has been designated as a UNESCO World Heritage Site. Located at its southern end, the early seventeenth century Imam mosque has the most beautiful onion-shaped dome I have ever seen. Towering high above the rest of the square, it's completely covered in turquoise mosaics with intricate geometric patterns and inscriptions.

Being a Friday, all mosques are closed to visitors except during prayers, so I miss out on seeing its reportedly stunning internal architecture. Instead, I make my way to the northern end of the square which leads to Bazar-e Bozorg. It's a rabbit warren comprising of hundreds of shops running along fully enclosed timeworn cobbled streets. Each street is covered by a series of arched shaped caverns formed from a honeycombed structure of tan coloured bricks. At the peak of each arch is a tiny round skylight that allows a sharp ray of sunlight to shine through, illuminating the whole street in a succession of brilliant beams of light. Once more, I have the place to myself, my footsteps echoing around the walls and doors of the closed shops.

Following my map to Jameh mosque, Esfahan's largest place of worship, I sit quietly in a corner and watch crowds arrive for prayers. The women, all in black, outnumber the men. They cross the main compound in large, chatting groups en route to their own separate female sanctuary in which they pray. None of the men seem to mind me being there. Many nod, smile or greet me with 'As-Salamu Alaykum' (literal meaning 'peace be upon you') as they pass. I watch as they perform wudu, the ritual ablution before prayers of washing face and arms then wiping the head and feet with the moisture on the hands. Here it takes place at a small fountain and flower-shaped pool, situated in the middle of the mosque, that the men patiently gather round.

While the worshippers prostrate themselves, a mullah recites prayers over the mosque's public address system. The sound of his light voice is peaceful and slightly mesmerising. There's much I still want to see and explore in Esfahan but it seems rude to get up and walk out in the middle of such devout worship. I quietly stay in my corner and leave as soon as the prayers end.

Being very low on rials, I eat and drink simply throughout the day. The banks are all closed and none of my debit or credit cards will work in an ATM due to the US-led trade embargo. Indeed, I've been unable to access my bank account or look at my online Paypal account in any internet cafe. Every time I have tried, a warning page comes up telling me that access from Iranian IP addresses is prohibited due to sanctions. It's frustrating for me as a visitor and I can't begin to imagine the effect on the Iranian economy.

I'm feeling increasingly uncomfortable as I've received so many emails and blog posts from people following my journey that time pressures have precluded me responding to. Furthermore, I've fallen behind with my blog to the point where friends and strangers alike are sending messages of concern. I find an internet cafe and make a concerted effort to catch up. For a writer, my typing speed leaves a lot to be desired and without realising it, nearly two hours pass in a jiffy whilst I hammer away at the keyboard. At the end of a second day's post, I come out of my state of deep concentration and check the time. I hurry over to the counter to pay, but find to my horror I've incurred more costs than I have rials left to pay with. It's only a matter of a few pence but I really should have been more careful. I have a US$1 note, which I offer to the attendant to cover my time, but he simply won't accept it. He takes the remainder of my rials, saying they'll be more than sufficient. Grateful, but feeling rather stupid, I return to my hotel where the manager kindly changes enough dollars to keep me going.

I spend time walking by the river which is fortuitously just a short walk from my hotel. There are several beautifully elegant pedestrian bridges, of which the hundred and fifty metre long Khaju bridge is my favourite. Built as a double-decker footbridge, many of its graceful stone arches have retained their original paintings and tiles dating back to 1650. The reflection of the walkway on the still waters formed by the bridge's lock gates is entrancing. Many Iranians sit under the arches on the shady downstream side, talking above the background noise of the river as it flows through the slightly open dam gates. A tall poet, with long dark hair tied in a ponytail, stands on the bridge reciting his work. His voice is intense and somewhat spellbinding, making his poem sound like a song.

After dinner I spend an hour in a riverside teashop talking with a man I meet there, Mohammed. He tells me that the famous Esfahan hookah pipes were banned from tea shops by the government last year. We discuss Iran's poor international image. Like several other young Iranians I have spoken with, he tells me he cannot understand the hardline rhetoric of the politicians and that they certainly don't reflect the viewpoints of most Iranian people. He would like to move overseas and start his own business, questioning me intently on whether a traditional Iranian teashop would be a success in London. It's hard for me to predict but I wish him luck and eventually say 'so long'.

I go to bed looking forward to tomorrow's breakfast. My hotel puts on a great spread including something which I have a penchant for, tahini, an exotic paste made from sesame seeds. It makes a welcome change from the awful jam I've eaten from Hobson's choice throughout Iran. It looks like marmalade but is made from carrots!

Day 23 Esfahan to Kupayeh, Iran
82 miles

The banks don't receive today's new exchange rates until 10 am, so there's no chance of an early start this morning. Whilst munching on toast and tahini I peruse my Royal Enfield maintenance book and find a couple of things I can do to use my time productively. One of the procedures it lists is putting a spot of oil on the contact breaker wick. The manual says this should be done every 3,000 miles and as there are now more than 5,000 miles on the clock, it's definitely overdue.

I remove the contact breaker unit and drip two droplets of engine oil onto the small felt wick. Holding the contact breaker in my hand, I mull over how such a rudimentary mechanism can be so important, nay vital, to the operation of the motorcycle. It comprises just two tiny discs of flat metal; one on the top of a short screw, the other at the end of a narrow steel arm about one inch long. The flat plates on the ends of these two simple components normally touch, but on every revolution of the engine are forced apart by a cam, allowing a powerful burst of electricity to arc across the spark plug at exactly the right moment. Over the years, the contact breaker has been replaced by electronic, transistorised and ultimately digital ignition control units, but I quite like the fact that my bike runs so well on such a basic, antiquated system. Technology at its best to my mind. I fix it all back into place and walk to the nearest bank to get some much-needed rials.

Once on my way, it takes a full hour to clear the busy city environs. I stop to fill up with benzine then ride onto a dual carriageway. As soon as I get up some real speed I detect a misfire. I try to kid myself that I'm imagining it, but after a few miles I have to stop and check it out. I find a deserted building that offers some shade and try to resolve the problem step by step. I change spark plug, plug cap, HT lead and air filter one at a time. After each change I start the engine but there's no improvement. The instant I open the throttle more than half way there's a pronounced cough and misfire. I drain and clean the carburettor, wondering if I've just bought a tank full of contaminated fuel. How I would tackle that particular problem out here is a real concern, but I put it out of mind and decide to try riding on.

I get under way but the problem persists. After a few miles at low revs I stop again, this time without shade. It's blistering hot and I break out into an instant sweat. I re-examine everything on the bike and notice the flat spring on the contact breaker arm faces the opposite way to the illustration in my parts book. My mistake from this morning's tinkerings! I reverse it, set off, and the problem seems to be cured.

My mind wanders as I ride. First I think about my paltry mechanical skills. I've always believed that if my bike fails to make it to India it will most likely be as a result of something I do wrong. Then I begin to take in the scenery of wild, scrubby desert and the fierce heat. This would be a terrible place to break down. Right on cue, the misfire returns, like a jolt through my body, only now far worse. I can't believe it!

I see a sign which shows the next town, Kuhpayeh, is 25 kilometres ahead. Managing to limp there at low revs in third gear, I turn off the main road and find shelter under a scraggy tree. Removing the HT pick up, I clean the magneto slip ring using a rag-covered screwdriver. My fingers are crossed as this would be a neat and tidy solution, and quite honestly, I feel I'm running out of ideas. However, when all is connected back up my endeavours make no difference. After more deliberations, I set about changing the contact breaker to my spare one. No matter how I try, I cannot set the gap to the right clearance, 0.012 inches. I seem to have opened the points gap as much as possible, yet it's still too tight for my feeler gauge to fit.

It's hard to concentrate as a crowd has gathered, mostly young men on Hondas and schoolboys on bicycles. At times as many as fifteen are present, some studiously watching my every move and trying to guess which tool to pass me next. Others, more interested in the occasion than the stranded Royal Enfield and its rider, cavort on their bikes, kick a football or just generally fool around.

A middle-aged man joins me, quietly sitting at my side. I have no idea where he has come from but he tells me he's a motorcycle mechanic. At least I think that's what he means, but it could be that his brother owns a motorcycle shop and he helps out at times. It's hard to tell with the noise of the boys and our language differences. He's perplexed by the new set of points too. After much head scratching we compare them with my old set. The new ones are somewhat longer, no wonder I can't get them to open. Together we polish the pitting on my old set, seemingly the cause of my problems, taking care not to round off the surfaces. After several minutes fitting them and resetting the gap, I apprehensively start the engine. My bated breath relaxes; the misfire has gone, this time for good.

It's getting quite late so I ask the crowd if there's a hotel here. It transpires that there is one in Kuhpayeh, but unanimously they encourage me to follow the mechanic to the village of Toudeshk where there's a tourist hotel. I shake a dozen or so hands and get ready to follow my helper. To my amazement he walks across the road and climbs into a battered old Payken where his wife and two children wait. I'm absolutely floored... I was completely unaware that they've been patiently sitting in that oven of a car for nearly two hours.

He leads me twenty kilometres further along the main road to Toudeshk. We stop beside the promised guesthouse but it's closed. Driving to a nearby shop, a man informs us that the hotel owner has gone to Tehran for several days on business. I'm faced with a tough decision: ride on another fifty five kilometres to the next town, Na'in, or backtrack to Kuhpayeh. Checking my watch, I estimate there's only twenty minutes of daylight left so I opt for the latter, closer option.

Being caught out in the desert at night was certainly not on my wish list of experiences for this trip. I say my thanks once again to the helpful mechanic and his family, check my head and taillights are working, then ride back out into the wilds. Whereas before the trip I'm sure I would have found my current predicament quite a scary one, I unexpectedly relish the journey. The sky has turned a deep purple, with whispery streaks of red on the western horizon. The surrounding dark wilderness, partially illuminated by the setting sun's afterglow, is awe-inspiring. My bike thumps along, effortlessly cruising at eighty kilometres an hour. The problems of the day now long behind me, I feel a tangible release of mental pressure. Loving the sensation of cool air flowing around me, I'm just thrilled to be riding a healthy bike again.

Off to the right I see the silhouette of a rocky outcrop. I'm sorely tempted to ride off-piste and sleep under the stars behind it. Stopping, I dismount and test the sand by the roadside. It seems firm enough, but it's just too dark to risk getting stuck in an unseen trough or soft patch. Ten minutes more light would have made all the difference. Sighing, I climb back on the bike and ride the final few kilometres into Kuhpayeh.

I find the hotel and under the guidance of the manager, push my bike into a neighbouring ironmongery for the night. The reason I was told to ride on to Toudeshk immediately becomes clear. The accommodation is a fleapit and its manager an absolute slob, with dishevelled hair and numerous stains down the front of his shirt. A stale smell of urine and sour sweat pervades my room and the bathroom is so disgusting that I'm compelled to nip down a back alley and hurriedly pee against a wall. I'm the only guest, which is no surprise.

Just as I set off on a hunt for food, a wiry, stressed-looking man comes running towards me.

“Are you the biker who came to my guesthouse in Toudeshk?’ he breathlessly asks. I cautiously reply,

“Yes”.

He introduces himself as Mohammad Jalali, the owner of the ‘closed’ guesthouse.

“My brother phoned me and told me a motorcycle had called then ridden back to here. The man who told you I was away is my enemy, and he does everything he can to spoil my business, including telling visitors that I am away.”

I now understand his agitation and begin to warm to him, more so when he tells me he has simply come to apologise to me and ask if I would like to call by in the morning to have breakfast with him, which I agree to.

The tough day doesn’t really get any better. The town has three eateries, all of which are now empty. Both Mohammad and the hotel manager escort me, thinking I’ll have a problem finding vegetarian food. They’re right. Each of the restaurants has a choice of meat, meat and more meat on display in oily metal containers.

At the third place I spy a large bowl of plain curd in a fridge. Via Mohammad, I ask to buy some. There’s a fair amount of debate between the restauranteur and the hotel manager as apparently there are no takeaway food containers I can use. Eventually, a small soup bowl is produced and handed to the hotel manager whilst the restauranteur goes to find a spoon to ladle the curd. The manager, who’s been coughing and sneezing with a bad cold ever since I arrived, blows into the bowl then wipes it with his grubby shirt. Before I can open my mouth to protest, the curd is spooned into the ‘infected’ bowl.

Groaning, I explain what has happened to Mohammad, who looks to the heavens in exasperation. I ask for another bowl, offering to pay for the first at the same time. The manager looks more bemused than insulted, but at last we all leave with me clutching a bowl of uncontaminated yoghurt and a bottle of mineral water.

Thanking Mohammad and promising to meet him for breakfast, I return to my none too pleasant room and eat the curd with some English muesli, wishing again I’d not left my search for prepared camp food until the last minute. I clean my teeth into the empty curd container and go to sleep in my sleeping bag on top of my camping mattress rather than on the scungy bed. As I drift off, I reflect on the old adage that the bad times make the good times feel better. Let’s hope so.

Day 24 Kupayeh to Rafsanjan, Iran
314 miles

The ironmongery is just opening its doors for business when I arrive to claim my bike. The three staff look quite taken aback by its presence, so I wheel it out as quickly as possible, thanking them profusely whilst cursing the hotel manager under my breath for not getting their permission.

I soon park up outside Mohammad Jalali's Toudeshk guesthouse and knock on the door. It's built from a converted village post office which was closed several years ago. Mohammad appears from around the back with a large flat loaf of bread tucked under his arm. He beckons me to follow him, which I do, pushing my bike across the road and leaving it on its sidestand outside a small shop which doubles as a café. I order peach tea and buy a small packet of cream cheese and a couple of portions of the ubiquitous carrot jam to eat with Mohammad's bread.

Unfortunately, because of Ramadan I have to eat alone, but my host doesn't seem to mind. He shows me a guestbook with messages from several foreign bicyclists that have stayed with him whilst cycling across Iran. He's a fascinating man; as well as running the guesthouse he works for an NGO that promotes the heritage of the old silk road (called Miras-e Yarane Jadeye Abrisham) and also runs tours into the desert, offering his guests an authentic Persian sand dune experience.

Whilst I chomp my way through the enormous loaf, we are visited by Mohammad's brother and father. The latter is totally enamoured with my bike, stroking all its surfaces then stepping backwards with a camera to photograph it. He tells me, via his son, that he owned BSAs and Ariels during the time that British businesses, mainly petroleum companies, were commonplace in Persia. Iranians love to touch my bike and up until now I've kept a close eye on them, sometimes asking them to stop when they begin to play with its controls. However, as Mr. Jalali senior is an old-school motorcyclist, I confidently leave him with the bike while I return with Mohammad to finish breakfast.

The next visitors are the police. Mohammad confides that he has a responsibility to report the arrival of every foreign national to the authorities, a mere formality he assures me. The two officers step out of their vehicle, a very American-looking police car, and enter the shop. After shaking my hand, they ask to see my passport and bike paperwork. They take them outside, radio my details in to some distant headquarters, then return both to me. Again they shake my hand, saying 'welcome' with real sincerity.

It would be pleasant sitting here all day, watching villagers going about their business and spending the evening in Mohammad's warm company. The village looks very traditional, with mostly mud-brick housing and badgirs (clever windcatchers that funnel cool air through buildings). Everyone I've met so far has been exceedingly welcoming too, but I covered so few miles yesterday that I really need to press on. Just as I'm preparing to depart, voices ring out in the road calling Mohammad's name. Two Czech tourists, hearing about Mohammad's desert tours in Esfahan, have just alighted from a bus. I'm glad he has paying guests, his first for nearly two weeks, and I tell the Czechs that they're in for a treat before I say my goodbyes to everyone else.

I bypass Yadz, a medium sized city with a renowned old quarter that had been yesterday's failed destination. The bike continues to run well but the heat is stifling, the hottest day of my journey yet. I want to stop to eat a snack but ride miles without finding a suitably quiet and shady area. On the far side of a village I spot a cluster of tall, ropey bushes. I park the bike and crouch under their shade. As I unpack my staple of bread, cheese and dates, I look down at movement on my boot. At first I think it's an enormous black ant, then see its long curled tail... it's a black scorpion! I shake it off, grab my food bag and make a hasty retreat.

I haven't been able to contact Jane and Jacques for a couple of days and don't want my silence to alarm them. The problem is that I haven't managed to get a signal for my mobile phone either in the desert or at my hovel of a hotel last night. Furthermore, I know Jacques has contracted a virus and I'm anxious to hear news of his health. Under the relentless sun I pull over at the outskirts of a succession of small towns: Sar-e-Yezd; Kermanshahan; Shemsh; Anar and Bayaz, but to no avail, my texts remain unsent

It's a day of gritting my teeth and riding long hours. My throat and nose begin to burn with the heat, so I wear my neckscarf wrapped around my face outlaw style. The desert remains scrubby but still the endemic sand is whipped up by a strong easterly wind. I'm heading south east so my right leg and foot get a thorough toasting; the outside baked by the sun and the inside cooked from the heat blown off the engine by the cross wind.

Fortunately, the roads are quiet and flat, enabling me to ride many miles standing on the footpegs. I try to eat a chocolate biscuit bar whilst riding but get into more mess than a three year old would. It has melted and the sticky chocolate gets everywhere, including on my goggles and in my now bushy beard. I leave the main road and ride into a small desert town to eat another one, clean up and buy more water. I've already drunk four litres and so stock up with the same amount again. Within a minute of leaving the fridge it's poured into my Camelbak. Almost immediately under way again, I experience a uniquely delicious sensation, riding in the suffocating heat whilst imbibing icy water.

Arriving at Rafsanjan at dusk, I'm guided along the city's wide boulevards by a succession of helpful pedestrians. The town has one central hotel, fortunately with a locked basement car park. The receptionist has a 400 cc Honda rocket ship, which I park my Bullet next to. He tells me he imported it privately from Japan. It's the only motorcycle I've seen in Iran that's larger than 125 cc and he's obviously very proud of it. After eating a meal in the hotel restaurant, his younger brother comes to give me a ride to an internet cafe on the back of his world-weary CG125. It rattles and shakes, the chain jolts every time he changes gear and the engine sounds as though it's about to implode. Without doubt it's the worst maintained motorcycle I've ever sat on, but I'm grateful for the lift.

Most importantly, the news from home is that Jacques, although still poorly, is definitely on the mend, I sleep better knowing my family will receive emails telling them I'm safe and well, if a little saddle-sore.

Day 25 Rafsanjan to Bam, Iran
208 miles

This morning I stop for benzine on the outskirts of the city of Kerman. Up until this point the day is going well. I climb off the bike and look down. The left hand side toolbox lid is wide open and rolling about in it are one oil filter and a bottle of Loctite Lock N' Seal. Three more oil filters and all my emergency repair kit, such as a tube of plastic metal, superglue, 2-pack glue and insulation tape, are gone. Hey-ho. I knew there was a risk of the flower bolt, which keeps the door locked, working its way loose and I'd even packed spares just in case I lost one. However, I'm surprised it has happened on these good roads and not the broken roads of Romania, Bulgaria or Turkey. I can't help but wonder if one of the many admirers who touch the bike has curiously turned the flower bolt, thus loosening it.

Petrol stations provide many encounters with Iranians. Without exception, I have to shake several hands each time I stop, answering the same questions again and again, mostly about my impressions of Iran and also the perceptions of people in my home country about Iran. The questions are always sincere and asked with genuine curiosity, and the friendliness of the askers is, at times, quite overwhelming. On two previous top-ups the petrol pump attendant had no black market ration card to allow me to buy petrol. Within moments a fellow customer generously proffered his card for me to use.

I secure the toolbox, and after a quick but futile check on the garage approach road for my lost spares, head off. Once clear of Kerman I begin to climb onto a high plateau, which peaks at 2,550 metres. The air is cool and my ears pop. Around me, the land is devoid of all life and mini tornados swirl across the desert. They fascinate me as they give the scenery the look of a wild west film set. One, about 10 m high with a diameter of 2 m at ground level, begins to cross the road ahead of me. I can't resist the urge to ride through it, accelerating to meet it head on. I get a face full of sand as my reward and have to stop to clean the air filter for good measure. Lesson learned.

It's mid afternoon by the time I descend from the plateau. A stiff cross wind becomes my companion again. I have to take shallow breaths to cope with the heat, guessing this is what it would feel like inside a fan assisted oven. Once I'm within fifty kilometres of my destination, the town of Bam, I meet an endless procession of trucks heading north. Each one puts out a shockwave of intensely hot, volatile air that rocks my motorcycle and all but wrenches my hands off the handlebars.

The road is now single lane and several times I'm run off it as trucks overtake each other, forcing me to hit the roadside gravel at just a second's notice. It's a sign of things to come in India, I'm sure, and it's a phenomenon that I have to reacquaint myself with rapidly in order to stay safe. I feel a great deal of indignation at being driven off the road and my European sensibilities make me feel I should stand my ground, so to speak, to make the oncoming traffic drive with more consideration to others. Thankfully, I inherently know that this course of action will lead to my untimely and rather gruesome death, so I hit the dirt, repeating as ever my mantra,

"I must survive this for Jacques."

I see Bam in the distance, my first sighting being a wall of green date palms, bearers of the boxed fruit that has kept me going for the last week. I make my way to the eponymous Akbar's Tourist Guest House where, as soon as I've stopped my engine, a young man comes over to say hello. He introduces himself as Leo, a twenty six year old engineering graduate from Paris. He tells me he arrived from Pakistan two days ago on a motorcycle he bought in India. I'm delighted to meet him, hear of his exploits and, most importantly, learn that the roads I will be taking in Pakistan are safe.

"There are police checkpoints everywhere," he tells me. "If ever it was getting late, they always offered me a bed and food. Anyway, every Pakistani I met was very friendly."

This is a big relief as I had been prepared to turn around at this point if the American insurgencies, recently promulgated on the news, had made the region less safe for tourists. He also tells me he spotted three BMWs heading to the border two days ago, which Akbar, who has joined us confirms, as they were also his guests

Leo turns out to be a mine of information and we even exchange money, my spare rials for his surplus Pakistan rupees. It's pleasing to know I'll now not have to deal with the money-changing sharks at the border. We sit around a large coffee table in Akbar's courtyard while Leo recounts tales from his adventures.

"I spontaneously bought the Honda in India for about 300 euros. I saw Royal Enfields there and loved them, but thought I would struggle if I bought one and it broke down. The Honda is so omnipresent that I knew every mechanic in the world could fix it."

This strikes me as an ideal way for Leo to travel, especially when he confides he has zero mechanical knowledge and carries no tools or spares, not even a spark plug or clutch cable.

His journey sounds equally impulsive but brilliantly exciting.

"I left the Honda in Peshawar (provincial capital of the North West Frontier Province and the gateway the the Khyber Pass) and crossed into Afghanistan. I kept well away from the south, which is really dangerous, but spent a month wandering around the north."

Blimey!

He certainly has a 'fly by the seat of your pants' approach to travel, illustrated no better than by his tale about entering Iran.

"My Pakistan visa expired when I was in Afghanistan, so I changed the date on it in my passport by a month. I had no problems getting into the country but the forgery was spotted when I came to leave a couple of days ago."

Leo goes on to describe in animated terms how the Pakistan authorities questioned him about his passport for three hours and refused to let him exit the country, adamant he would have to travel nearly fifteen hundred kilometres north to the capital, Islamabad, to get a new visa.

I ask the obvious question,

"So how come you're here?"

He gives a typically gaelic shrug and answers,

"The immigration staff went to the mosque for prayers, leaving me on my own in an interview room. I just walked around for a bit, then went outside, got on my bike and rode to the Iranian entry barrier. No one noticed I hadn't been stamped out of Pakistan and here I am!"

At 5.30 pm he gets ready to ride north. He's certainly a fascinating character, not less, an unconventional motorcyclist. He's tall and gangly, with real boyish good looks, and bounces around with seemingly limitless joie de vivre. We walk together to his motorcycle. It's a 125 cc Indian Hero Honda in a fairly beat up state. He straps his backpack onto the pillion portion of his seat with rope and puts on his riding jacket... a green long-sleeved cotton shirt! His trousers are regular lightweight cotton affairs and on his feet are ordinary city shoes. But it's his 'gloves' that take the biscuit, leaving me open-mouthed. They are just strips of thin cloth that he wraps around his knuckles to stop the sun burning them too much.

Sitting astride his Honda, he tells me that the motorcycling part of his eighteen month travels is just a whim. He doesn't have a driving licence and the bike's paperwork is still in its former Indian keeper's name. He intends to ride in the cool of the evening and spend the night simply where he lands.

“I really want to see northern Iraq, so I plan to cross into it from Iran, then continue east through Syria to the Lebanon,” he tells me whilst starting his bike.

Although his method of travel appears pretty cavalier, if not reckless, I like him and his carefree spirit immensely. The place feels empty when he leaves. It's not that I'm now the only guest; it's the departure of Leo's positive, buoyant energy which leaves a vacuum.

Day 26 Bam, Iran
0 miles

Bam is famous as the site of the world's largest adobe structure, the Arg-e Bam, a magnificent fortified town at the edge of the Persian desert. In 2004, an earthquake measuring 7.2 hit the town. Thirty one thousand people lost their lives and the Arg was turned to dust.

I breakfast with Akbar, over which he tells me his sad memories of the disaster. His prosperous guesthouse was demolished and two of his guests killed. One of them, an Englishman called Gavin, was riding a Bullet from India to the UK. Akbar takes me to see the remains of the bike which are in a corner of his garden. It's the first Royal Enfield I've seen since Hungary and it's a particularly sad sight. Sitting forlornly in an area builders have used when reconstructing the neighbouring house, it's covered in dust, mud and splattered plaster. The front crashbars and petrol tank are stoved in and the rear shock absorbers are buckled. There's a hole in the primary cover and the headlight is missing. I stand looking at it for quite a while. Having spent so much time on this journey reflecting on my family, how much they value me and I them, I cannot begin to imagine the impact of this man's death on his loved ones.

One day, I hope, someone will see the bike who has the desire and determination to get it going again. Akbar agrees,

"I look upon myself as its guardian. When someone comes along who is serious about taking it home to restore it, I'll happily let it go... for a small donation to the reconstruction of my guest house, of course."

Akbar acts as an impromptu taxi service, driving me to the remains of the Arg. All around are huge supporting scaffolding structures that prop up leaning mud brick walls. I walk in deep dust that has the consistency of talcum powder, instantly turning my boots and trouser bottoms a light sand colour. There's very little left of the ancient oasis fort but a fifteen year restoration project is underway. It's an enormous task as I estimate the site is the size of eight football fields. Furthermore, the Arg was built over centuries, with layers added in various styles using different techniques of mud brick making. It's a painstaking task to recreate just one building, and in the four years since the disaster, only a couple of squares and their surrounding edifices have been partially rebuilt. Incredibly, there are still many areas where the rubble hasn't yet been touched.

I see around fifty workmen at the ruins. All are very welcoming, giving me waves, smiles and the obligatory, "which country?" It's still early in the morning but they're already grey with dust from head to toe as a result of moving debris and making piles of the few bricks that have somehow remained solid.

After lunch at Akbar's, I spend a couple of contented hours preparing my Enfield for the rigours of Pakistan's roads. Apart from the customary nut and bolt checks, I examine both tyres for nails or glass, noting that the rear tyre is starting to show wear, and have another go at tightening the steering head. I've given up on the dynamo, making use of the battery charger on an almost daily basis, but I pay special attention today to the contact breakers, making sure they are clean and correctly set. I empty my one litre aluminium oil can, which contains Turkish 20/50, over Gavin's Bullet's engine to protect it. Then I transfer the last few drops of my valuable Penrite straight 50 from the 5 litre petrol can into the now empty smaller container, deciding that from tomorrow it will be wise to carry spare fuel.

Venturing out in the late afternoon to explore the city further, I stock up on provisions and make use of an internet cafe. The seismic devastation is evident on every single street. Gaping spaces mark where buildings were levelled, piles of rubble and crushed possessions litter street corners and many shopkeepers trade from sea freight containers haphazardly arranged around partially reconstructed buildings. I can't help wondering where they sleep at night, hoping that it's not in the depths of the containers. I read a report that thousands of people lived in tents for months after the quake, resulting in even more deaths when the winter desert temperature dropped well below freezing.

I return to Akbar's to find him sitting on the front step to his guesthouse. A former English and Persian history schoolmaster, he now looks brooding and despondent, quietly watching the street in the vain hope that more tourists will show up and help pay his bills. None have today. He takes me on a tour of his new premises, which adjoin the rooms and courtyard where I'm presently staying. The breeze-bloc three storey building is devoid of all windows and doors, except for one corner where three rooms have been completed. Akbar explains,

"I ran out of money. All those three rooms require are new beds, bedding and curtains, then I can let them out. As for the rest of the place, there are nineteen rooms with ensuite bathrooms in total, plus a restaurant and bar. When I'll finish is Allah's will."

It's a real chicken and egg conundrum, with Bam's now low tourist numbers the root cause of his problems.

I return to the less salubrious part of the complex to shower and get ready for dinner. The place reminds me of the bottom-of-the-range backpackers haunts I frequented twenty years ago when I travelled on a shoestring. There are two petite communal showers with squat toilets incorporated inside them, a small shared lounge, complete with fridge, and half a dozen very basic rooms with makeshift walls constructed from tatty cardboard and floors covered in colourful but threadbare rag carpets. Since my recent tour of the new hostel, I now see this place in a new light and cannot help but sympathise with Akbar.

I spend a very strange evening with a 24-year-old Iranian man called Emad. Sporting a well-developed black goatee beard, he looks very untypical of his countrymen. He wears a Mettalica heavy metal t-shirt, ripped jeans and earrings. We eat at a pizza shop as it's the only restaurant in town he believes will cater for vegetarians. The waiter is somewhat baffled by my request for a non-meat special and his first offering has chicken on it, which in his opinion mustn't qualify as meat. We try again, and this time I get the weirdest concoction yet, reconstituted grilled mashed potato on a thick tomato base.... mmmm.

If the food is unusual, the conversation with Emad is even more so. He asks me to write my name, which I do in my notebook

"Ah, like Gordon Brown," he says, smiling. He continues, "I don't like Gordon Brown; he's never happy, he always looks sad. I like Tony Blair. He's a strong, handsome man. I think he is attractive. Yes, a very attractive, handsome man."

This is all said with the utmost sincerity. I'm lost for words!

After dinner, we relax in a nearby subterranean internet cafe with a group of his former school mates who run the place. For some unknown technical fault, none of the computers can get internet access except for the server which sits on the manager's desk. He has a crowd of young Iranian women, some with their fathers, around him. Emad explains that it's university entrance time and that all these girls are seeking help filling in their applications online. I watch a couple of intense debates before hanging out in a corner with some of Emad's pals. They all seem very friendly and, fortunately, display no predilection for European Prime Ministers, whether former or current. The cafe closes just after 10 pm, so Emad and I share a Paykan taxi back to Akbar's where we say goodnight and Bon Voyage.

Day 27 Bam to Mirjaveh Border, Iran
274 miles

Akbar didn't tell me a fixed room rate when I checked in. Instead, he told me to pay what I could afford. The present accommodation standard is very poor, worth only a few dollars a night, which makes Akbar's pricing strategy a very sound one. How could anyone not want to give him more as a 'contribution' to his and the guest house's survival? I fork out a good deal extra, telling him I truly hope he is able to get his new building complete in the near future.

I'm on the road by 8 am as I need to be through Iranian immigration by 3 pm at the latest to get into Pakistan today. The first two hundred miles are plain sailing; good straight roads across endless desert, the Dasht-e Lut. It's baking hot and I ride virtually non-stop. The wide open plains are punctuated with sharp volcanic ridges that magnificently rise several hundred metres into the air and the silence, when I briefly stop to have a pee, is eerie. Just a couple of hundred kilometres north of my route, in the very heart of the desert, a NASA satellite recorded the highest temperature ever seen on the earth's surface: 71 °C (159 °F). I don't know how my air-cooled engine is coping with the intense heat today, but thank my lucky stars it's not anything like that phenomenal temperature.

Highlight of the day is spotting three wonderful camels trekking across the empty plains. The first two are a sandy brown colour but the third is a beautiful rich chestnut. They look so noble as they quietly continue on their way seemingly impervious to me and my noisy motorcycle. I have read that some drug traffickers teach camels how to 'home' across the Afghan / Iran border, then surgically implant heroin in their humps. These three are heading in the wrong direction to be carriers, but it does emphasise the problems faced by the estimated forty thousand Iranian border guards who do constant battle with the smugglers.

There's no crosswind, for once, and although the roads are single lane I make very good time. I'm on the outskirts of the city of Zahedan just after midday with only seventy five kilometres to run to the border. I've been warned to keep well clear of the city as more than eighty percent of all drugs smuggled out of Afghanistan and Pakistan are reported to pass through this part of Iranian Baluchistan. Local drug smugglers, some of the richest people in the country, have a reputation for kidnapping people to bargain for the release of their accomplices and foreigners are not exempt from this. At the present time, a Japanese tourist has been held by kidnappers for more than three months. As a consequence, any foreigner showing face in Zahedan gets a twenty four hour police escort. No thank you.

On the city bypass I call in at a benzine station. It turns out to be a garage for trucks and they only sell diesel. I use the petrol from my five litre spare can which I fortunately filled to the brim in Bam this morning; it'll certainly be enough to get me to the frontier. I'm surrounded by the usual crowd of kids, station attendants and young men who shake my hand and practise their English. After a few minutes an enormous new white Mercedes pulls in. Not only is it the first Mercedes I've seen in Iran, it's also by far the most opulent car I've come across. Two suited men get out. One is short and round, quietly spoken and very suave. The other is a giant; at least 6' 6". with a thick black moustache. He's dressed like a stereotypical TV mobster: expensive dark suit, burgundy shirt, dark silk tie. They look so incongruous next to all the other Iranians around me. They are also quietly intimidating.

Deference seems the wisest course of action. I take a step forward to shake their hands, saying it's a pleasure to meet them. The tall one immediately asks me if I am American. It's the first time I've been asked that in Iran, so I laugh and say no. They stand watching as I strap the now empty fuel can onto the bike. Trying not to rush, I climb aboard and offer my hand to them first before shaking the petrol attendant's hand. They just stand and stare as I give a big wave and, with all the false confidence I can muster, ride out of the station. I think I'm possibly being a little paranoid but for all that I'm mighty relieved to get away from them.

Fun and games begin at a police checkpost ten kilometres later. Two guards take my passport and keep me waiting thirty infuriating minutes while it's being inspected and logged. I keep looking at my watch, urgently pointing to it when I can catch anyone's attention. Finally I'm told I'll need an escort to the border. A young paramilitary policeman emerges from the blockhouse offices, shows me my passport is in his pocket and indicates I am to follow him. He goes to the road, waves at a car that appears to be waiting for him and climbs in.

I follow... at least I try to follow. They set off at breakneck pace and I see nothing more of them for the next twenty minutes. They wait for me at a road junction and surprisingly turn right towards the border town of Mirjaveh as I approach, instead of continuing directly to the frontier which is signposted as being fifteen kilometres straight ahead. I can't believe it, but have to follow because of my passport. My escort climbs out of the car in the town centre and stands at the roadside trying to flag down another lift. I'm dumbstruck; I realise my escort is hitching his way to the border! He soon gets a ride for another couple of kilometres, then has to wait quite some time before a van stops for him. I'm now really fretting about making the border crossing today as well as thinking what a strange set up it is that the police don't seem to have any vehicles.

He climbs out of the van at another police station. It's 2.50 pm and just five kilometres to the border. He hands me over to a sergeant who disappears with my passport. I sit in the sun on my bike, getting very angry at this seemingly needless time wasting. The Bullet's engine is running very hot and I'm sweating profusely. After twenty minutes I try to enter the building to get things moving. A soldier blocks my way. I try to explain about the border closing but he just shrugs. I lose my temper and shout that I want my passport. A couple of men come out when they hear my raised voice but it makes no difference, it's still another fifteen minutes before I get a new escort. This one is very young and totally inept at flagging down the few cars that pass. They all swing into the middle of the road at speed to avoid him, continuing on their way without even braking.

It's almost four o'clock when we reach the border post. I'm checked through the gatehouse and pointed to a building five hundred metres away. With my hopes very much raised, I hastily put my helmet on and ride there, imagining that for some unknown reason the immigration department is working late today. My hopes are soon dashed, it turns out to be a restaurant with a few rooms attached. The keeper tells me the border is closed, that I must stay there for the night and go to the nearby immigration building first thing in the morning.

I ride back to the gatehouse but it's already closed and empty. Worst still, there's a lock and chain on the gates. I park the bike under a tree and spend an hour calming down before I return to my enforced quarters for the night. I'm the only 'guest'.

Later I wander around the compound to pass some time. and see three artics that are also captives for the night. One driver, who has put his bedroll on the tarmac next to his cab, boils a kettle on a small paraffin stove. He signals for me to join him for chai, which I do, sitting cross legged on the ground opposite him. Neither of us can understand the other, but we share the sweet milky tea in companionable silence. As I stroll back to the restaurant, I watch him get up and wander over to the other truck drivers who are playing cards round a flickering lantern.

The restaurant offers an uninspiring choice of kebabs or kebabs, so dinner is more of my emergency breakfast supply of muesli and powdered milk from my bag. As I unpack it, that phrase 'to cap it all' comes to mind. Half the contents of the bag are coated in green slime... the top has come off my bottle of clothes washing liquid. What a day!

Departing Tony & Jan's, Folkestone, having just ridden through the hole in their hedge.

With the team at Royal Enfield UK, Day 1.

With Ferenc & Bullet, Bekescaba, Hungary.

Michal & Ural, Czech Replublic.

Entering Turkey after 2,300 miles.

Tombs hewn into the cliffs, Amasya, Turkey

Faruk (right) and friend, Safranbolu.

The earthquake damaged Bullet, Bam.

The magnificent 17th Century Khaju pedestrian bridge in the early evening, Esfahan, Iran.

The incomparable Imam mosque, Esfahan.

My police escort, Sukkur, Pakistan.

Little wonder hotels turned me away!

A police checkpost on the road to Quetta, the toughest day's ride.

The stunning desert road between Dalbandin and Quetta, Baluchistan, Pakistan.

Long John Gordon, the Golden Temple, Amritsar, India.

The JBF Informal School morning class. Teacher Sandhya (L) and aid Prabhakar (R).

The JBF Mobile Cattle Clinic. Sharafat, Dr. Sashanka, Yogesh and Anil (left to right).

Lalli Singh (with turban), Imran (standing far right) and the Inder Motors team, Delhi.

Joney's Place, Agra, 1988 (left) and 2008 (right). He still serves amazing chocolate lassi.

The morning of the foiled robbery, MP, India.

A life-changing Wateraid pump, Warangal.

'Porden' with the surprise reception committee at the Wateraid project, Pamnuur, India.

With the Madras Bulls at the Hotel Ashoka, Chennai, feeling both elated and relieved.

At the Royal Enfield factory, Chennai, just before the bike is packed into a shipping crate.

Day 28 Mirjaveh Border to Dalbandin, Pakistan 186 miles

Exiting Iran goes smoothly, as does entering Pakistan. The air-conditioned Iranian immigration and customs offices are relatively modern if nondescript and are manned by civilian staff who, without exception, wear shirts and ties. On the Pakistan side, the offices don't look as though they've changed in possibly fifty years. I sit on an ancient scalloped sofa finished in worn purple and orange chenille. A ceiling fan whirrs overhead and paperwork is completed on a battered wooden coffee table. The immigration staff wear lightly coloured salwar kameez, the traditional baggy trousers and long tunic typically worn in the region. The police wear the same style of garments but the cloth has a pronounced woven texture and is dark grey.

Seeing these outfits worn by absolutely every man in sight brings up a memory from my first visit to Pakistan in 1988. In the north western town of Chitral, I met a young British man of Pakistani descent. It was his first visit to his ancestral home and he was self-consciously wearing pale blue salwar kameez.

"I wore these things as nightwear when I was a boy. Now it feels like I'm walking down the street in the middle of the day in my pyjamas!" he had told me with a laugh.

Still, they make wonderfully practical attire, especially in the heat of the desert.

I have to ride my bike to the customs buildings, which lie half a kilometre away from the immigration post. After finding it easily, I go inside past a long line of truckers to complete formalities for my motorcycle. Here too, it's like stepping back in time. A long row of battered wooden desks are lined up, each with a slowly whooshing ceiling fan directly overhead. There must be a dozen officials in the room, most of whom are reading newspapers or sitting around chatting. Again I'm directed to a large, ancient sofa where I wait until my carnet is stamped. My details are entered into a enormously thick leather-bound ledger which looks as though it's been in service since before Partition. I'm quickly free to go.

It always amazes me that a line on a map, or in the sand, as it were, marks such a difference in people, culture and lifestyle. This is no more so apparent than in the border town of Taftan. I make a whistlestop visit to the bazaar to buy smuggled Iranian benzine, which is poured from opaque plastic four litre containers into my tank through a capacious funnel. The top of the funnel has a muslin cloth spread over it to act as a primitive filter. The weave is so open and tattered that I'm not sure what it's trying to prevent from entering my tank... a dead mouse? Tank full, I ride out into the desert.

Today's wilderness is made up of golden sand. I see enormous dunes on each side of the road that are staggeringly beautiful, real *Lawrence of Arabia* scenery. The tarmac has been recently upgraded, making it a fantastic road to ride and I thoroughly enjoy myself. After three weeks on the right I'm now back on the left side of the road. It feels totally natural to make the change. Huge Pakistani trucks trundle past me heading south roughly every ten minutes, brashly decorated all over in bright coloured vinyl applique, paintings and jingling trinkets. A couple of cars overtake me, but that's all I see for the first hour.

I stop at a police checkpoint. It's nothing more than a single room blockhouse next to a chain that's suspended across the road. Opposite are the remains of a glorious desert fortress with crumbling ramparts. It's awesome... again, the stuff of film sets. The lone policeman gets me to record my passport details in his book then invites me to sit in his cool room and relax. At least my motorcycle has a chance to cool down somewhat whilst sheltered in the breezy shade of the building.

Moving again, I'm just thinking the road is in terrific condition when I come across a stretch that's been eroded by wind and sand, and have to ride around it on shingle for a couple of minutes. Then I encounter several sand drifts on the road. Some are ten feet high on my side of the centerline but there's always a thin line of tarmac to squeeze by on the other side. A few kilometres later I come across a couple that have formed almost perfect sand dunes, but the sand is only a couple of inches thick on the right side of the road and I get through with nothing more than a slight wobble..

I crash my bike roughly ninety kilometres north of Taftan. It all happens so quickly. Coming over a rise at 50 MPH, I see a big sand dune in the road. It has a mound roughly eight feet high on the left and is around thirty foot long. This time the sand on the right is quite deep too, at least a foot thick, but it appears to have been flattened by cars and trucks driving over it. I have little time to make a decision. I make a bad one. Slowing down slightly, I drive at it somewhere between 30 and 40 MPH, thinking I don't want to get bogged down in it.

Immediately, I lose control, but somehow stay on until the other side of the dune. By now the handlebars are violently jerking from side to side...

a tank-slapper. I hit the tarmac hard with my left elbow, head and hip. I hear my beautiful motorcycle crash down on one side then catch a glance of it flipping over and turning around all in one movement. It comes down on top of my left leg, but most of the blow is absorbed by the crashbars. All is silent.

I lie there and say,

"You're OK. You're OK Gordon. You're OK."

I know I have no broken bones and the crash helmet has safely absorbed the blow from my head hitting the road. My left leg is twisted under a pannier box. The knee is painful and I can't move it because my boot is hooked underneath, pressed against the exhaust pipe. It's very hot on my big toe, which begins to burn. Because of the twist in my leg I can't even touch the bike, let alone try to move it.

I think PETROL, but I can't smell any. I lie and wait. I know someone will come along to help and feel strangely calm.

Not more than five minutes later a southbound truck comes to a halt and its Baluchi driver runs over to me. He's stronger than he looks. He lifts the bike upright in one movement. I get to my feet but end up back on the ground as my now flaccid left leg numbly gives way. He pushes my bike to the other side of the road and gets it onto its centre stand. I hobble around looking at the damage, more concerned about the bike than about myself. The front mudguard is pressed against the tyre, the numberplate scratched and twisted. The headlamp is pointing skywards, the glass pushed in but not broken. One of the rear crashbars is noticeably bent and a pannier box dented. A footpeg points upwards at an acute angle.

Then I see the forks are twisted. When the front wheel is straight the left side of the handlebar is about three inches ahead of the right.

“That's bad”, I say out loud.

I inspect myself. My jacket is torn at the left elbow and pocket and my elbow is bleeding but not seriously. There’s a road burn on my left hip which I suspect will also come up in a big bruise. My knee is very painful and so is the top left hand side of my chest. I keep my Leatherman multipurpose tool in my jacket’s left breast pocket. It’s been indispensable until now, but I must have landed on it and pushed it into my ribs.

For a short while I think the game’s over, that surely the bike won’t be rideable with twisted forks, but during the next couple of hours a succession of three lots of people help me fix it up. At one point I am on my own. I cry. I can't stop thinking about my son and how I have to make it home to him.

The final problem is a nut on the left pannier frame that rubs against the rear wheel. If I ride like this it will certainly shred the tyre. In the midst of a hideous but thankfully short sandstorm, a passing motorist helps me remove it. I use three cable ties in its place; what a marvellous invention! Sand gets everywhere, in my tools, up my nose and in my mouth, down my neck, onto my bloodied elbow. It's an exceedingly grim experience.

Everyone who has stopped to help has made one thing very clear; I have to get the bike running and ride it out of here. I'm fairly numb from shock... it is, after all, the first crash I've had in twenty four years, but it eventually sinks in. I have read this road is safe by day but notorious for banditry by night. It's also only fifty kilometres south of the Helman Province of Afghanistan, an especially troubled spot at present. My final helper refuses to leave me alone until he sees me riding the bike. I become determined to get moving.

That wonderful, adorable machine starts second kick! With help from my motorist friend, I struggle onto it and set off. It's rideable! The steering feels odd but stable. The brakes work. Fuel, air and spark all do their thing.

It's an emotional and physically tough twenty kilometres ride to the desert village of Nok Kundi. At the checkpost on the outskirts, the policeman tells me there's no hotel in the village. I stop at an open-fronted roadside shop to buy water and a cold Coke. As I limp out of the shop a man accosts me and asks me to give him my Camelbak as a gift, which I politely refuse to do. Sensing there will be no respite for me here, I climb back on the bike and set out for Dalbandin which my map shows as 167 km east. At least I know there will be accommodation available as I remember Jonny Krause writing about it in his blog.

I just grit my teeth and ride. Thankfully, the road is in terrific condition and I don't encounter another sand drift, but do have to pass through two fierce sandstorms. There isn't any shelter and I have no option but to tough them out from the saddle. I worry about my air filter becoming clogged but don't have the energy to stop and change it. It's also hard to know where to put my left leg so that it's comfortable and the ache in my ribs is intensifying.

My relief at seeing the 'Dalbandin 5 KM' sign is almost palpable. The town is in the midst of a grey dust storm when I arrive, but I easily spot the hotel. It's three stories high, by far the tallest building on the main strip. Stopping my Bullet on its forecourt, I stiffly push the sidestand into position with my aching left limb and climb off. The leg immediately gives way and I end up in a heap on the ground. The crowd that already surrounds me seem nonplussed. One helps me stand. He tells me that he works in the hotel, but unfortunately it's closed for a complete renovation.

Every room has been gutted.

"But you are injured," he says. "You must stay with us. Your bike will be safe in our restaurant, which is closed anyway, and you can sleep on a mattress on the roof with me."

This man, Shoki Khan, must be my fourth Good Samaritan today. He helps me unload the bike, provides me with cold drinks and sends out for food. He even fixes a temporary shower in a partially renovated bathroom. He's kind, very understanding and has a fine sense of humour, jovially kidding me that I'll have to stay in Dalbandin for at least a week to recover from my injuries.

Shoki tells me the hotel, about to be renamed the *Al-Dawood*, has had many foreign visitors in the past. There's a team of twenty workmen, who keep going until midnight, plastering, wiring in new electrics and manually shifting rubble down the stairwell. Each and every one shakes my hand.

I finally bathe, dress my bloody bits and tentatively climb out onto the roof. Shoki has prepared a foam mattress and pillow for me. It's painful getting horizontal but once my leg adjusts to the new position, I feel surprisingly comfortable. With a strange quirk of timing, the town is struck by a power cut as I settle myself. This makes the dancing lights of the moonless heavens seem even more alive. I watch the transporting vista of glittering stars for a while then sink somewhat sublimely into oblivion.

Day 29 Dalbandin to Quetta, Pakistan
214 miles

It's wonderful to be woken just before 7 am by the sunrise. The air temperature is still warm and it smells fresh and clear. My knee feels stronger for the rest but my ribs and hip ache acutely. I make up my mind to press on, thinking that a day spent lazing around may just cause everything to stiffen more. Furthermore, if I do require medical help, I'm much more likely to find what I need in my next destination, the city of Quetta.

I feel as though I'm moving around in slow motion, creeping through an open window into the husk of the hotel then hobbling around whilst making breakfast (good ol' UK muesli again) and checking my bike over. There's not much I can easily do within the dark and dusty confines of the restaurant, so I content myself that all is still bolted together and there are no major leaks. It's 10 am by the time I've eaten and loaded the bike. I take a couple of Ibuprofen to loosen everything up and go to say my thanks to the staff. Shoki left before I woke, but has given a note to another staff member.

It reads, "Bed, no charge. Take care and happy journey!"

Mounting my motorcycle, I feel apprehensive about the day ahead, mostly around whether the rear subframe will stay clear of the wheel should the roads get bumpy and to a lesser extent, whether my body will be up to the journey. I kick the bike over and it fires first attempt, an auspicious start I tell myself.

The first twenty kilometres are easy going, then the road turns sharply left to run parallel with the stark, granite-like Raskoh mountain range. Gradually two lanes become one, which means I have to slow and get off the road when anything comes the other way. Buses and trucks are okay as they travel sedately on what is a steadily worsening surface. Not so for Land Cruisers and the like which tear along kicking up palls of stony dust that results in me hitting dirt at the side of the road in double-quick time. Quetta-bound trucks shake along at 15 to 20 KMPH. I can't stay in their murky, choking wake as it's hard to breath and at this pace, I'd never make Quetta today. Feeling that I'm putting myself at risk, I have no option but to bump past them in the rough, sandy edges.

2.15 pm. I stop at a remote police checkpost where I eat a handful of nuts and quickly check the bike over. It's been an absolutely awe inspiring ride thus far with jaw-dropping, barren scenery and a feeling of being completely alone much of the time. I check my progress on my odometer and can't believe I've only covered eighty six miles in over four hours! I ask the officer in charge and his two newspaper-reading friends about the road ahead.

"Bad for ninety kilometres," responds the policeman, "then smooth to Quetta".

Time for more Ibuprofen methinks.

Bad is the kind of gross understatement that should land the offending policeman in court! Those ninety kilometres take another three back-breaking hours. It is by far the most formidable road I have ever experienced and I can only describe it as a mangled, stony, potholed farm track with short, sharply rising sleeping policemen seemingly every hundred metres or so. It just goes on... and on... and on. The sun beats down interminably and the surrounding plains of bare rock and dust appear fluid as they dance behind the constantly shimmering heat haze. It's impossible for me to guess the temperature, but I'm certain I could fry an egg on the front mudguard.

I can't believe that my motorcycle can take this punishment; it's jolted, rattled, shaken and battered. Both horns stop working. The indicator switch turns upside down and the advance/retard lever unwinds itself. The speedo reads 0 MPH and the mirrors face the ground. The engine, smeared in oil by yesterday's crash, is completely covered in sand. Only occasionally do I manage to get into second gear, yet it somehow splendidly plods on, never missing a beat.

I pass several villages where all the kids come running out asking for pens, almost as if they're waiting for today's foolhardy biker to arrive. In some villages they're highly organised: the children run out and form a chain across the road when they hear my bike approaching. Quite a few are armed with stones which they throw as I keep rolling, desperately taking care to hurt no one as I ride my way though the crowd. None hit, but it's no fun. I feel quite demoralised and curse the 'numpty' that passed through these parts handing pens out to the children. I only have two pens and really need them, but in any case, how could I give to one child and not their twenty friends.

I finally reach the promised 'good' road. Hmmm. In an attempt to cheer myself I sing the Tigger song from *Winnie The Pooh* as I bounce along it:

"The most wonderful thing about Tiggers,
is Tiggers are wonderful things.
Their tops are made out of rubber,
their bottoms are made out of springs.
They're bouncy, trouncy, flouncy, pouncy, Fun! Fun! Fun!".

I suppose that, in relative terms, third gear is at least possible and hopefully the increased air circulation will help the engine cool.

The road crosses another craggy mountain range, following a sequence of hairpin bends. Next I crawl over two dry river beds where the bridges have been washed away during some recent floods. It's unbelievably difficult to stay upright. I come across my last police checkpost of the day, where this time I'm invited into a tent for chai.

After the much needed refreshment, I ride off in search of a place to stop for a call of nature. I haven't seen any other traffic for quite some time, but as sod's law would have it, a bike and a car, each coming from opposite directions, converge on my motorcycle whilst I'm in full flow. Both driver and rider are understanding, only stopping to check I'm okay and have no mechanical problems. The motorcyclist, on such a beat-up moped that its manufacturer's name is illegible, is keen to swap email addresses so we can exchange photographs of ourselves and our bikes. He touchingly rides off thrilled to have my contact details hurriedly written on the back of a Turkish hotel receipt.

The final approach to Quetta is horrendous. I climb then quickly descend a large rocky hill. The road has been stripped of tarmac in preparation for resurfacing and speeding cars and minibuses create whopping clouds of chalky dust as they wildly race past me. It's nearly dark and almost impossible to see where I'm going.

"Too much. Too much," I say over and over again, feeling absolutely shattered.

It's now pitch dark and I'm somewhere in the cantonment area of Quetta, utterly exhausted. I stop next to an auto-rickshaw and try to persuade him to lead me to my chosen hotel. A crowd forms and everything becomes confusing as the driver fails to understand why I need his services.

"Can I be of assistance?" asks a well-spoken, smartly dressed older man.

I ask him if he can explain my request to the rickshaw driver.

"That will not be necessary," he replies. "You must follow me. I will show you to your hotel."

I thank him profusely.

"Please. It is my duty," he humbly responds.

Fifteen minutes later I pump his hand very hard. We are outside the gates of the Bloom Star Hotel. His name is Mohammed and he tells me he is an author of books on Pakistani culture. I tell him he's a real gentleman too, but he merely waves me away with a shy laugh.

Entering the hotel, I'm met by the manager. He beams from ear to ear and warmly welcomes me. I walk to the reception desk like an arthritic old man. I'm covered from head to toe in grime, sand and white dust. My eyes and mouth are dry and gritty and the painkillers have most definitely worn off. The bike and every bag on it is absolutely caked in muck. I explain I have stopped for no more than a total of thirty minutes in ten hours and that I have only eaten snacks. Is it possible to get some food?

"Fresh food will be prepared for you to eat in our garden. You can have a shower first," he says with a big smile. Then he says something I never expected to hear:

"We also have a special licence from the government to serve foreigners with alcohol. Would you like me to put a beer in the freezer for you?"

After the toughest, most challenging ride of my life, it was as if the portals to my very own Shangri-la had opened.

Day 30 Quetta, Pakistan
0 miles

I sleep late then take a leisurely breakfast under a shady tree in the Bloom Star garden. Birds chirp all around and I can smell the fragrance wafting my way from nearby rose bushes. The hotel feels completely cut off from the thriving city that surrounds it, a real oasis of tranquillity.

Today is supposed to be a day off, but tell that to my brain. All I can think about is my bike and how I might strengthen it for the rest of the journey. I uncover it, sit on the ground with my back propped up by the car park wall, and spend ten minutes simply looking at it, hoping for inspiration. I cover it up again and set off to explore Quetta.

Outside the hotel I flag down an auto rickshaw, asking the driver to take me to a specific bank that the Bloom Star receptionist assures me has an ATM. I don't know what it is about rickshaws and me, but I seem to have an unconscious attraction to duds. I crashed in one in Thailand and in India and Nepal caught two that subsequently broke down. Today's journey, which is only two kilometres at the very most, takes a good thirty minutes.

We've only travelled five hundred metres when the little 2-stroker comes to a grinding halt... in the middle of a busy intersection. The traffic lights change and a line of quickly accelerating cars, bikes and other rickshaws come careering towards us, horns blaring. My driver hops out and begins to push his machine, with me inside, to the other side of the junction. Once safe, he rummages around under his seat and produces an adjustable spanner. Giving me an apology by means of a shrug, he disappears around the back of the rickshaw, lies on the ground, and begins working away underneath.

I'm in no real hurry so decide to stay put and see if he can fix the problem easily. A few minutes later he appears at the front of the cab and begins to loosen a nut that holds one end of the windscreen in place. Once done, he demonstrates the problem by pressing his foot up and down on the accelerator pedal - it uselessly flops around. Back under the rear of the vehicle, he uses the filched nut to reattach the accelerator rod to the engine.

We progress no more than three hundred metres when the engine begins to cough, splutter and then cuts out. I feel sorry for the hapless driver, who's looking very harassed by now. He signals me to wait in the cab, reaches for an empty plastic water bottle from under his seat and disappears across the road at a trot. I calmly wait, enjoying the chance to unobtrusively 'people-watch' from the shade of the cab. My cabbie returns ten minutes later with half a litre of petrol in his bottle which he proceeds to pour into the tank. We're off... for all of two minutes before the accelerator fails again. Once more my driver prostrates himself under the engine and makes his repairs, before the final leg to the bank. The poor guy is hot, filthy and looks very embarrassed by the whole experience. I give him the biggest tip I think I've ever given a taxi driver; he needs it!

Quetta is a fascinating place. Almost completely ringed by desolate hills, it sits in the centre of a vast desert amphitheatre. It's the provincial capital of Baluchistan and a key trading point between Pakistan and Afghanistan. The streets are chock-full with locally farmed fruits, textiles and crafts accompanied by a constant hubbub of wheeling and dealing amongst the traders and their customers. The population is officially quoted as half a million, but the real number of inhabitants could be as much as three times that due to the large number of Afghan immigrants and refugees.

I wander the streets after successfully extracting cash from the bank. Many people smile and say hello. I really enjoy taking the initiative when meeting people.

"As-Salamu Alaykum" I say to one man in a pharmacy. Three or four at once heartily respond,

"Alaykum As-Salamu" with handshakes all round.

I like this too, observing that men shake hands with people they see every day as part of their greeting ritual. The pharmacy has a 'phone which I use to make international calls at the bargain rate of three rupees per minute. I call Jane and my parents to warn them about the accident before I write anything on my blog. One of the staff, who hears me talking about my painful knee, produces a wooden stool for me to sit on. When I finish the last call, the manager signals for me to walk behind the counter, where he offers me a seat and a heavenly glass of cold mango juice taken from the medicinal fridge. I drink it out of sight of passers-by so as not to cause any offence, then offer to pay for it. The manager will have nothing of it, not for the first time on my journey explaining that it's his duty to offer hospitality to strangers.

The pavements and streets are vibrantly packed with all forms of life: donkeys and carts; a flock of goats, herded by a boy using a long staff; fruit sellers; cobblers; children running errands; women in bright and colourful traditional skirts and headscarves; buzzing rickshaws; random cyclists heading the wrong way against the flow of traffic; laundry wallahs pushing shaky wooden handcarts, returning piles of freshly pressed garments to their customers. There's a cacophony of voices and road noise too. It's mesmerising. The men are mostly imposing, long-bearded Pashtuns, who wear loose turbans on their heads and carry themselves with great poise and dignity, or Baluchis, wearing small, red, embroidered skull caps.

I rest at the hotel, talking with a couple of fellow guests. One, Ahmed, spends time telling me about Islam and the major role Jesus Christ plays in it. It makes me realise just how little I know about the religion, and it's fascinating to hear that Muslims also call Jesus 'Messiah'. According to Ahmed, who's both articulate and erudite, they too believe Jesus was raised to heaven by God (Allah) and that he will, at the 'end of time' be resurrected to reunite good against evil.

I find Ahmed both exceedingly interesting and very humane. We discuss Pakistan's problems and how it's portrayed by CNN and other global TV news channels. He talks about the images usually shown of extremists or terrorists, tearing around the Afghan border regions in open-topped jeeps, heavy machine guns cocked and ready to fire. He then points to himself; he has the clothes, the long beard, the headwear, the open sandals.

"All I need is a bandolier of bullets around my shoulder and I could be your Taliban, Al-Qaeda or any other form of extremist militant" he says.

We laugh together. Like so many others I've met in my short stay in Pakistan, he is an open, genuine man with a very big heart. He gives me a friendly hug as we part.

Returning to my bike, I try to straighten the front forks by loosening all the pinch bolts and the steering head, but no matter how much I strain at the handlebars, I cannot shift them. Reflecting that it's still possible to ride with them as they are, I transfer my attention to the rear end. The now brown back tyre has a jet black ring around its drive-side edge where it has rubbed on the subframe when bouncing along the Quetta road. I replace the cable ties with a shorter bolt put on in reverse, resulting in a couple of millimetres extra clearance. Then I remove the panniers and jack the rear suspension up another notch to its hardest setting, adding another centimetre to the unloaded height of the rear mudguard. I fail to get either of my two horns to work, but at least make sure the headlight glass and the handlebar fixings are fully secured.

In the cool of the evening I sit in the garden talking to another guest. He's a feudal landowner and farmer from the southern Sindh province. I find his openness refreshing as he discusses a long line of topics from agreements with his tenant farmers (a 50% share in their crops) to his successful arranged marriage with his second cousin. Their three gorgeous children play around the garden edge for some of the time, coming over to gravely shake my hand at their father's request.

Just as our conversation is drawing to a close, a new guest, completely dressed in black bike gear, arrives and is shown to a room on the far side of the hotel gardens. As he walks past he says,

"Hi Gordon. I'll come and talk in a minute"

I'm intrigued, not having a clue who could possibly know me here. I go to the reception area and see a crash helmet plonked on a chair. Outside is a huge BMW 1200 cc cruiser. The rider comes back, warmly shakes my hand and tells me his name is Cem (pronounced Chem) from Switzerland.

He explains that he's been riding one day behind me and has seen my name at the bottom of the list at every police checkpoint he has stopped at. He then saw my name as the only foreigner registered at the hotel. It's great to compare notes with him over a beer, and he confirms that today was the hardest ride of his life, but like me, it's a day's journey he will always look back on with great satisfaction.

I decide to stay another day in Quetta as my aches seem to be getting worse, not better, and it'll be enjoyable to have the company of another motorcyclist into the bargain.

Day 31 Quetta, Pakistan
0 miles

What a strange experience, waking slowly and not needing to busy myself with bike riding preparations. It makes me realise just how quickly my days on the road have become the norm. Thoughts of routine chores and work at home are virtually non-existent and although I do miss people, I'm so completely 'in the moment' when I'm travelling that it thoroughly dominates my thoughts. Although a further day of rest seems necessary, I go and look at my bike straight after breakfast and yearn to be back on it again.

My knee has benefited from another night's rest and is definitely improving. The bruising on my hip is at its most colourful but the road burn has now scabbed over and looks clear of infection. The sores on my elbow are suppurating and I have to painfully clean them and apply more antiseptic cream. However, my ribcage is the greatest concern. I caught a cold in Esfahan so I 'm still coughing and sneezing; not exactly the kind of respite my bruised ribs need.

Cem to the rescue. He's an engineer and has just completed a three month assignment in Taiwan. Whilst there he bought some large *Tiger Balm* patches, which he swears will cure all manner of ailments. They're at least six inches square and inimitably suitable for the job. I put one on my chest and Cem commences to bandage it firmly in place. It's the middle of the afternoon and very hot so I immediately apologise for any unpleasant odours as I lift my arms.

"Not a problem," says Cem. "Hey, we're bikers, right" he adds with a fake macho voice.

He kindly gives me a handful of patches to take with me, saying he doesn't plan to crash his bike and certainly won't need them all. The heat generated by the *Tiger Balm* has an almost instant soothing effect.

We spend a couple of companionable hours working on our bikes. I'm truly impressed by Cem's BMW, it's a beautifully engineered machine with smooth, flowing lines. He bought it new in California in 2000 whilst on secondment there and shipped it home to Switzerland two years later. Famous for stunts in the James Bond film T*omorrow Never Dies*, I'm surprised when Cem tells me that only forty thousand R1200 US export cruisers were ever made. I agree with him that it could one day be regarded as a classic, with its winning combination of contemporary design, sound engineering such as anti-dive front suspension and ABS brakes, plus its solid good performance. It's a hundred kilograms heavier than my Bullet and must have been a major test of Cem's riding skills to manhandle it over the road from Dalbandin. He shrugs; like me, he loves his bike and couldn't imagine making the journey on anything else.

On close inspection, we notice that my rear tyre is even more noticeably wearing. In my panniers I have a bottle of *Slime*, a fluoro green gooey liquid used to help prevent punctures. Together we remove my inner tube valve core and squeeze the solution into the tyre. Cem has a very efficient foot pump and in no time the tyre is back to full pressure and the job done. I hope it lasts to Chennai, which is still more than three thousand five hundred miles away. There is the option of exchanging it with my front tyre, but as that wheel's grip under braking is so crucial, I'm loathe to do it.

Cem plans to stay tomorrow then head north to the Karakoram Highway, the precipitous route north through the Hindu Kush to Kashgar in China via the remarkable Khunjerab Pass. After that he hopes to backtrack south to Lahore where he'll cross into India then motor east to his final destination, Nepal. I'm sorely tempted to stay another day in Quetta as it's so restful hanging out in the Bloom Star garden, but I don't want to put myself under the extra pressure of having to make up time in India. I decide I'll move on tomorrow.

There are two routes I can take. The shorter northern route is mountainous with very poor roads, passing through Loralai, Mekhtar, Fort Munro and Dera Ghazi Khan en route to Multan. It crosses a tribal area, the Loralai District, where Pakistani law has no force. I'm told by the hotel receptionist, who is a mine of local travel knowledge, that in theory I'm supposed to have a permit to pass through that region and will undoubtedly be picked up by the police at the district boundary and given an escort. I'd like to give it a go, as I understand the scenery is very beautiful and the mountainous route appeals to my sense of adventure. However, for the sake of my bike and body I opt for the three hundred kilometre longer southern route, which I'm promised will take me on roads 'as smooth as the reception desk'. We shall see!

Towards the end of the day Cem finds me and warns there has been a suicide bombing at the Marriott Hotel in Islamabad, resulting in at least fifty deaths.

"I was planning to stay there," he says, explaining that his company frequently uses that American hotel chain and he has amassed a considerable number of Reward Points. "I guess I'd better think about staying somewhere else," he concludes.

I like Pakistani food very much, it's flavoursome but not overly spicy hot. However it doesn't like me very much. All the curries are swimming in oil which has quite a loosening effect on my gut. The Bloom Star's cook must go through litres of it every evening, so I decide to venture out to a recommended top class restaurant where the chef may be more responsive to my appeals for dry(ish) food. Along with Cem, I set off to look for a rickshaw but before we can flag one down, a large car pulls up at the hotel gates. Its driver, a good friend of the Bloom Star's owner, winds down his window and offers us a lift, which we gratefully accept.

The car is a luxury Japanese import. Its interiors are all soft leather, with ambient lighting and icy air conditioning. The dashboard, illuminated in green and blue, resembles a modern airliner cockpit and the music that emits from the quality Hi-Fi sounds sublime. It's like travelling in a bubble of modernity, completely cut off from the real, if somewhat harsher, world on the outside. It serves as a timely reminder of just how much riding a motorcycle puts you right in the thick of things, and intensifies all the experiences of travel. Glad as I am for the lift, I know which method of transport I prefer.

The meal is all that I anticipated; tasty without being awash with oil. It's amazing just how important the quality of your food becomes when travelling. Cem and I spend the evening talking about future overland bike trips we would each like to make: Africa; Mongolia; the Pan American Highway; North Cape... aggghhh!

Day 32 Quetta to Sukkur, Pakistan
248 miles

It's great to be moving again and I find my way out of Quetta with surprising ease. True to form, the locals that I check my navigation with are both congenial and helpful. At first I struggle to pronounce my destination, Sukkur, correctly. I try a few variations, pointing first at my map then along the road ahead:

"Sukaar...? Sookoor...? Suk-Kor...?" but have no joy.

Then someone clicks on to my destination.

"SUCKER! SUCKER!" he calls out.

Oh well, I guess it had to be.

Roughly thirty miles on, the road enters a deep ravine. I'm stopped at a police checkpost that consists of little more than a couple of old army issue canvas tents next to a chain across the road. After a few minutes, two policemen mount a motorcycle and tell me the road ahead is very dangerous and they are to be my escort for the next twenty kilometres. The pillion has a Kalashnikov in his hands. I don't like guns and am a firm believer that violence perpetuates violence. Still, I have little option but to follow my guards.

It reminds me of a motorcycle magazine test I did in Northern Ireland during the latter years of that province's 'troubles'. I was puttering down a country road in the shadow of the Mountains of Mourne on a 1949 350cc British bike, searching for places to stop to photograph the machine. I swept round a bend to find myself right up against the tail of a British Army Saracen armoured personnel carrier. I braked hard and dropped down a gear to match my pace to that of the military vehicle. The young soldier in the turret was facing my way, his finger on the trigger of a roof-mounted heavy machine gun. It was pointing straight at the middle of my chest. Thinking it would look suspicious if I immediately stopped, I lifted my hand to give a wave and followed the armoured car for at least ten minutes. A cold sweat overcame my body as I fretted that a bump in the road might cause the soldier to fire accidently, or that the armoured car was in itself a prime target and that I didn't want to get caught up in anyone else's fights.

I'm relieved when we exit the rocky valley and stop beside a police Toyota truck with a canvas back. There are two police in the cab and two armed guards riding shotgun in the back. My reprieve is short-lived, they are my next escort.

Each one says "As-Salamu Alaykum" and warmly shakes my hand.

Again I have no choice but to follow them, this time over a bridge at least a kilometre long which crosses wide, bone-dry flood plains. They take me to the end of their jurisdiction, probably another fifteen kilometres, where they sharply pull in to the side and wave me on. I'm amazed to see that my next team of protectors are already rolling ahead and think to myself that their organisation, which must be happening via walkie-talkie as I ride, is superlative.

This sequence of events continues for a couple of hours until I get ahead of a slow escort on a fast stretch of road. Their Toyota jeep looks well past its use-by date, painfully graunching through its gear changes until it rattles along at a top speed of 50 KMPH. I surge ahead and they simply cannot keep up with my motorcycle as I weave in and out overtaking a long line of trucks, figuring I'm in no imminent danger on this excellent stretch of dual-carriageway. I think they must give up on me as it's the last I see of them.

Some time later I stop and haul my bike under the partial shade of a thorn tree. A farmer sits on an ageing tractor under a nearby tree, smoking a cigarette and listening to loud, wailing music on a crackly transistor radio. I go over and ask his permission to rest here. He's dressed in dusty, threadbare salwar kameez and his dark skin is dry and wrinkled by the hours he spends outdoors. He speaks no English but understands my request nevertheless. Hand on heart, he gestures that I am very welcome on his land. Lunch today consists of banana on bread, a childhood favourite of mine, some fresh dates from Bam, which surprisingly (and thankfully) haven't gone off in the heat, together with a handful of almonds. After a quarter of an hour I wave cheerio to the farmer, who, starting his engine, decides it's time to get back to work too. What work he plans to carry out on this crusty, parched land is hard to imagine.

I'm soon picked up by another police patrol. They're heading west looking for me and do a sliding stop and action-thriller U-turn to come after me. They overtake and with big smiles but firm hand actions, indicate that I'm to stay behind them. The super efficient system of rolling hand-overs continues throughout the afternoon, with no retinue taking me more than twenty kilometres before smilingly waving me past in a slick transfer to my next bodyguards.

The police take some interesting detours to avoid the busy central areas of towns we pass through. I see places where people live very basic, simple, rustic lives, with livestock wandering the streets and feed piled up around their single room homes. Yet they're not more than a few hundred metres from the very heart of towns with populations I estimate of between fifty and a hundred thousand people. Naked infants play at the edge of the road and older children chase each other or play football whilst dodging traffic. The streets are full of slow-moving vehicles, everything from wide, lumbering buses to farmers pushing handcarts weighed down with produce or feed. I make slow, if fascinating, progress.

The land changes dramatically as I enter the fertile Indus valley. Over just a few kilometres, dry, arid rocks and sand transform into bountiful fields of crops fed by immense flowing waterways and a convoluted network of irrigation ditches. After more than two weeks of dusty high plain and desert it's very soothing to my eyes.

Following my final escort in the dark, I reach Sukkur at 8.30 pm. I'm dead beat, having ridden over nine and a half hours with just that single fifteen minute stop. I can only guess at the number of police units that have cosseted me; somewhere between thirty and thirty five. I feel guilty about taking up so much valuable police time, but they're insistent that I need protection after yesterday's Marriott Hotel bombing.

We pull up outside Sukkur's most expensive hotel, The Forum Inn, a relatively modern tower block in the city centre. It looks well above my accommodation budget. Although my stay here appears to the police as a done deal, I refuse to let them unload my bike until I've checked out the room rates. I'm next in the queue to two UN field workers who pulled up in their white Land Rover just seconds before me. They're obviously Europeans, although I can't tell by their accents where they originate from. As I suspected, the tariff is fairly steep, so I thank the receptionist for his time and head for the door.

My escort are nonplussed when I tell them I must find a cheaper hotel. A sergeant gets straight onto his walkie-talkie and, after a quick-fire conversation, asks me to wait beside my bike. I'm keen to just ride off and find somewhere for myself, but it's made very clear to me that this is not an option. Ten minutes later a rather rotund plain-clothes police inspector gets out of the back of a police car and introduces himself.

"Why do you not want to stay here?" he begins.

I explain that the hotel is too expensive and that I would like to find somewhere cheaper.

"Do you not have any money?" he asks with concern.

"Yes, of course," I reply, "but this hotel charges more than I want to pay. I usually stay in small hotels or guest houses."

"But there is a bank with an ATM across the road. You can get more money there," he persists.

"Yes, but I don't want to spend so much money," I retort.

The conversation comes to a grinding halt, both of us quite stubbornly sticking to our guns.

The inspector talks in Urdu to his sergeant. Several times I pick up the English words, 'guest house' and 'security risk'. After one more failed attempt to persuade me to cough up more money for the Forum Inn, to which I reply that staying in a more expensive hotel doesn't guarantee safety, vis a vis the Marriott, he huffily marches inside. A few minutes later I'm summoned to the reception desk where the inspector and hotel manager make a proposition; I can have a room at a specially reduced rate if I will agree to stay there. They then ask how much I wish to pay, to which I suggest a price twice what I paid in Quetta but just over half of this hotel's rate. A deal is made.

The police escort and all the hotel staff must think me their nightmare customer. They tell me to park my bike across the road in a parking lot. It's not exactly safe, indeed, far from it as children are currently playing football amongst the cars parked there. The long suffering senior police officer is called upon again, only this time he immediately orders his subordinates to assist me in humping my Enfield up a broad flight of steps that lead to the automated hotel door. I can park it next to the foyer plate glass window where I'm assured a night guard will be able to keep an eye on it. I can't help imagining his thoughts of 'anything to get this damned motorcyclist out of my hair!' and have to force myself not to laugh out loud.

I'm almost too embarrassed by all the fuss to show my face in the hotel restaurant some thirty minutes later, but I'm spared as the other diners have finished their meals and left. The staff treat me with good grace and the vegetable Jalfrezi that I'm deftly served is excellent. Without leaving the 'safe' bosom of the hotel, I head back to my room and fall asleep watching an old American cowboy film on television.

Day 33 Sukkur to Bahawalpur, Pakistan
236 miles

Today's first escort is patiently waiting for me in the hotel lobby, but before we can leave I have to do the daily maintenance on my motorcycle. This causes them great concern.

"There is a problem? What is wrong?" they ask.

The concept of maintenance goes right over their heads, which is no surprise. Most bikes I've seen from Turkey onwards are run until they break down, at which point they're fixed. Today I have to adjust the rear chain. I managed to get my Iwis Megalife shortened to the correct length in Iran and it's done two thousand miles since then. As promised, it has stayed very clean despite all the sand and dust I've ridden through and this is the first adjustment I've had to make.

With the help of four strapping officers, I soon bounce the bike down the hotel steps, load up and set off. I only ride a hundred metres before I spot a petrol station. My guards fail to see me indicating left and continue merrily on their way, only to come back frantically searching for me a few minutes later. I fill up with fuel, which seems to be getting cheaper the further east I head, then make another start.

The troop lead me across the Sukkur Barrage, an enormous series of sluice gates built on the Indus by the British in the time of the Raj. The hotel receptionist told me this morning that the barrage controls the irrigation of three million hectares of prime Sindh agricultural land. The mighty Indus looks immensely powerful as it silently slides underneath the road I roar along atop of the dam, but it's impossible to stop and enjoy the moment as my escort constantly watch my movements, urging me to catch up whenever I slow down.

One of my fondest memories of visiting Pakistan in 1988 is the trucks, and in particular the 1960's British Bedford trucks made under licence here. These venerable old thumpers were covered inside and out in the most sparkling, whimsical artwork imaginable. I remember hitching a lift in one close to Gilgit, a major settlement at the edge of the Himalayas. Access to the cab was through two flatly opening carved wooden doors. The driver's area was just as crazy as the outside of the vehicle, with tin baubles and twinkling mirrors dangling from the ceiling and the dashboard covered in intricate, loudly-coloured applique.

Although Pakistan's omnipresent trucks have gone on to achieve new heights in garish and gaudy design, many professionally created at a cost equivalent to two years of their driver's salary, I've been slightly disappointed thus far to see the base vehicles are modern Hinos and Isuzus. Today, however, all that changes, with my first sighting of a traditional Bedford.

"Aha!" I shout out jubilantly.

Its sidepanels are painted with Dali-esque landscapes of lakes and mountains, but in stark contrast, the back sports a faded image of the assassinated Gereral Zia. The truck can hardly move, it's so ludicrously overloaded with hay held in place by a stretched white tarpaulin secured over the top. It has burgeoned outrageously above the cargo bay like a loaf of bread growing to three times the size of its baking tin.

From this point on, Bedfords become more common than the modern alternatives, obviously part of several old fleets that work this region's highways. It's such a thrill to see them again, no matter how much they resemble an ear-popping mobile disco that assaults my senses as I pass.

Squads of police await my arrival along the highway. Like yesterday, there's no stopping. I can't remember ever seeing a Pakistan team in the Olympics 4 x 400 metre relay race but these guys should consider putting one together. Their handovers are superbly choreographed and the baton, i.e. one man on an old motorcycle, is never dropped.

Around half past one I'm brought to a halt at a major checkpoint. This is the state border between Sindh and the Punjab. I wait for over an hour whilst the Punjabi police coordinate their forces. I spend the time eating my lunch (you guessed it, the same as yesterday) and chatting with the Sindh policeman. All the uniformed officers appear to defer to a tall civilian in business trousers and a plain white shirt. Wiping his forehead with a handkerchief, he comes over to say hello.

"I'm a plain-clothes member of the security services," he begins after we've shaken hands. He produces an ID card to validate his credentials. Taking down all my details in a notebook, he then explains the need for this over-the-top security.

"To be honest, you are perfectly safe travelling on your own. It is a part of Pakistan's culture, and also Islam, that we are to offer hospitality to strangers and travellers." He continues, "But our government is very keen that no harm should come to any foreign national after the bombing in Islamabad, and we have received instructions to ensure that any foreigner travelling on our roads is to be accompanied by the police for the time being."

It makes sense, but I do feel very uneasy about taking up so much of their time.

"Please, do not concern yourself," says the officer.

Right on cue my first Punjabi escort arrives in a practically new jeep. I'm introduced to my latest group of protectors; they're quite different from the men I have had with me up to this point. The Baluchistan and Sindh officers wore smartly pressed beige trousers, a grey or navy shirt with police epaulettes and sometimes a beret-style hat. They were regular police, often middle-aged with paunches. My new escorts are young, lean and fit. They wear black combat trousers and training shoes. Their black t-shirts have a large shield screenprinted on the front with an image of two crossed handguns in the middle. 'Elite Force', 'Commando' and 'No Fear' are emblazoned in bold white script on the front, back and sleeves. At first I can't believe they're for real and am tempted to ask if they had the t-shirts printed at the bazaar for a bit of fun. I quickly decide that might be a bit tactless as they do look remarkably focussed. They must be what their t-shirts say they are... even their vehicle has 'Elite Police' painted on its doors and tailgate.

After saying farewell to my final set of Sindh officers, I set off in hot pursuit of my 'commando' unit. The motorway, a dual carriageway mostly used by trucks, is just as smooth as promised by the Bloom Star staff. When passing through towns it becomes the main street and I have to slow for rickshaws, bicycles, herds of wandering long-eared sheep, goats and water buffalo, food-stall holders pushing their glass-topped carts and a host of 50 cc motorcycles that buzz around in all directions. It's a very colourful if somewhat slow ride.

I especially like the water buffalo; they seem such a gentle animal. Then I get stuck behind a small truck with two immense adult buffs in the back. They're so large that their rumps protrude over the tailgate, their tails swishing from side to side. I'm hemmed in on both sides and can't slow down as a petrol tanker is millimetres from my rear numberplate. There's no way round, so I have to keep my position in the road at the mercy of these two enormous creatures' bowels. With relief, I'm spared from that slapstick fate.

When I stop for fuel, I notice that an unmarked car that's been hovering somewhere in my mirrors for the last few miles also pulls in. One of the Elite Forces' officers goes over and converses with the driver through his window. I ask another of the team who the car belongs to.

"He's a government official who's travelling with us to make sure everything goes okay" I'm told.

Blimey Charlie!

After the motorway stretch, which lasts for a hundred and thirty kilometres, I'm relayed on to regular police who tag team me all the way to the city of Bahawalpur and the 'Luxury Hotel'. The mystery government official stays somewhere in the background along the way, but vanishes from sight when I pull up outside my hotel. Today's ride took about nine hours, with just the one hour stop at the state border. Again I'm extremely fatigued, but need to do some maintenance on my bike, especially the tappets and points. Thankfully, the police, who must think I'm safe here, leave me to get on with it in peace.

I go out for pizza as the hotel restaurant, lacking a single clean tablecloth and sporting an even filthier floor, looks like a considerable health risk. Catching an auto-rickshaw, which for once works and has enough fuel, I arrive safely at Pan Pizza. It's a strange, dark restaurant, with tables built on brick platforms so thick that it's virtually impossible to sit front on without grazing my knees. To my delight their menu offers vegetarian pizza. When it arrives, it tastes like last night's vegetable Jalfrezi curry that's been simmered down to a thick paste and spread on a roti with a mound of goats cheese melted on top. Strange, but unexpectedly enjoyable.

Day 34 Bahawalpur to Lahore, Pakistan
270 miles

For reasons unknown I have no police escort at all today; I've mysteriously slipped through the net.

I leave the inaptly named Luxury Hotel and head north. At traffic lights I ask a young motorcyclist if I'm on the right road.

"Follow me," he responds.

Like many riders in Iran and Pakistan, this man enjoys a good conversation whilst riding side-by-side with a companion. I find this particularly unnerving as traffic is heavy and coming at me from all directions. My new friend tells me his name is Lillee. His father is a big cricket fan and named him after legendary Australian cricket fast bowler, Dennis Lillee.

Now he's hit on a subject close to my heart. I tell him I'm a big New Zealand cricket fan and have watched several thrilling one-day games between our two countries. This goes down a storm and I'm delighted when he begins to list back to me his favourite New Zealand cricketers, some of whom were probably playing before he was born... Richard Hadlee, Glenn Turner, John Wright, Martin Crowe, Stephen Fleming, Danny Vettori... music to my ears! It's with some regret that we part at the beginning of the expressway, him to Bahawalpur University for classes and me in the direction of Lahore.

Heading north for a while, I then take a shortcut to bypass the large city of Multan. It's a poor choice. The road is ninety kilometres long with more than fifty percent of it under repair. I'm reduced to a slow crawl and eventually to a halt. There's a complete log jam of buses, trucks and rickshaws ahead. Nothing moves. The sun beats down and I feel like I'm beginning to melt.

All the other motorcyclists head off road and ride in the sand and gravel at the side. It looks treacherous and I'm reluctant to try to manhandle my bike over the verge. After ten static minutes with horns blaring all around I know what I must do. I turn my bike at right angles to the road, rev it through shingle and bounce over the edge before zigzagging backwards and forwards to make myself once again parallel with the road. Ahead lie acres of sandy, rocky wasteland that I have to navigate with extreme care, standing high on my footpegs to keep my bike's centre of gravity as low as possible.

All goes well for a couple of kilometres until my route is blocked by huge piles of gravel being shovelled from dumper trucks by wiry, tough looking men, stripped to the waist and sweating profusely. The motorcyclist ahead bumps himself back onto the road, weaves between a couple of stationary wagons, then hops over the verge at the other side. I try to follow but my bike gets stuck in the sand. I stamp my left foot down but it sinks deep, failing to find any leverage. It's not in the most graceful manner that I fall off, but at least this time I'm not underneath the bike.

A couple of workmen rush over to help me right the Enfield. One grabs the throttle grip and yanks it straight off the handlebars. Together they try again and this time have more success. With their help I push the bike across the road and park up on more solid ground. There's no damage, but I'm panting with exertion. It takes just a couple of minutes to straighten a twisted mirror and brake lever, rethread the throttle cable onto the twist grip and restart the engine. The crowd of workmen, truckers and passers-by applaud when my bike starts third kick.

Five minutes of easier riding sees me clear of the traffic jam. I stop to buy some fruit from a village foodstall, then find a shady tree to eat under. As I sit on the baked earth, sipping water and munching on a saved piece of last night's curried pizza (which tastes even better today... like all good curries do), I realise that I haven't even inspected my 'pride and joy' for scratches or dents caused by this morning's drop. I stay where I am and smile to myself, thinking my obsessive need for my bike's perfection has been literally knocked out of me. Over the course of the journey, it has transformed from a much-prized artefact to a valiant workhorse.

It takes nearly three hours to regain the motorway. I'm dead beat and my eyes begin to close. I try standing on the footpegs, drinking some water, even shouting at myself, but nothing works. I'm falling asleep. Pulling off the highway at a convenient petrol station, I see there's a small shaded lawn in one corner. I park next to it, groggily climb off the bike, and as usual am quickly surrounded by a small crowd. Without hesitation or comment, I walk a few paces onto the grass, make a mound from my jacket, helmet and back protector, rest head and shoulder on it and am almost instantly asleep.

In *Jupiter's Travels*, Ted Simon says he developed a totally reliable intuition about when he and his belongings were safe. For some reason I know this applies to me today. As my eyes close I see the onlookers walk away from my bike. When I awake some thirty minutes later, it sits by itself, my gear untouched. Casually stowed in easily accessible bags are a couple of thousand pounds worth of electronics: digital camera; video camera; lenses and microphone; satellite navigation; mobile phone. I was so groggy when I arrived that I didn't even put a padlock and chain around the wheel and the bike doesn't have an ignition lock so anyone could have kicked it over and ridden away. I feel rather pleased with both the soundness of my intuition and the trustworthiness of the people hereabouts.

A man approaches and asks if I'm all right.

"I'm fine, thank you. Just very tired," I reply, pretending to force my eyelids open with my fingers to illustrate my sleepiness.

He leaves but soon returns with a cold Coke. It's a gift. He tells me he's a truck driver and I thank him for his kindness. I then pay him a compliment along with a thumbs up signal,

"Pakistani truck drivers are the best."

He smiles, not sure if I'm being serious, but from my experience it's true. These rolling works of art outnumber cars at least ten to one so they've been my constant companions since entering the country. More than this; the drivers have been extremely friendly and helpful, moving aside to let me pass, giving me space to manoeuvre and more often than not tooting their horns and waving to me.

It's late by the time I eventually reach the outskirts of Lahore. Before leaving the UK I made it a rule to never ride at night. Today I'm forced to break my rule yet again. I simply cannot see a hotel on the approaches to the city so as the sun dips below the horizon, I switch on my lights and press on. The headlamp works fine, although its beam still angles heavenwards from my altercation with the sand dune, but the tail lamp is dead, broken at the point where the bulb makes contact with the wiring. I presume it's another victim of the pounding the bike received on the road to Quetta. I'm not in the best shape to safely continue, but have no choice.

Following signposts through Lahore for the Wagah border post, I take a straightforward but dimly lit route along the banks of a canal. I constantly look out for a hotel and after thirty tense minutes spot one to the left. It looks like a 5-star establishment but I'm desperate to get off the road so decide to check it out. Not only am I fearful that a speeding car will crash into the back of me, I'm just as concerned that I'll plough into the back of an unlighted cycle rickshaw, bullock cart or one of the many mopeds that tear around with their lights off, presumably to extend the lives of their bulbs!

No matter how I try, I can't find a way back to the hotel and nearly run into the rear of a donkey cart carrying large blocks of ice in the process. Then three cars in a row muscle past, all with their lights turned off, but at least they spot me and briefly flash their headlights on to alert me of their intentions. This isn't an enjoyable experience and I curse myself for the 'short-cut' this morning that resulted in me being so late.

I stop nine kilometres from the border beside a police car. The officers tell me there's no accommodation near the frontier, but direct me to a hotel about a kilometre back that I passed without noticing. It's another fleapit, The Red Rose, but at least I've survived the journey and they allow me to wheel my motorcycle into the reception area for the night. For the life of me I cannot understand how the hotel stays in business. There don't appear to be any other guests and the reception area has a group of middle aged men, probably friends of the hotel manager, sitting around smoking hashish.

I've ridden for almost eleven hours today, one and a half of them in the dark. I'm so filthy that I don't know where to begin cleaning myself, especially as the shower doesn't work and the sink wobbles dangerously when I turn on the tap. I go for a walk in search of food. The hotel is on the edge of a guarded residential compound and I see one house with a night guard sitting on a stool beside its garden gate, a pump-action shotgun casually lying across his knees. I smile and wave as I walk past him, thinking he's not someone I'd like to get on the wrong side of.

There are no local restaurants so dinner is the last of my muesli with some yoghurt and biscuits from a small shop. To relax, I lie on my bed and listen to an English music programme on my wind-up radio. I've used it purely as a torch up until now, but tonight, in this dowdy, damp room, it gives me some much needed company, even if the station's favoured brand of 80's American pop-rock is almost unbearably slushy.

Day 35 Lahore to Amritsar, India
32 miles

The hotel staff are still asleep at 8 am and I have to wake them to get into the reception area. It takes several journeys for me to carry my gear down three floors before I can load the bike, making it almost 9 am before I'm ready to depart. I nip back upstairs to my room for a final check that I've left nothing behind, noting that a man and woman, whom I'd just seen in the reception area, are being shown into a room next to mine. Funny, I think, checking in so early in the day without any luggage. As they walk past me they look sheepishly away from my gaze. It suddenly makes sense how this hotel makes most of its money. For want of a better term, I guess it's called a 'knocking shop', renting rooms by the hour. This explains why my rather below par room was so expensive for a whole night!

I arrive at the Pakistan Immigration and Customs hall just before 10 am. The only other vehicle parked there is a bright pink long-wheelbase Land Rover towing a large trailer. It's well set up for overland expeditions, with an extended engine breather pipe to allow it to ford rivers, a substantial winch on the front and a couple of spare wheels on the roof. The tour group, consisting of seven Swedes, comes over to say hello. They're a friendly bunch and most intrigued with my Royal Enfield.

"You must be the guy we hung around for yesterday!" says one of the group, in mock accusation.

He goes on to tell me that they've been escorted by the police for the last three days but that yesterday they were made to wait for half an hour whilst the police searched for a lone motorcyclist in Bahawalpur to join them. Oops!

I apologise, but explain that no police were waiting at my hotel yesterday morning so I just set off. They're good humoured about it, moving quickly on to having their photographs taken posing with my bike. Their journey turns out to be even more fast-paced than mine. Bound for Tibet, which they must enter within five days before their visas expire, their whole tour, which started in Stockholm, lasts only 35 days. There's a certain symmetry to that number as today is the 35th day of my journey.

Once I've wished them all luck and vice versa, I enter the Customs hall. It doesn't take long to get processed, the procedure with my carnet being the fastest to date. The only other migrant in the hall is one of the most bizarre travellers I have ever met. He's a thin, balding Japanese man wearing clothes more suitable for gardening than travelling... not that

I can talk! His luggage comprises the smallest of holdalls, roughly the size of a school lunch bag, and a folding bicycle with tiny white wheels that he sits astride whist having his passport stamped.

He doesn't speak any English and my Japanese these days has shrunk to little more than Konnichiwa and Sayonara, but he conveys that he's travelled overland from Shanghai through China and India and is heading to Europe. I'm unable to ascertain if he's actually cycling the whole way (surely not on that bike) or whether he uses trains and buses. Whichever, I'm more than impressed with his journey if a little baffled by his appearance and modus operandi.

I make a short trip across no-mans-land heading for the Indian border control offices. The stretch of tarmac between the two countries' border posts is remarkable. Along one side of the road is a two hundred metre long strip of grandstand seating, separated in the middle by a wire fence. It's here that the border closing ceremony takes place every day,

The ritual, in which troops of Indian and Pakistani soldiers fervently try to outshine each other, has been a daily occurrence since 1948. With goose-stepping marches that emulate John Cleese's iconic funny walk in the *Fawlty Towers* episode, 'The Germans', the opposing soldiers endeavour to out-salute, out-march and out-shout each other as part of the flag lowering spectacle. Visitors are able to watch the event from the grandstands and I've read that it's very popular amongst tourists as well as patriots of the two countries. It's a shame that I won't see it as the atmosphere of pomp and rivalry is almost tangible when I slowly ride my bike beside the stands.

The immigration process on the Indian side is straightforward too, although I am pointed to sit at a desk opposite a sleeping man for ten minutes. The man, I guess to be a manager close to retirement age, snores heavily, a newspaper open on his lap fluttering in the draught caused by his personal free-standing electric fan. I'm not really sure why I'm here, wondering if I'm supposed to wake him so he can review my paperwork or if it's more diplomatic to patiently wait until he stirs. It transpires that neither of these guesses is right. It's the man who sent me to this seat that will process my application. He was just being kind by offering me somewhere to sit whilst he dealt with an Indian holidaymaker.

Soon after, I'm questioned quite closely about my Royal Enfield. Several customs officers gather round, my paperwork in hand. None of them knew that Royal Enfields were once made in the UK; they only think of it as an Indian motorcycle. I give them a potted history and I receive in return a stamp in my carnet and a ticket that allows me to clear the compound gatehouse.

At 12.10 pm precisely, a pair of heavy wrought iron gates are opened for me and I enter India. I check my odometer; I've ridden 6,390 miles from Manchester.

Last night was a long one with a bad stomach and I'd been feeling pretty ropey in the Indian immigration hall too, reluctantly popping a couple of pills to calm everything down. As I gun the engine and accelerate away, my nausea evaporates. I feel an upswell of joy. Laughing out loud, I pat my bike's tank several times. My brilliant motorcycle has brought me all this way, overland to India. As usual it responds with a hearty roar.

It's not long before I spot my first Indian Bullet, two in fact; one black, one silver. Both are parked at the side of the road, their young riders stopped for a chat. They look up as I ride past and I give them a big thumbs-up. They respond with bemused looks, but it goes right over my head... I'm grinning like the Cheshire Cat.

I follow the Grand Trunk Road thirty kilometres to Amritsar where I call it a day. My chosen accommodation, The Grand Hotel, is easy to spot as I approach the city centre. Fantastic. There's nothing worse than endlessly chugging around crowded city streets searching for a bed for the night. I'm cooling down under a shower no more than half an hour after entering the country.

Following a light lunch in the hotel garden cafe, I catch a cycle rickshaw to the Golden Temple. I always try to patronise these pedal-powered rickshaw wallahs when possible. They work so hard and seem to be right at the bottom of the automotive pecking order, harassed by buses, cars and auto rickshaws alike. Nevertheless, I tend to feel a little guilty as they sweat and toil to haul me around. This afternoon we have to go up a steep ramp to a roundabout which is too much for my man, who climbs off and starts pushing. I feel even guiltier than before, so jump off and walk beside him to the top.

We reach the perimeter of the Golden Temple complex. I take off my shoes and am given an orange headscarf to wear. I'm horrified when I catch sight of my reflection in a shop window; I look like a fancy-dress pirate with the headscarf, my beard and earrings! I decide a shave is needed very soon, having not attempted one since the demise of my razor in Bulgaria.

The temple is culturally the most important as well as the oldest gudwara (place of worship) for Sikhs. The main temple area is a wide, white tiled walkway built around a square lake. In the middle, along a causeway, is Harmandir Sahib, the Golden Temple itself. It's considered most holy by Sikhs as they believe the eternal Guru of Sikhism, Sri Guru Granth Sahib, is always present within.

The sun is low in the sky and the temple glows as though it were on fire. It's stunningly beautiful. Thousands of worshippers and pilgrims move around the water's edge. Most of the male Sikhs are clothed in white with vibrant coloured turbans, many wearing a kirpan, a small strapped silver sword. Some strip and bathe in the lake too.

I follow a long line of devotees in an orderly queue along the causeway and into the ornately decorated temple. There's a reverent atmosphere. A large group sit praying in the middle and a small cluster of musicians play subtle music and chant incantations. Quietly standing in a corner, I absorb the holy ambience.

When I came here in 1988, it was under completely different circumstances and the changes are immense. Then, Amritsar was off limits to foreigners due to armed militant activity. I'd found myself there totally by accident, having been stranded on a diverted train from Kashmir to Delhi by severe monsoon flooding. Along with three others, Jude and I were given shelter in the city's top 5-star hotel by the Chief of Police, as well as an armed escort for the three days we were trapped by the high waters.

Our escort's leader, a charming lieutenant, accompanied us to the Golden Temple. Already four years had passed since Operation Blue Star, the raiding of the temple by the Indian army on the instructions of then Prime Minister Indira Ghandi. The ensuing battle, which lasted four days, resulted in the deaths of four hundred and ninety two civilians and eighty three soldiers and ultimately the assignation of Mrs. Ghandi by her Sikh bodyguards in October of the same year. Despite the passing of time, the temple walls were riddled with lines of bullet holes caused by automatic weapons fire and the temple complex was grey and deserted but for us.

Today the temple throngs with vibrant life and colour. Although some reconstruction is underway along one wall, the majority of the buildings look to be in fine condition with no traces remaining of the bloody battle that once raged here. It does actually feel like it was originally intended to, a place of worship where people of all religions are free to meditate or listen to prayers of peace.

At night I indulge in two Kingfisher beers to celebrate my arrival in India. My stomach malady has settled so I eat dhal and tandoori paneer tikka. I remember the parting words of a friend,

"It's a long way to go for a good curry, Gordon."

It is, but I can honestly say it's worth it.

Day 36 Amritsar to Ludhiana, India
88 miles

Delhi lies four hundred and sixty kilometres south east of Amritsar. I decide it's too much to attempt in one day on Indian roads, so I'll break the journey in two. This decision has the effect of relaxing me so much that I set off without a care in the world.

I soon stop for directions.

"Grand Trunk Road? Delhi?" I ask, pointing hopefully forwards.

"Yes, certainly, that's the GT road. Just follow it straight," I'm told.

Abbreviating names and places to initials is something I've noticed before in India. States such as Uttar Pradesh and Andhra Pradesh are known as UP and AP. I've also heard people call themselves and others by their initials, such as VJ and RT. I like it very much but I'm not sure I'll adopt it... GG somehow doesn't have the same ring to it.

I become part of the perpetual dance that takes place on all Indian roads. Traffic moves like a surging wave and there's no mercy shown to those who don't ride it; you join in or get swatted aside very quickly. Aged Tata and Ashok Leyland trucks, no matter how heavy and slow, hog the middle of the road or the right-hand lane on a dual carriageway. They belch out palls of dense, sooty exhaust fumes and I, like everyone else, have to forge my way around them.

Buses and cars take precedence. Bus drivers steer like *The Terminator*, ready to crash everything off the road at the least provocation. Then, just as they pass me, they dive to the inside and come to a screeching halt to pick up a passenger. Car drivers incessantly demand to be let through. They accelerate hard up to my tail, horn blaring and lights flashing. It makes no difference that there's a long slow line of cars and trucks ahead that will plainly be impossible to pass; I'm merely a motorcycle, middling in the road hierarchy, and have to move aside.

At traffic lights all the small motorcycles and Bajaj scooters squeeze their way to the front. The same happens at railway crossings where most riders lean their bikes right over and manhandle them under both stop barriers. The train hoots loud as it nears the crossing and the trespassers becoming frenetic in their efforts to safely reach the other side.

Bottom of the pile are bicycles, cycle rickshaws and any form of animal-powered vehicle. Bizarrely, their riders and drivers seem totally unflustered by the mayhem that encircles and thus threatens to eradicate them.

Thrown into the mix are cars driving the wrong way down a dual carriageway, every kind of vehicle doing impromptu U-turns, tractors swinging out into the middle of the road for no apparent reason, a swarm of buzzing black and gold rickshaws around every large village and town, pedestrians turning their backs to the traffic as they cross the road, livestock wandering hither and thither, sometimes herded, sometimes with their young, and police occasionally waving vehicles to the side, berating their owners for no apparent reason.

It’s at junctions that this seething drove of wheeled madness is most evidently like some chaotically choreographed massed fandango. No one slows, they simply weave at speed, timing their run through the maelstrom of motorists to perfection. Vehicles criss-cross diagonally or straight on, front wheels missing other’s rear wheels by inches, or more accurately, as timing is everything, by milliseconds. Rudolf Nureyev eat your heart out.

Every minute I'm forced to make a dozen life or death decisions. Where's he going? Is that a water buffalo backing out of the central reservation? Have those two on the bicycle seen me? Is that truck moving aside to let me past, is he just avoiding a pot hole or is he going to wildly swing across the carriageway to a gap in the central reservation in an impromptu U-turn? It's tumultuous, edge of your seat stuff. Sometimes I love it, sometimes I hate it, but it’s never dull.

I spot the faded grand facade of a large government hotel in extensive grounds a few kilometres before Ludhiana. It has a rose garden with wooden park benches and each room boasts a balcony facing a large lawned area. At less than £8 a night it’s perfect. After a quick shower, the crimson-turbaned Sikh receptionist offers me a lift to the nearest internet cafe on the back of his Hero Honda. The cafe is situated in a small area of shops at the northern edge of the city close to one of its most prominent landmarks, an imposing clock tower dating from the days of the Raj.

Before I update my blog, I scroll through my mail inbox. I find two emails from people in Ludhiana, both saying it would be great to meet if I’m passing through. As I have more free time than usual today, I reply to one, Paul, and write down the name and cellphone number of the other, Davinder. Both appear to be British but either live in, or at least frequently visit, Ludhiana. I spend an hour blogging, pay my bill and ask for directions to the nearest PCO (Public Call Office) to phone Davinder. A tall Sikh enters the cafe as I'm leaving. His face creases into a grin.

"Hey, you must be Gordon," he says.

It's Davinder, the man I’m about to telephone! It transpires that he and

Paul are cousins; both from Huddersfield in the UK. Paul received my email at home, sent a text to Davinder, who hightailed it to my hotel and was subsequently directed here to find me. Twenty first century communication at its best, I smile to myself, remembering that just two decades ago when I first came to India, I actually sent a telegram home!

Davinder tells me that as well as being cousins, he and Paul are business partners in the UK and are also building a house together in Ludhiana. We hop into his car, a locally produced Tata version of a Range Rover come Land Cruiser, and set off to see the partially built dwelling. Accompanying Davinder is another cousin, known as Kirnku. He's a very likeable, quietly-spoken young man who understands English but doesn't speak it very well.

The half-built house turns out to be a major development. It's on four levels with a central staircase leading to a plethora of sitting rooms, bathrooms, offices, staff quarters and even a rooftop area that will eventually be gardened, However, the single-skinned construction, poor quality bricks and antiquated building methods and materials are a major concern for Davinder, who tells me he's been pulling his hair out trying to get the job done to UK standards...

"It freezes here in winter but no one builds cavity walls. Then there's the electrics. Power spikes are commonplace in India but you simply cannot buy 3-phase wiring; I've had to import it all by the roll from England."

Building a dream home from afar seems a complicated and difficult process, but it appears to be coming together, with windows due to be put in soon. These should transform the red brick shell into something much more like a house.

Parked in a basement garage is Davinder's Royal Enfield, a silver Thunderbird cruiser with a Lean Burn engine. He tells me that he and Paul bought identical bikes last year, but have so far only taken them on one long run, a trip north to Chandigarh.

"But all that changes next year. Along with Paul and a couple of other mates, we're going to do a six week road trip around India, starting at the very south and making our way here via as many historic and religious places of interest as possible."

There's a real edge of excitement in his voice at the prospect.

I spend the evening with Davinder and Krinku, commencing with a brief twilight tour of Ludhiana. There are modern shopping malls, clubs and restaurants, well-heeled pedestrians and many up-market foreign-made cars, evidential of much prosperity.

"The Punjab is the powerhouse of India and one of the wealthiest states," my host informs me. "The shopping malls in the centre are just as good as those in an American or European city."

It's certainly not what I was expecting to see on my second night in India.

We progress to a restaurant and bar. The food is superb, the clientele young and obviously upwardly-mobile. It's interesting to hear about Davinder's life. He's an NRI (Non Resident Indian) which means he's able to get a five year multiple entry Indian visa in his UK passport. Born in England, he's proud to be British but has a deep affinity for India, telling me that as a wind-up he supports the England cricket team when he's with his Indian father and the India team when out with his English mates. He's done well for himself in business and is rightly proud of his achievements. It's a side of India I've not experienced before and I have a fascinating time hearing about life in the Punjab from a man with a Yorkshire accent.

More Kingfisher is consumed than a Delhi-bound motorcyclist should drink. At the end of the night, when he drops me back at my now hushed hotel, we agree to meet again in the UK, this time over a pint of Yorkshire-brewed John Smiths.

Day 37 Ludhiana to Delhi, India
212 miles

The road to Delhi is busy and slow going. It's a dual carriageway reduced to single lane traffic a good deal of the way by incomplete roadworks. I repeatedly experience another phenomenon of Indian roads; the 'might is right' principle. Most commonly this occurs when the road is narrow and opposing traffic is bigger than me. They invariably hog the slender tarmac strip and, at the last second, I have to brake hard then dive offroad into dirt and rocks to avoid a collision.

A potentially far more deadly set of circumstances occurs when the oncoming vehicles overtake each other. A case in point is a cycle rickshaw being passed by a truck. There's still enough room for me even though the truck is on my side of the road. All of a sudden a car swings out from behind the truck and I'm faced with a fast approaching wall of heavy metal and nowhere to go but into the potholed, rough edges.

It's tough going, but my incredible bike just soaks up the punishment hour after hour. I thank Royal Enfield, not for the first nor last time, for good brakes, springy suspension and a flexible engine.

Davinder told me there were many service stations on the road to Delhi, but recommended one in particular, Haveli Dhaba services near Karnal in the state of Haryana. After a couple of false turns, I finally spot it a hundred metres before the Karnal motorway toll booths. I'm immediately impressed; there's a large carpark with friendly security guards that check every vehicle in and out and agree to keep a close eye on my loaded bike.

The set up is like a small holiday village, with entertainment, including a ride-on fun railway, for kids. Several eateries are located around a large square where people sit beside a pool, watch entertainers or browse shops. I choose the main restaurant, a voluminous affair ornately decorated to a very high standard in a classical Indian restaurant style. The walls are brick with recessed gold-rimmed Moghul arches, the polished wooden tables have delicately carved fluted edges and the high-backed turned chairs are upholstered in luxurious vermillion and gilt silk. Strategically dotted around the central area are copper or brass urns, coffee-pots and Alibaba oil lamps. In one corner is the masterpiece... a brightly-painted vintage Tata truck.

The waiters, resplendent in crimson shirts with gold brocade waistcoats, are efficient and helpful, bringing me a delicious, freshly prepared curry, naan bread and fruit juice in double-quick time. The bill is accompanied by a bowl of digestive, comprising fennel seeds and crystallised sugar. I'm seated, served and billed in under twenty minutes. The bill gets my approval too - just under £2.

I remember seeing flickering black and white TV footage of the first service station to open in the UK, at Newport Pagnell on the M1, in the 1960s. The documentary showed the restaurant, describing it as *the* place to be seen dining. Indeed, at the time it was common for people to travel at least an hour north from London on the motorway simply to dine out at this fantastic new restaurant complex. By comparison, today's British service station experience is a pretty dull affair and I think I'm not alone in saying that I would go hungry rather than eat in one. The Haveli Dhaba is without doubt the most superb roadside rest place and restaurant I have seen anywhere, period.

Back on my bike, I see an unusual method of road repairs being undertaken. Small gangs of wiry, sun baked women, still in their saris, fill potholes with steamy black tar. Traffic moves around the workforce at speed, their only protection being a man with a red flag in front of them. They stamp the tar flat with their feet, which appear to be protected by clogs made from discarded car tyres, then another man pushes a small roller over the top. Finally a team of workers trample leaves and grass onto the tar to protect the patch until it dries. I ride over many of these primitive, make-do repairs that must have been done some time earlier. They're surprisingly effective at levelling the road.

At the outskirts of Delhi I begin to look for a PCO so I can call my contact from JBF (aha, I'm really getting into the swing of these abbreviations). The roads into the capital are so wide and busy that I simply cannot see anywhere to phone from. I know the JBF projects are in the southern part of the city so I initially follow signs that will take me close to the centre: the Red Fort, Central Railway Station and ultimately, Connaught Place. Daylight is fading fast and traffic is moving at a crawl, causing my engine to overheat to the point of meltdown. I stop outside a police station but still cannot find a phone. Clutching a handful of rupees, I stop a man walking past, try to explain my plight and ask if I can quickly use his cell phone. He's happy to help and flatly refuses payment.

About forty minutes later a Royal Enfield pulls up beside me. It has two bright yellow pannier boxes on the back bearing the JBF logo. A very affable Dr. Sashanka introduces himself, telling me he's been quite worried as it's almost dark and he thought I would have reached Delhi much sooner. I explain about the traffic and the lowly speeds my old motorcycle cruises at. He's accompanied by one of the JBF field workers,

Anil, and together they lead me south for half an hour to a residential area where Jonny Krause keeps a small room for his visits to India.

It's a simple one-room tin roofed shack built onto the flat concreted rooftop of an old colonial building. It is very plain, cooled by a fan and has a blockhouse washroom opposite. I take a shower by dipping a plastic jug into a large drum of cold water and throwing it over myself. It's remarkably refreshing and I'm comfortable to be staying in such humble accommodation in view of the projects I will visit tomorrow.

Sashanka has patiently waited for me to clean up so that we can go for dinner together. We spend an hour discussing tomorrow's schedule, which sounds very interesting. It will be World Rabies Day and the JBF school, which is usually closed on Sundays, is holding a special session to teach the children about the disease. I am invited to attend and go to bed very much looking forward to finally meeting them all.

Day 38 Delhi, India
15 miles

I'm picked up by Anil on the JBF Bullet at 9 am. To get to the school we must ride past the Viklang Basti slum where the school children live. It's a shambles. We have to travel very slowly as the road is rutted, quite muddy and strewn with garbage. I try really hard not to stare but the conditions these people live in are truly appalling. Their temporary homes are made from tree branches and scrap metal with rags and polythene sheets on the sides and roofs. There is rubbish everywhere. Great ugly mounds of it. People are sifting through and sorting it into piles of plastic, cardboard and rags. It's all been collected from a rubbish dump, often by the children, and can be recycled for a few rupees.

The school is right at the end of the slum dwellings. It's a simple wooden structure with sides and roof of woven palm and corrugated iron. It's bright and cheerful looking, a complete contrast to the long line of wretchedness I've just passed. The classroom is L-shaped with the rest of the space taken up by a small clinic, also operated by the charity, that gives free medical treatment to the slum inhabitants two hours a week.

I step through the open door and see about fifty children quietly sitting cross-legged on raffia mats on the floor. They all wear bright yellow JBF school uniforms and are looking expectantly my way.

"Good Morning, Mr. Gordon" their sing-song voices proclaim in unison.

"Good morning everyone," I reply.

There are lots of big smiles all round. I'm first introduced to the teacher, Madam Sandhya, who's been with the school since it opened four years ago. Her eyes sparkle and I can immediately see that she's adored by the children. Dr. Sashanka is there, as is his wife, Dr. Smriti. Sashanka is the managing trustee of JBF and Smriti works at the National Institute of Animal Welfare but gives most of her spare time to JBF. Both are qualified vets and it's quite apparent that they are genuine, kind people who care very deeply about the school and the children.

Two drawing competitions are organised for the children. The older ones are given messages about rabies in English that they copy then make into placards. The younger ones are handed outline drawings on the same subject with a collection of colouring pens to creatively use. Half an hour passes in intense concentration and the results are exceedingly good. There are three other guests, all from Delhi, who judge the competition and present simple prizes.

Next up, Smriti gives a presentation on her laptop about the dangers of rabies and the benefits of vaccinating animals. It goes down a storm, the children gathering round her become very animated as they shout out the names of animals they see on her computer. Then the teacher, Sandhya, sits in a chair and tells a story with animal puppets. There's a hushed silence, the children are completely mesmerised by the tale. I have to pinch myself as I watch their entranced faces, thinking that this could be any school in the world but for the appalling conditions that the children will soon return to.

Finally, they are fed a healthy meal which is a daily occurrence at the school. For most, if not all of them, it's their only meal today. There's rice, dhal, and a vegetable curry which they eat off metal thali plates. Every morsel is wolfed down. I have one of the meals too, it's plain fare but very nutritious. Unfortunately, I have to leave before the children as my bike is booked in for repairs, but I'll return tomorrow for regular classes.

Another JBF worker, Yogesh, kindly offers to lead me across Delhi to the Karol Bagh district. It's a tightly packed, crowded area overflowing with motorcycle dealers and spare parts suppliers. I've arranged to have some work done on my bike by Lalli Singh and his team. Lalli has a first class reputation for supplying many tour companies with Royal Enfields as well as leasing them short and long-term to independent travellers. It doesn't take long to find his premises. As soon as we pull up in the motorcycle district and ask a dealer where we can find Lalli Singh, three sets of hands simultaneously point and issue instructions that lead us right to his doorstep.

My bike is wheeled down a steep ramp to a basement workshop where four other Bullets, all in various stages of repair, are lined up with mechanics hard at work on them. It's Lalli's son's sixth birthday and he's at his birthday party for the afternoon, but I'm well looked after by a senior mechanic, Imram. My Bullet gets a wash, then much needed engine and gearbox oil changes. Imran's a methodical worker, using precise, careful movements to remove all the sump plugs and deftly clean the oil compartment out with a paraffin soaked rag. Filters are changed and a new set of points and spark plug fitted.

The broken wire on my tail light is sent out to be soldered and my tappet clearances given an accurate check. A new horn is fitted to replace the two that 'gave up the ghost' on the road to Quetta and Imran assures me that as this one is built to withstand Indian road conditions, it will last a lifetime. We look at the forks and decide to leave them as they are, they're quite twisted but spares for these old-style forks are not readily available in India. We reason that they've made it thus far; they should get me to Chennai. The rest of the bike gets a thorough going over too.

Lalli arrives in the early evening. He's a tall, slender Sikh dressed in blue jeans, t-shirt and a white turban. He's going grey but it's impossible to guess his age as he has such a strong life-force. His eyes seem to laugh as he talks, giving him a vibrancy somehow incongruent with his quiet, soft voice. It's a joy to sit and talk Royal Enfields with him as he not only deals in them but rides one every day as his regular transport. He's deeply passionate about ensuring the visitors who lease bikes from him have a wonderful time in India and even gives short courses in Bullet maintenance before the holidaymakers set off on their journeys. His desk and wall are covered in photographs, letters and gifts from clients, including an enormous New Zealand flag.

Lalli makes sure Yogesh, who has patiently waited for me, gets something to eat then listens with interest about the school I visited this morning. We move on to my bill for the afternoon's work. I hand over payment, commenting that the charges are very reasonable. Lalli says,

"I would like to take this money and give it to the charity you have told me about."

He hands my full payment over to Yogesh as a gift for the school. My heart fills with joy but I get tongue-tied and can't think of anything to say except 'thank-you'.

He then asks my permission to perform a puja, a small blessing, for my bike and the rest of my journey. He sends out for a garland of marigold flowers and some sweets. There are six or seven workers left at his premises and all gather round my bike. The garland is draped over the headlamp and a sandalwood incense stick trapped in the brake lever. It sends a plume of heady, sweetly-scented smoke skywards. Lalli says some prayers then invites me to say a few words. I sincerely thank them all for their kind wishes and for taking such good care of me and my bike today.

We all share the sweets, then two small stickers are put on my bike. One is of Ganesha, the Hindu deity in the form of an elephant, the other is the Om symbol. I've kept my bike a sticker-free zone despite several requests from businesses to have stickers with their logos and brand names put on my pannier boxes. Today, and in this company, I feel it's altogether appropriate to let these two gifts of mystical stickers adorn my Enfield.

Lalli insists on escorting me back to my room, a good half hour ride away. He leads the way on his 500 cc Royal Enfield. Like me, he wears a pair of Halcyon goggles but his are propped up on his turban. He looks an awesome sight.

It's past 9 pm. I quickly shower and travel to Sashanka and Smriti's home. They live in a simple two-room rented apartment with their four-year-old daughter, Hiya (pronounced Heeya). They tell me accommodation is hard to come by in Delhi and one of their two rooms houses a desk and computer from which Sashanka does much of JBF's administrative work. The family comes from the state of Assam in north-eastern India, moving to Delhi four years ago to work with JBF.

I'm fed a scrumptious meal of traditional Assam food that Smriti has specially prepared. There are small bowls of three different curries, all are tasty and for India, very subtly spiced. We spend the rest of the night talking, laughing and playing with Hiya, who is a lively, bright girl. It's a relaxed and friendly atmosphere and I feel privileged to spend this time in their home. It's after midnight when I finally return to my room, reflecting that I've just experienced one of the most special days of my life.

Day 39 Delhi, India
0 miles

I reach the JBF Informal School just as classes begin. The morning class, from 9 am to 1 pm, is for smaller children and the afternoon class, between 3 pm and 5 pm, is held for older students. I'm met by Dr. Sashanka who first takes me behind the school to see the rear of the slum which backs onto a vile open sewer. The stench is awful, making my stomach turn. Four communal toilets hang over the slow-moving waters which are shared by the fifteen hundred or so inhabitants of the shantytown. Sashanka tells me there's no drinking water available; residents walk nearly a kilometre to a public toilet to collect it.

Back in the school I watch the lessons. The children learn to count and speak English by participating in songs and exercises with the teacher. It's fun and their pleasure is obvious. The school doesn't set out to provide a formal education as state schools are able to do that. However, street children and those raised in slums tend not to do well in regular government schools; they don't know how to behave, how to learn, how to fit in with the other kids. A high percentage never attend any lessons and spend most of their time on the streets begging.

JBF's primary aim is to help these children develop in such a way that they'll want to, and also have the social skills to be able to, attend state school. It works. Sashanka tells me he is really proud of their achievements: more than seventy children have progressed from the JBF school into formal education.

"It gives them a chance to break the cycle of begging and living in the slum with no hope of anything better," he says. "They learn how to behave with others and how to learn. Hopefully that will give them the chance of getting a job when they're older."

The school is non-denominational so children learn about many religions, celebrating most of the major Hindu, Muslim and Christian festivals. In a couple of days time it will be Eid ul-Fitr, the Muslim celebration that marks the end of Ramadan. All the children make Eid cards, which they will take home. The teacher, Madam Sandhya, moves around demonstrating painting techniques, which in this instance involves dragging bright paint-sodden knitting wool through a tightly folded card. The children are thrilled with the results. Again I think to myself, 'they look just the same as happy, care-free schoolchildren anywhere in the world.' It's amazing what some positive input, guidance and love can do.

Two highlights of the morning really impact on me. The first is when the children sing. One particularly touching rendition is the modern adaptation of Charles Tindley's gospel song *We Shall Overcome*. A small, dark-skinned girl with an open face and beautiful clear eyes, made all the more striking by the contrast of her canary-yellow JBF school dress, stands up to lead the singing.

"We shall overcome
We shall overcome
We shall overcome some day

Oh, deep in my heart
I do believe
We shall overcome some day

We'll walk hand in hand
We'll walk hand in hand
We'll walk hand in hand some day

Oh, deep in my heart...

We shall all be free
We shall all be free
We shall all be free some day

Oh, deep in my heart...

We are not afraid
We are not afraid
We are not afraid some day

Oh, deep in my heart...

We are not alone
We are not alone
We are not alone some day...

Oh, deep in my heart... etc"

It's very moving and at the end I applaud until my hands hurt.

The other high point relates to my stomach (what else!). For their mid-morning snack the children each receive a glass of lassi, a popular Indian yoghurt drink. It's ladled straight out of a tin urn and is so thick and creamy that I suspect it was only collected from a water buffalo this morning. Ambrosia! It is without question the most delectable, mouth-watering drink I've ever tasted.

When the children have lunch I set off with Sashanka to see another part of JBF's work. They also run an animal welfare project, focusing on the cattle that wander the streets of Delhi which Sashanka estimates number around forty thousand. His team work within an area that has about five thousand cows. We go to an open sewer the size of a small river. The stench makes me heave. The banks are so filthy that I don't know where to put my feet. There are roughly twenty cattle around me, all looking utterly miserable. They wander in the piles of rubbish, picking at scraps amongst the rotting sludge and fly-blown excrement. Some drink from the sewer. It's utterly sickening. I shift from foot to foot, feeling desperately distressed.

Many of these pitiable creatures suffer from wounds to their horns and hooves, chiefly caused by rummaging in rubbish that contains tins and broken glass. Three JBF assistants tend to a large cow with a wound on its heel at the edge of the sewer bank. The lesion is the size of a human hand and is yellow and festering. Using a time-honoured technique, the team bring it to the ground with ropes then clean out the infected area, squirting puss onto the ground until scarlet blood flows. Antiseptic dressings are applied and the cow gets an antibiotic injection. It's released then limps away.

"We'll try to find it again in another week or two so we can keep tabs on the infection," Sashanka informs me.

We then travel to see a cow that's just had a calf. It has an old wound that the team re-dress. The calf looks to be okay, but I can't help wondering what a miserable, sorry existence lies ahead for it. It really upsets me to see the hideous conditions in which these poor animals somehow survive.

Sashanka tells me that JBF's goal is simple; to make the lives of these animals more bearable and free from pain caused by injuries.

"Scavenging for scraps in a busy city is completely the wrong environment for these creatures," Sashanka says with feeling. "Without doubt they belong in the countryside. But they are here, and we do what we can to make their existence tolerable."

He goes on to tell me that contributors to JBF are always asked where they would like their donations to go: to the Viklang Basti school and community project or to the animal care programme.

Back at the school I catch the class for the older children. Many are now in formal education but continue to come to JBF for extra support and a quiet place where they can concentrate. Sandhya moves around, helping them with their homework, giving encouragement and advice. Some younger children are there too... it's better than being out on the streets begging.

Today is Dr. Smriti's birthday. She's at work but has sent two large birthday cakes for the children to eat. At 4.30 pm all the younger children from morning class come to collect their slice. The schoolroom is packed as we all sing "Happy Birthday" to Smriti down a cellphone. It's a magical moment.

As they leave the school at the end of the day, each child is handed an apple which they run outside to eat. I feel sad to be saying farewell to the children, but at the same time, feel very hopeful for them. Despite its shoestring budget, JBF is undoubtedly making a huge difference to their lives.

I spend a very enjoyable evening with Sashanka, Smriti, Hiya and three of the JBF animal welfare team, Anil, Yogesh and Sharafat. More delicious birthday cake is consumed and Hiya enjoys having so many guests to play with. But the talk naturally returns to the subject of the school and cattle care.

"Do you know, Gordon, that just two weeks after we built the school it was completely flattened in a huge storm. We had to start all over again." Smriti tells me.

"But it's built stronger now," adds Sashanka.

I'm really impressed to hear that the slum community, rightly suspicious of the charity at first, have been completely won over by the project.

"We leave all the valuables inside at night, from medicine to teacher aids." says Sashanka. "One small padlock holds the sliding front door closed and the key to it is held by one of the slum residents. It's never been broken into because the people now see the value in having their children safe, positively occupied and hopefully getting the chance for a better life."

I'm really interested in this feeling of ownership.

"It's helped by the weekly evening classes we organise in women's literacy and sewing skills at the school. It really makes a difference to the lives of the people who want to escape the slum," explains Smriti.

The evening passes quickly and my mind can't help but think about my journey which will resume tomorrow.

"I wish I was coming with you," says Sashanka with feeling as we say goodnight. "I used to ride my bike at least fifty kilometres a day before I moved to Delhi and I miss travelling on open roads with the feel of the wind in my hair."

On the way back to my room I call in at a barbershop for a much-needed haircut and an even more imperative shave. It's been over four weeks. The barber leaves me with a thick moustache that wraps round the corner of my lips. It's hilarious; very 1970s. In fact, I decide that I look like a cross between one of The Village People and former Aussie batsman, David Boon. I quickly insist he shaves it off! After the shave comes ice, face balm and possibly the most eye-watering, lip-curling aftershave ever invented. I ask the barber if he picked up a bottle of battery acid by mistake, but he just laughs and says,

"It's good for the skin".

Yeah right; minutes later it still smarts like pure alcohol and my yelps attract quite a crowd at the shop door.

Day 40 Delhi to Agra, India
133 miles

My escape from Delhi's rush hour traffic takes longer than I'd hoped. I have breakfast with Sashanka in a South Indian restaurant which serves freshly ground coffee, a very welcome change from the *Nescafe* I've had to drink since Turkey. Afterwards, I do battle with chaotic Delhi congestion for over an hour. I follow Sashanka on his motorcycle to the city limits, which I'm very grateful for as signposts are few and I'd otherwise have almost certainly become lost.

Unfortunately, I lose sight of him amongst a mass of trucks before we have the chance to say goodbye and can't work out if he's behind or in front of me. Traffic gradually thins and I manage to build up speed whilst keeping an eye on the roadside for the missing vet and his motorcycle. He's not anywhere to be seen. After fifteen kilometres I pull in, convinced I'm well ahead of him. I find a PCO and whilst quenching my thirst with a bottle of Limca, a fizzy sweet lemon drink, call his mobile. Fortunately, he stopped just a couple of kilometres back at the building where Smitri works, which, as luck would have it, is smack bang on the Delhi to Agra road.

Soon finding them, I thank my two hosts for their wonderful hospitality before we say our goodbyes. Sashanka heads back into the city and his duties, which often keep him working late into the night, especially when an emergency call comes through about an injured animal. I head on south.

The route to Agra follows a well made dual carriageway. Twenty years ago, when I first came to India, I rode my shiny red 350 Bullet along this very highway, which was my first experience of Indian driving conditions. My memory is of a quiet, well paved broadway, probably the best made road I travelled in India during that trip. It's been superbly maintained and is just as smooth to ride along today. What has changed, however, is the volume of traffic. In 1988 there were buses, trucks, and a few motorcycles but cars were quite rare. The only models available at the time were the Hindustan Ambassador, a copy of the 1950's Morris Oxford which was, and still is, a veritable automotive dinosaur, together with a cute 1960's Fiat built in India under the PAL badge.

Now there are scores of different cars, including many small two door family vehicles and a considerable number of early 90's Land Cruiser lookalikes which appear to be used as collective taxis. The majority appear to be manufactured by truck giant, Tata, but I do see a number of

European luxury sedans too, a sight that was not even a consideration on India's roads two decades ago. There are also far more auto-rickshaws around towns and villages than I remember and to stay safe I have to concentrate intensely every second of the journey.

I see a sign that tells me Agra is just twelve kilometres ahead. To the east of my route brew colossal black storm clouds. Thinking I'll just manage to skirt around them, the road takes an unexpected turn and leads me directly into their path. The heavens open in a tumultuous, pounding downpour. Within moments, all bicycles and motorcycles have vanished into thin air. Cars, buses and trucks, however, still plough ahead at breakneck speed. It's impossible to see where I'm going and far too dangerous to continue, so I stop.

There's no shelter, not even a small tree to hide under. I'm already pretty wet so there's little point struggling into my rain suit. I sit on the bike, leaning slightly forward so that my chest rests on the tank bag, and let the rain pelt down on me. A strong wind gets up and the rain bounces high off the road, creating wisps of steam as it evaporates. My Cromwell crash helmet has a stainless steel shell, a feature I like very much as it's hard-wearing and still looks great after all these miles. Today, the raindrops are so huge they create a melody of metallic ringing sounds as they hit my head.

It takes over an hour for the storm to pass. I'm soaked to the bone and quite chilled when I eventually crawl into Agra. To make matters worse, the bike, which was only cleaned a couple of days ago, is grimy and mud-splattered once again. As I pass the famous Red Fort, I see the incomparable Taj Mahal. Even from this side-on angle it looks absolutely magnificent, its ivory marble illuminated by the setting sun. It sits on the banks of the river Yamuni, whose dark waters act as a backdrop against which the Taj looks other-worldly. Traffic is too heavy to stop for a photograph so I freeze-frame the scene in my mind.

I saw the Taj twice on my first visit to Agra, at sunrise and sunset. Completed in the mid-sixteen hundreds, it was built by grief-stricken Moghul emperor, Shah Jahan, as a mausoleum for his third wife, Mumtaz Mahal, who died during the birth of his fourteenth child. Many myths surround the Taj, including the supposed brutal murders of its architects to ensure a similar building was never constructed elsewhere as well as the tale of a second, identical mausoleum which was planned for the opposite bank of the Yamuni. This one, legend has it, was to be made from black marble. What is known is that Shah Jahan was deposed by one of his sons just after the mausoleum was completed and imprisoned for the rest of his life in Agra Fort, from where he could look down on the Taj from afar. After his death, he was laid to rest next to his wife inside the now famous white tomb.

Finding a suitable hotel, more by good luck than good judgement, I decide to visit the Taj early in the morning. I put on dry clothes and go in search of dinner. Climbing into an auto-rickshaw, I ask to be taken to the busy tourist area, Taj Ganj. My driver, who races through the slippery, tight city lanes at reckless speed, seems rather distracted. Looking left and right as if in search of someone, he completely fails to notice a car come to a sudden halt immediately ahead and crashes directly into its back.

We bounce straight backwards off its bumper, a sensation not dissimilar to hitting another dodgem car in a fairground, and abruptly stall. For pity's sake... rickshaws again! My ribs hurt where I was jolted forward onto the rail that separates me from the driver, but apart from that I'm thankfully undamaged. I expect to see the driver of the car we hit, a new-looking VW, jump out and give my driver what for. Nothing happens, it's bizarre. My driver restarts his engine, angles around the side of the still stationary car and heads off at speed.

"Hey, stop!" I shout. "You need to go back and see if that driver's OK."

"It's not a problem," he cooly retorts, "things like this happen in India all the time."

"But what about damage to the car and your auto?" I ask with consternation. "Don't you need to sort out insurance details?"

The driver simply shrugs and drives on. By now we have reached the main restaurant area of the city and he pulls over for me to climb out. Feeling very concerned, I pay my fare and stand watching his wake for quite some time, wondering if I could have done something else.

By-and-by I start walking. Rounding a corner, I can hardly believe my eyes. A small café, the eponymous *Joney's Place*, lies straight ahead across a small square. Its pink signs and fascia are faded but the dazzling cerise plastic furniture looks new. In 1988 I ate breakfast, lunch and dinner here both times I came to Agra. Even then, the zany owner was a legend amongst travellers and I remember taking a photograph of him and his cohorts posing in front of the café. I can picture it in my mind as I stand here now. Despite contracting food poisoning during my second visit, I look back over time with great fondness for the place.

I recognise Joney the second I enter. We must both be around the same age and he's aged well. I tell him about my twenty-year-old photograph and he agrees to my request for an update. To my delight he strikes an almost identical pose in the doorway. I decline dinner... my trip's too short to risk it... but succumb to a chilled chocolate lassi. It's divine, so curdled and syrupy that I have to eat it with a spoon. As I leave, I promise to email both old and new photographs and spend the rest of the evening feeling very nostalgic for my happy-go-lucky travels of twenty years ago.

Day 41 Agra to Orchha, India
146 miles

My alarm clock wakes me at 5.45 am. It's my intention to visit the Taj at sunrise, but I have a raging sore throat, a temperature and a completely blocked nose... the result of yesterday's soaking, no doubt. I decide a recuperative sleep is more important than tourism, take a couple of paracetamol and doze until 9.30. By the time I've breakfasted on milky porridge (I have to remind myself this is India not Scotland!), done my daily maintenance and loaded the bike, it's 11.00 am. Chennai lies over two thousand kilometres south and I worry about how long it might take to get there at this rate.

The road is good at first, but deteriorates as I leave the state of Uttar Pradesh (UP) and enter Madhya Pradesh (MP). In Ludhiana, Davinder warned me these states are amongst the poorest in India and never to ride through them at night. He said it was very common for gangs to create roadblocks by felling trees then holding up the first motorist that comes along.

"Banditry? In India?" I'd asked, somewhat astonished, but I heed his warning.

I certainly plan to reach my revised destination for today, the temple complex of Orchha, well before sundown.

The final fifty kilometres are hell. The sun is low in the sky and leafy trees each side of the road cast a mosaic pattern of shadows ahead of me. My front mudguard is driven all the way up into the bike's frame as I smash into a huge pothole. The same happens again and again as I hit speed breakers and great ruts in the tarmac camouflaged by the dappled shade effect. My wrists, arms and shoulders tense up and ache and I have to slow right down. Fifty kilometres takes nearly an hour and a half.

I enter the town of Jhansi and stop to ask directions at a large roundabout. A smart young man, dressed in a fine blue cotton shirt and immaculately pressed trousers passes by, carrying a laptop bag. He spots me struggling to communicate with a couple of men who stand next to a barrow selling incense sticks.

"Can I help?" he enquires in perfect BBC English.

"Oh, thank you," I reply. "Please can you tell me which way to head for Orchha?"

He does, issuing perfectly clear directions. We shake hands then he tells me to pull out quickly while there's a lull in the traffic.

Thanking him, I launch forwards onto the roundabout. I get perhaps twenty metres when a large, bristling policeman steps forward, walking towards me with both arms spread out wide and assertively signalling me to stop. As he blocks my path I have no option but to come to a rapid halt. He shouts at me, his cheeks turning crimson as he builds up a real temper. In his right hand he holds a long, brass-tipped cane which he waves aggressively around. I deduce that I've inadvertently entered the roundabout against his signals so I gesture with open arms and hands that I was unaware and hadn't seen him. My mild protests seem to enrage him still more and he shouts even louder. As he builds up to a crescendo, spittle forms on his top lip and hangs underneath his bushy moustache. The situation is getting out of control. He now intimidatingly stands side-by-side with the bike, bellowing in my face.

At that moment the smart young man who had helped with directions comes running over and begins to calm the policeman down. Within a few moments the fire visibly dies down in his eyes. Taking a couple of paces back he then, almost sheepishly, waves for me to ride on.

"These guys have a very tough job controlling the traffic," explains my helper. "But he shouldn't shout at you like that. I told him the mistake was mine as I urged you to set off quickly. He also should learn how to treat tourists better."

I gratefully shake his hand again, this time for coming to my rescue in such a timely fashion.

My luck changes when I find a fabulous hotel, the Sheesh Mahal, at the top of a steep rise half a kilometre along a dirt track from the village of Orchha. It's part of an imposing, weather-beaten fort that dominates the surrounding flatlands. The fort contains my hotel together with the Raja Rammandir Palace, which has numerous green parrots cavorting around its tall, plain walls, and the crumbling but nonetheless stunning sixteenth century Jehangir Mahal Palace.

I enter the swish hotel, which charges the princely sum of £12 per night. The lobby has silk covered sofas and armchairs set around ornately carved tables. My room is sublime. There's a small four poster bed with an embroidered pale blue brocade bedcover and dark wooden furniture adorned with delicate carvings. There are even silk wall hangings. The porter opens two shutters right next to my bed to let in fresh air. There's no glass, just a fine mesh. The view of the surrounding plains, dotted with crumbling temples and fields of ripe crops, is breathtaking. I know I'll sleep with the shutters open so I can be cooled by the soft breeze during the night and awoken by the sunrise.

I spend a very contented hour wandering around the temple ruins while the sun sets. Most temples, tombs and mausolea date from the seventeenth century, when under the rule of Mughal emperor Jahangir the region was at the peak of its power and influence. Although nearly all the buildings are in a decaying state of repair, they make an enchanting sight as I wander around them completely alone.

A wizened old woman, dressed in a saffron coloured sari, emerges from behind some rocks, herding her water buffalo amongst the overgrown grass, weeds and bushes that surround each temple. As I approach, she puts her long staff on the ground and presses her hands together into namaste. I do the same in return, which causes her to smile hugely. She looks at least seventy, her face wrinkled and her tied-up hair almost white, yet she's timelessly and naturally beautiful. It's a magical moment.

I have dinner in the village then return to my palatial hotel for a cold Kingfisher in the lobby. Hearing a noise outside, unmistakably another Bullet arriving, I get up and hurry over to the entrance where I see two silhouetted figures on an Enfield. I'm so excited, I can't wait to hear where they've been and what sort of adventures they've had on their bike! I go outside to say hello but am somewhat taken aback. It's a man and a woman and they're riding at night with no crash helmets. All they wear are t-shirts, Bermuda shorts and sandals. A pair of backpacks are strapped onto luggage racks each side of the rear wheel making it appear dangerously tail heavy.

I say hello but get no response. Trying again...

"Have you come far?" I ask.

This time I get a grunt from the man. One last try,

"I have one too," I say, pointing at my Bullet under its cover. "Where have you ridden from?"

The man speaks at last.

"We just hired it in Delhi. Man it's so hot when you stop riding."

They walk away from me and enter the hotel reception. I spend a couple of minutes looking at the bike then return inside to my beer.

I hear the woman tell the receptionist they are from Israel. I feel I should warn them about the dangers of riding at night in this area. I ought to tell them about the risk of riding without crash helmets and protective clothing; how I would certainly have been a hospital case in Pakistan without all the gear I was wearing. But I sense my words won't be well received; they're not even interested in a quick chat with a fellow two-wheel traveller. I relax backwards in my chair and enjoy the live music and traditional dancing show that soon starts. They go to their room and don't return, a porter carries in their backpacks. It's a disappointment, they're the only foreigners touring on an Enfield I have seen to date.

Finally I go to my wonderful room and drift off to sleep looking at the moon and listening to distant music through my open window.

Day 42 Orccha to Khajuraho, India
176 miles

My first target today is the small provincial town of Tikamgarh so I follow my map south. The route seems to be straightforward and I experience two and a half hours of the most marvellous motorcycling imaginable. The roads are often narrow but virtually devoid of all other vehicles. What utterly captivates me is the slice of rural India that I pass through. Many of the villages seem to have less than a hundred dwellings, with a large percentage of the rudimentary single-room houses made from mud bricks with thatched grass roofs. One even has a functional milling circle next to it complete with a muscular ox which drags a weighty millstone slowly around as I pass.

Women in a wonderful array of alluringly coloured saris walk purposefully at the roadside, some with brass water jugs balanced on their heads. They appear precarious, but the women seem to be in total control, their backs ramrod straight. The roads are a veritable four-legged highway. Countless herds of goats with rich, lustrous bronze coloured coats, are moved to one side so I can pass. Many leggy kids, cute and frisky, bounce along towards the rear of the flocks. Water buffalo, cows and donkeys are plentiful too, and I overtake numerous bullock carts pulled by brawny, humped Brahmin cattle, their huge horns gaily painted a cornucopia of rainbow colours.

A crop I'm unable to identify grows in abundance on both sides of the road. Many farmers have covered great sections of tarmac with piles of it so that passing traffic can do the threshing for them. I try to join in the fun but the bike's centrestand acts as a hook on my first attempt, dragging a great chunk of leafy stalks behind me. Picking my way around the edges of many more of these large green patches slows my progress considerably but the experience is worth far more than a little lost time. It's quintessential rural India and I'm thrilled to be able to experience it on my motorcycle.

My next waypoint is the town of Damoh. The map shows a straight road; no forks or junctions. It's wildly inaccurate. I have to ask directions again and again as the route passes through small towns, with more than one choice of direction for me to follow. I know from experience that people will often wave you on rather than admit they don't know the place you seek, so after each set of directions I try to stop and get corroboration.

"Damoh? Damoh?" I ask at least a dozen times.

I follow where I am pointed and judging by the sun's position in the sky, it's usually in a southerly direction, which seems right.

After nearly two hours of this I come to a T-junction which is definitely not shown on my map. Two men loiter nearby so I repeat my now familiar "Damoh, Damoh?" chant. They point left so I head that way.

The road is deserted and I ride for fifteen minutes without seeing anyone who can verify my last set of directions, let alone another vehicle, and the sky has clouded over so I can't even tell which way I'm heading. It's soon down to a single lane, indeed it's so narrow I doubt a bus or truck could move along it.

I round a sharp bend and see a long straight road on a gentle incline. Standing in the middle of it are a group of men; at least seven of them. Braking sharply to a halt forty or so metres short of them, I observe they've blocked the road with felled tree trunks. The lane is far too narrow for me to do a U-turn. I sit still and look at them with Davinder's words of warning about bandits clear in my mind.

I'm not conscious of calculating my options but it's what I do. The verges are too bumpy and narrow to pass at any speed. They would easily reach me before I could complete a three-point turn. There are two tree trunks, each at least one and a half metres long, and I can see where they're butted together in the middle of the road. I also notice that two of the men have long, thick canes in their hands. Not good, I think.

A man in the middle of the group signals me to approach with his right hand. I sit and stare, showing no reaction. He starts to walk towards me, still signalling, and quickly covers half the ground between us. The gang behind him, seeing my inactivity and presumably thinking I'm frozen with fear, all set off at once. They begin walking quickly but after a few paces break into a trot. The leader gets within a couple of metres; the rest are more than half way now. I act instinctively. Letting out the clutch, I drive straight at them as hard as I can. My bike surges forward, catching them all by surprise.

Flailing hands try to grab me. I can half see them reaching out but their attempts are completely ineffective as simultaneously, the men are jumping out of the way of my roaring bike and its potentially leg-breaking crash bars and panniers. I ride straight at the join in the two tree trunks and crash through. My motorcycle doesn't even wobble. I'm in second gear and pulling strongly away as a couple of stones bounce down the road alongside me. Fortunately, the throwers are as inept at this as they are at highway robbery and I make my escape at speed.

Within a kilometre I come to a small village. There's a fork in the road but I don't stop for directions in case some of the villagers are in cahoots with the gang. I choose the major looking option, which more or less heads straight on. It's at least thirty minutes before I eventually stop. I've been repeatedly going over events in my mind. I can't believe so many men would've been content with the rupees in my pocket and feel sure they would have taken everything, maybe even my bike. I had felt a cold calmness at the roadblock but now I start to shake. I talk sternly to myself, put the bike into gear and ride on. I soon reach a town, thinking, 'thank goodness, Damoh at long last!'.

Sadly not; when I ask for directions the crowd that gathers around me point in unison back to the way I've just come. One man speaks English. He tells me I have to backtrack thirty kilometres before I can join the Damoh road. That means driving along the robber's road... I think not!

I establish where I am and where my present road leads. Drat, I'm heading north east when I need to be going south. I weigh up my options, which takes all of a couple of seconds, then ask if the road ahead is safe. My guide laughs,

"Of course," he replies.

Just then a bus arrives from the north. That makes up my mind, if there's public transport on the road it has to be reasonably free of danger, so, somewhat reluctantly I set off in that direction.

Two hours later I reach Khajuraho, a small village famous for medieval Hindu and Jain temples which have erotic stone carvings. Built between 950 and 1050 AD, the complex was abandoned and concealed in dense jungle by the time of the early Moghul conquests that destroyed so many of India's ancient temples. It wasn't until the mid nineteenth century that it was discovered by the British, totally overgrown and forgotten. Now a UNESCO World Heritage Site, it's one of the most popular tourist attractions in India. Located eleven kilometres off Highway 75, which runs from Jhansi towards Kolkata (Calcutta), the village has expanded considerably in recent years, with the addition of several large hotel chains such as Ramada and Holiday Inn to cater for all the visitors.

I rode my Enfield to here twenty years ago, indeed celebrated my twenty fourth birthday in the temple grounds. I never thought I'd be back again, certainly not in these circumstances. I spot the Hotel Surya. Jacques has a sister by that name, surely a good omen, and so it proves to be. I shower then watch the sunset from my balcony. I'm in no mood to visit the temples, my mind too preoccupied with brigands and highwaymen to be bothered with viewing stone effigies of copulating people and animals. I know I'm being unnecessarily dismissive of one of the best preserved temple sites in the world, but the day's events completely dominate my mind. I look at my map in irritation; I could have ridden directly here from Orchha in just two or three hours instead of the eight hours it actually took me.

I finally relax as I look over the hotel's considerable private gardens, illuminated by the sun's purple afterglow. My bike sits safely parked below me and more than that I've survived. I let go of my uptightness... tomorrow's another day.

As I head to the restaurant for dinner, I tell the hotel manager about my day.

"You were very lucky," he says. "My advice is to stay on the large national highways from now on."

It's counsel I intend to follow.

Day 43 Khajuraho to Seoni, India
249 miles

Starting afresh with my map over breakfast, I plot a course first east then due south. My revised route begins by following a national highway through a tiger reserve. When an hour or so later I reach it, I eagerly look from side to side but of course see nothing large and stripy on the prowl. I do, however, see my first monkeys of the trip. Mostly in small troops, some cheekily swagger across the road in front of me whilst others scamper into the bush on hearing my approach.

It isn't long before I'm faced with my first navigational challenge and test of courage. The main highway heads east for ninety-five kilometres before I can turn south. There's a short-cut off to the right which takes a diagonal route cross-country, saving me at least a hundred kilometres and a couple of hour's riding. I pull up at the intersection and ponder my choices. Before yesterday's bad scare I would have taken the shorter, scenic way without question. It appears to be a fairly busy road and I see first a car then a small lorry set off down it. I spy a small hotel nearby so go to seek advice.

The simple establishment has only one member of staff, but he fortunately speaks good English and his polite demeanour engenders my trust.

"This way is very safe," he adamantly confirms. "All traffic heading south go this direction; no one would drive all that way east to then turn south." he adds as I show him my map.

A man on a scooter, spotting my motorcycle, dismounts and comes to join in the conversation. He's well dressed and again seems trustworthy.

"Please go this way," he says. "You will not be in danger."

I make up my mind, and still with some nerves and trepidation, take the short cut.

The road is not dissimilar to yesterday's, except that it climbs onto a plain where the crops have already been harvested and disposed of and the villages are far fewer in number. However, I'm in no state of mind to enjoy the scenery or the road. I push on, riding even more purposefully than usual, determined not to stop until I reach the main road again. Traffic is sparse, but I do see a bus or a truck every ten minutes or so which gives me some comfort.

A significant Hindu festival, the Durga Puja, is in full swing in these parts. I've seen several temporary temples erected in towns and villages to the super-heroine goddess, Durga, who has ten arms and is the embodiment of self-sufficient, feminine force. In the shadow of these temples and accompanied by pumping music through loudspeakers, I've also observed people collecting alms for the temple, About half way along my shortcut I speed over a rise in the the road and motor down a long straight stretch. Ahead of me, next to a small shack erected immediately before some minor crossroads, are two tall wooden posts that form a makeshift gateway in the road. Without seeming to pay any heed to my noisy and fast approach, two men pick something up off the ground and walk straight out into the middle of the road. It soon becomes apparent that they're carrying a large white festival banner, which they turn front on across my path.

In normal circumstances I wouldn't question their intention to raise the banner high above the road. The wailing music that encircles the area and their colourful festival attire add weight to their credibility. Nonetheless, we are out in the 'back of beyond' and their actions do appear deliberately timed to form a roadblock.

In a flash my brain concurrently produces the words 'Not today you don't!' and 'you're being paranoid Gordon!'. The former thought wins. Keeping my speed up and pressing my horn continuously to make my intentions clear, I ride straight at them. They stand still, looking like rabbits caught in car headlights as it dawns on them that I'm not slowing and certainly have no intention of stopping. At the very last moment and much to my relief, they drop the banner to the ground, narrowly avoiding a *Keystone Cops* or *Laurel and Hardy* scenario of me crashing straight through it. I hardly feel it under my tyres as I glide over its surface, my heart beating hard and fast. Guiltily checking my mirrors, I see the two protagonists standing stock still, seemingly transfixed by my rapidly diminishing form.

It takes a couple of tense but thankfully trouble-free hours to reach Highway 7, which is one of India's major north-south freeways. I intend to follow it for several days. At first I'm very impressed by the standard of the road, that is until I come to a toll plaza beyond which the tarmac deteriorates into a pitted and potholed mess which persists for the next hour. I reach the outskirts of the large city of Jabalpur at one o'clock. It was to have been yesterday's destination but today I elect to bypass it on a well-signposted ringroad. It turns out to be something of a mistake. The road is used exclusively by trucks and is exceedingly busy. With severely broken tarmac, it's virtually impossible to get out of first gear, let alone try to overtake any of these lumbering steel giants. I pull my neckerchief up over my face and tough it out for nearly two bone-jarring hours, covering no more than thirty paltry kilometres.

I've come to realise that my days always seem to be divided into three or four phases. Today, a new phase begins as the ringroad ends. The hundreds of trucks that have plagued my progress all but vanish. Road quality improves dramatically and in no time I'm cruising at speed through refreshingly cool forests. There are sweeping bends and small hills with panoramic views of the surrounding countryside and the treetops. What a transformation... it's again an absolute joy to be riding my motorcycle.

As I hurtle round a sweeping right-hand bend, I'm straightaway faced with a solid mass of thundering metal monsters bearing down on me. One especially large truck is overtaking another round the bend. Unwaveringly, he hits his horn and continues to drive straight at me. I dive for the roadside, a feat that's non too easy because of the direction of my lean into the bend. The overtaking truck misses me by inches and I stall my bike as I bounce over roots and mud-filled ruts in the slippery edge of the forest. It's a seriously close shave and makes me pause for thought. When I set off again, it's with that renewed caution which so often emerges after an 'adrenalin' incident.

True to form, phase four begins a couple of hours later. There is a series of roadworks on the highway and once again, I'm slowed right down. The sun is low in the sky and there's probably only an hour of daylight left. I would love to reach the Pench National Park tonight, but it's a least another sixty kilometres south and the patchy road prohibits fast cruising. Pench is the backdrop for Rudyard Kipling's most well-known work, *The Jungle Book*. I've watched the movie several times with my son and we both loved it. I can't help thinking how brilliant it would be if I can tell him I've slept at the real home of Mowgli and Baloo. As I approach the city of Seoni, I'm in two minds about what to do: push on for Pench and risk being out in the dark or play it safe and stay in the city. I opt for the bypass on the premise that I can assess the situation once I rejoin Highway 7 south of the city. If it's nearly dark I can always turn back and find a bed in Seoni.

I ride for five minutes, the road and surrounding fields are empty. Seemingly out of nowhere, a group of men, six or seven strong, run out onto the road at the top of a hill and stand in a line across my path, maybe one hundred and fifty metres ahead. One man stands in front of them waving a red flag on a long stick. They must have a ghetto blaster as I can hear loud music playing, but there are no temples, banners or any sign that this is a pukka festival site. I haul on the brakes, thinking this is all too redolent of yesterday. This time the road is wide so I don't even stop the bike; in one fluid movement I make a tight U-turn and accelerate away without as much as a glance behind me.

Five minutes later I drive back through the bypass toll booth. The single operator gives me a bemused look. Turning left, I head for Seoni. Within twenty minutes I'm safely ensconced in a central hotel, my bike tucked away in its underground car park. After dinner in the adjoining restaurant, which exclusively serves South Indian vegetarian fare, I wander the streets.

Celebrations of the Durga Puja are well under way. Several brightly lit temporary temples have been erected on the main drag and loud music blares out through antiquated horn-shaped loudspeakers. I notice strings of blue, red and green fairy lights hanging above a narrow passageway. Like following a mystical trail to an enchanted fairy grotto, I walk underneath them until I reach an open-air stage. Here I stand and watch a noisy theatre performance with a crowd of very excited children and their parents. The larger-than-life papier-mâché characters are wheeled out onto the stage on small railway tracks then jiggled around to simulate movement. The narrative is pre-recorded and played over a deafening PA system. It's impossible for me to follow the storyline but the atmosphere makes it a magical experience.

On the way back to my hotel I encounter two small but preposterously well-hung donkeys having an altercation, see three pigs causing traffic to screech to a halt as they unconcernedly amble across the busy central thoroughfare, dodge a cow that suddenly backs away from nibbling the flowers at a roadside offering to a Hindu deity and finally watch a goat steal an apple from a small fruit stand while the stall-holder is distracted by a beggar. Only in India!

Day 44 Seoni to Adilabad, India 205 miles

Early in the morning I follow an isolated road through dense, steamy jungle that makes my bike's engine and exhaust sound exaggeratedly loud. Briefly stopping to check my bags are secure, the pulsating vibrations of thousands of cicadas engulf me and a couple of green parrots squawk noisily as they fly overhead. It's a little eerie but very exotic and extraordinarily thrilling to be amongst.

Setting off again, I come to a screeching halt within minutes to admire an enormous elephant that's being lead in the opposite direction by its aged dhoti-wearing keeper. What a magnificent sight! It's impossible to tell if it's a resident of Pench or one of the many working animals still to be found in India; all I can do is sit on my bike and stare in wonder as it pads its giant feet along the tarmac past me.

Thinking this is something really special to tell Jacques about, I smile as I remember Colonel Hathi and his elephant dawn patrol in the *Jungle Book* film. For a while I talk to myself in my best impression of his upper crust parade-ground voice.

"Bullet, accelerate! To the left... wait for it ... steer!"

It's amazing what you do to pass the time on a long motorcycle ride.

The episode with the elephant does bring home to me one of the mistakes I've made on this trip. I love taking photographs but have found that by the time I've safely parked the bike (which isn't easy as the sidestand seems to have bent out of shape), removed goggles and gloves, unstrapped and unzipped my luggage and eventually extricated my rather large camera, the moment has passed. Not for the first time I tell myself that I must get a compact 'point-and-shoot' digital camera that'll easily fit in my jacket pocket for future journeys.

I somehow miss signs for the ringroad round the city of Nagpur, so have to drive straight through its centre. Being Saturday lunchtime, the streets are jam-packed with all manner of vehicles, except for trucks which are conspicuous by their absence. Perhaps there's a daytime or Saturday ban, I reason. I can't believe how many times I hit red traffic lights and my repeated stop-start-stop progress becomes rather wearisome. Along with twenty or thirty other bikes, I weave my way past buses and cars to the head of the queue, wait for a change to green, then roar ahead for all of a hundred metres to the next static junction.

It takes about an hour and a half to get completely clear of the city, but

I feel quite pleased with both my bike and myself. I remember crossing London the second day of the journey. Gracelessly making very heavy work of it, I overheated both the engine and myself. My congested city riding technique has improved immeasurably since then; I'm much more relaxed and hence able to put my motorcycle under far less stress.

Emerging back onto National Highway 7 almost results in me coming a major cropper. Building up speed, I overtake a succession of cumbersome wagons, happily motoring along at 80 KMPH. My next target is a wide bus that's moving just a little slower than me. Steering to the centre of the road, I check for oncoming traffic; there's none. I flick on my indicator and pull out to pass, thumbing my horn for good measure.

When I'm half way down the side of the bus, I see an elderly turbaned man standing in a large gravelled area wave his arm to flag it down... only he's on what would normally be considered the wrong side of the road for a south-bound bus. This doesn't deter the driver, who completely unaware of me, angles across the road towards him. I'm past the point of no return; if I brake the tail of the bus will certainly side-swipe me into oblivion.

As the bus rapidly decelerates, I open my throttle and try to complete my overtaking manoeuvre before being driven off the road. Braking and turning even more sharply, the front of the bus reaches the gravel on the north-facing side of the highway. I do too, and as the surprisingly nimble waiting passenger hurriedly jumps back out of our way, I somehow manage to squeeze past the front bumper, perilously skidding across the front of the bus's radiator grill. I clip some bushes at the far end of the gravelled area and miraculously bounce my way back onto the highway unscathed. Thankfully, the northbound lane is still empty as I lurch across it back onto the southbound side of the road.

"You bloody idiot!" I shout at myself as much as at the careless bus driver. "You'll get yourself killed" I mutter as I drive off.

Whilst technically I'd done nothing wrong and have safely overtaken literally thousands of vehicles on the journey to date, the incident serves to illustrate that in India you have to expect the unexpected and predict the unpredictable if you want to survive. 80 KMPH is just 50 MPH, not a crazy speed by any means. However, as I repeat my mantra of surviving the journey for Jacques once again, I know I'll have to keep my guard up and be much more careful about my speed on the last few days of the journey.

I spend the whole afternoon riding through some of the most horrendous roadworks I've ever encountered; they're at least one hundred and fifty kilometres long. Judging from the short sections of Highway 7 that are left untouched, the upgrade is more than overdue, but as usual the methodology of doing it all at once rather than piecemeal makes for energy sapping riding.

Some blissfully runway-like stretches have been completed, but these often only last a few hundred metres, at most a kilometre, before a sharp ridge bounces me back onto patches of old potholed road. The long cruddy stretches where the surface has been burnt off are particularly bad. My fellow road users' tyres dig into these hellish areas of loose rock, stone and dust and kick everything backwards over me and my poor Enfield. But from a motorcyclist's perspective, sections where new ballast has been laid are the worst. I snake my way along their edges, clinging to my handlebars as they shimmy from side to side in the thick but loosely laid aggregate that threatens to whip the bike from under me at any moment.

The low point of the day occurs when I begin to overtake an old Ashok Leyland dumper truck. There's plenty of room to pass and the road ahead is perfectly clear, but because of the poor road surface my progress alongside the wagon is slow. Like the majority of commercial vehicles in India, the driver's door folds completely back on itself and latches flat against the rear side of the cab. As I'm just pulling up beside it, the driver, who has obviously not heard my horn and certainly not looked in his mirrors (nobody does in India!), leans towards his open door and power-spits out a whole mouthful of red-stained water.

Because of the sweltering heat this afternoon I'm not wearing my neckerchief over my mouth and nose. I catch the full flow of vile liquid straight in my face, I wobbly brake then pull over to the side of the road, spitting and cursing 'yuk!... yuk!'. I unquestionably know why the water was red stained... paan.

This odious concoction is a curse of most South East Asian countries, but especially India. Made from chopped areca nut which, along with caustic lime, is wrapped in betel leaf, Paan (commonly incorrectly referred to as Betelnut) is a mild stimulant causing raised alertness. It's also quite addictive. Paan 'users' are easily spotted by their lurid-red rotting gums, a horrible sight, and many Indian streets, walls and doorways are splattered with unsightly red saliva stains where the remnants of chewed paan have been spat out. The driver of the truck I just tried overtaking was obviously rinsing his mouth out after chewing a wad of the vile stuff. I hop off my bike and use my spare litre bottle of water to vigourously rinse my face and shoulders clean.

After another gruelling day of about nine hours in the saddle, I'm more than ready to stop for the night in the town of Adilabad. As usual I find a hotel, unload the bike, quickly shower and go in search of dinner. Tonight I have the pleasure of dining at *Davey's Family Restaurant*, an unusually dimly lit establishment where the food, which I would need my torch to see, is nevertheless plentiful and flavoursome.

It's already quarter past eight by the time I've finished. I ask for directions to an internet cafe which, as chance would have it, is just a minute's walk from my hotel. It closes at nine and there's a queue for the limited number of terminals, a situation I've encountered several times already in India. By the time I've waited my turn then quickly checked emails, the cafe is ready to close. I'm now more than a week behind with my blog and once again feel concerned that people will think I'm 'road-kill'. However, as the cafe doesn't reopen until midday and the proprietor claims his to be the only one in town, it'll just have to wait.

Day 45 Adilabad to Warangal, India
239 miles

The day staff at my hotel comprises of five young men who all appear to be the best of friends. They gather around my bike as I load it, arms around each other's shoulders, laughing and enjoying the moment. They're curious about me and my bike and their instant friendship is genuine and very warm. They request a group photo and give me their email addresses. Their uninhibited camaraderie and sense of humour is heartwarming and gets my day off to a great start.

I have exactly 149 KM of Highway 7 left to travel. Like yesterday, it's virtually continuous roadworks. Just after noon I thankfully turn off it and head east, feeling that a major challenge has been met. Hurray! My new route follows a much smaller, quieter road. It's also well surfaced. Great joy! The surrounding fields are dedicated to corn production and it must be harvest time. I see huge pyramids of corn cobs built up against the sides of houses. The road is used as a communal drying facility too, with hundreds of metres at a time covered in a golden layer of kernels desiccating in the sun. It's spectacular.

Half an hour later, a storm approaches fast from the north. I hurriedly park and duck into a large bus shelter, where several other folk appear to be waiting for the bad weather to pass. I finally feel that I'm in south India. The people have darker skin than northern Indians and two of the men wear longis, the traditional sarong-like garment often worn in the south. One speaks English. He advises me to brave the rain as the sky looks clear further east.

"It can rain for hours once it sets in here," he warns.

I buckle up my Barbour's collar and cuffs, pull my neckerchief up over my face and make a dash for it.

The rain falls in huge droplets that hammer the bike. But, as predicted, I'm able to skirt round the periphery of the squall and within a few minutes I'm drying off as I ride under clear blue skies.

Stopping for water around lunchtime, I spot a small open-fronted general store near an intersection, its owner sitting cross-legged behind a low counter. I park up next to the doorway and ask for water and a couple of bars of chocolate. A boy and girl inquisitively come out of the back room when they hear my voice and are fascinated by the procedure of filling up the Camelbak. The boy, who is twelve, speaks excellent English. He confidently approaches me and holds out his hand to shake mine.

"I'm in year five at school," he begins, "and I really enjoy learning English. When I grow up I want to be a businessman and travel the world making money so that my family are not poor any more."

He speaks with such sincerity and conviction that I readily believe anything is possible for him. His sister comes by his side and holds his hand, their father looks proudly on despite not being able follow our conversation.

Another customer arrives and buys a couple of coconuts from a pile at the shop entrance. The shopkeeper removes their hairy dark brown husks with a short machete then drops them into a plastic carrier bag. I indicate that I would like one too and ask, via the boy, if he can crack it open for me. His efficiently does this, handing me the nut with a straw so I can drink its delicious, clear milk. I think of Jacques, who recently won a similar coconut at a fairground in England only to be bitterly disappointed when I split it open to find the the milk had gone off. I ask the boy how long the fruit will stay fresh, thinking that possibly I can take one home for him.

"Only two or three days after it is cut from the tree," he replies, "then the milk goes sour."

Another of life's mysteries explained; bet they wouldn't know that at Asda! I spend a very relaxing ten minutes sitting on crates of soap powder stacked on the shop's steps, chomping the heavenly flesh of the coconut and soaking up the ambience of the quiet village. As I finally get ready to leave, the future businessman shakes my hand and says.

"A pleasure to meet you."

I arrive at the large town of Karimnagar and seek directions.

"Warangal? Warangal?" I ask people.

Four or five times I receive hand signals waving me straight on. A TVS moped cuts right across the front of me, its rider fully occupied typing a text message. I haul on my brakes to avoid crashing into him, cursing loudly as I stall my engine.

Then comes a bit of a shock. When I try to kick my bike over, the kickstarter spins round quite freely. I've lost virtually all compression. Dismayed, I push my bike into some shade, take off helmet, jacket and gloves, then sit on the kerb, head in hands. I try to work through possible causes and solutions in my mind. When I take my hands away and open my eyes, I find I'm surrounded by a crowd numbering at least fifteen and growing fast.

My nose is blocked by the cold I caught in Agra, I'm saturated in sweat and my bike is poorly. It's too much. I ask an English speaker if I can be left alone. I might as well ask for the Koh-i-nor; I'm without doubt the best entertainment in town today if not this week. No one moves so I try to blot all the inquisitive faces out and munch on some nuts and a bar of chocolate. Thank goodness Cadbury's Fruit & Nut is made in India; its energising properties are a veritable lifesaver, redeeming the moment.

I look round my engine. It's impossible to tell if the cylinder head gasket is blown as crankcases, barrel and cylinder head are completely coated in a fine film of oil. It looks like the engine has been sweating the stuff. I check out the decompressor unit and clutch but they both seem fine. I'm out of options. To my left is a Public Call Office. It offers the full gamut of services, mercifully including ISD calls. I get out my address book, gather my riding gear and make ready to call Andy Berry. At the last moment I decide to give the bike another try, figuring at least I'll be better able to describe my dilemma to him. It turns over top dead centre without me using the decompressor. I tickle the carburettor then give the kickstarter a firm kick. It immediately bursts into life. I rev it. It sounds fine. Somewhat bemused, I get myself organised, wave to my audience, and set off.

I'm absolutely amazed, the bike pulls and accelerates just as well as on day one. I don't want to tempt fate by stopping and trying to restart it, so I head south for Warangal.

The ride is longer than my estimation. It's turning dark as I approach the city limits but I spy a hotel almost immediately. It's called The Grand Central and looks far more expensive than my usual level of accommodation. I deserve it, I tell myself. Parking up under the watchful eye of a doorman, I take off my helmet and enter the foyer. A besuited receptionist confirms rooms are available and asks when I would like to check out. He's joined by his manager who looks me up and down with unguarded concern.

"I'm sorry, sir, but we are full," he says.

His assistant looks confused. I question him, but he remains firm. I leave.

All becomes clear when outside I see my reflection in the hotel's windows. My jacket and trousers are blackened with oil and weeks of road grime and my boots are crusted with dust. My hands are black and my fingernails a major health risk. Moving up to my face, probably the most scary bit, the factor 50 sunblock I liberally applied to it this morning has transformed from white cream to a greasy dark grey paste. There are also red lines around my forehead and nose where my goggles have rubbed. The piece de resistance that completes my tramp-like appearance has to be the absence of one arm on my glasses which I unwittingly stood on yesterday...!

It takes half an hour to find suitable lodgings near to the railway station. Another Hotel Surya provides a safe haven for the night. Patting my bike, I thank it for yet one more safe and enjoyable day. It has run beautifully all afternoon despite the scare I received in Karimnagar. I stop and start it several times. Compression remains poor yet it fires up first kick and runs sweetly. There are only three more days ride left to Chennai. I hope we will make it!

Day 46 Warangal to Vijayawada, India
186 miles

I begin the day somewhat bleary-eyed. I'm met outside my hotel at quarter past seven and led to the offices of MARI (Modern Architects for Rural India). MARI run many projects in the Warangal region that aid impoverished villages with clean water, improved sanitation and educational activities. It also administers several Wateraid projects, two of which I'm going to visit.

I meet with Mr. Murali at the MARI headquarters. He's a highly educated, erudite man, passionate about making a difference in the region. He tells me that MARI's aims include the empowerment of some of the poorest people in Andhra Pradesh, to make local government more accountable for its spending on rural development and to demonstrate how simple new technologies can be used to bring safe water and sanitation to small communities. It's inspiring stuff.

We're joined for breakfast by two journalists and a photographer. Mr. Murali tells me he thinks that newspaper articles about my visit may help raise awareness of their work. As a former biker, he admits that he has a secondary agenda; he hopes that news of my ride will inspire some local young men to get on their bikes and see other parts of India, and possibly the world, for themselves. I agree to the interviews, but it all gets a bit surreal.

We quickly progress from my ride and support of Wateraid and MARI, to subjects I'm not qualified to comment on, such as youth problems in European society, the breakdown of family values and the proliferation of pornographic material on the internet, which they claim mostly originates in the UK and USA! I don't know who these two characters think I am. I explain that I'm just a regular bloke undertaking a six week motorcycle journey... journalists! Mr Murali apologises to me when they leave, but he really has no need and we quickly turn the subject of discussion back, for us, to far more important things.

Wateraid supports work in thirty one villages in the region and I'm keen to see the results. I'm escorted to the first village, Pamnuur, by two MARI staff on a lightweight motorcycle. It's a thirty kilometre ride on the main road to Hyderabad. We eventually turn off the highway and head down a narrow country lane. I round a bend to find the road blocked by a large crowd; upwards of a hundred people. There are three drummers, an old man carrying a spear and excited children running this way and that. A young woman wearing a beautiful blue sari holds garlands of red flowers. Over the last two weeks I've seen several Hindu festivals on the streets of India, so I come to a gradual halt and wait for the crowd to pass by. They don't, instead they gather closer in on me. I see a large placard being held up high. It reads 'Welcome to Porden'.

I think to myself, "Oh, this village must be called Porden. Doesn't sound a typically Indian name," and I look around to see who they're welcoming.

My guides have parked their bike and are encouraging me to do the same. Maybe I'm a bit dim but I blame it on the early start. It gradually dawns on me that Porden actually means Gordon. Three garlands of deep red carnations are ceremoniously draped around my neck and I'm asked to make a short speech. I'm embarrassed as I've only really come to see some water pumps and toilet blocks and I'm certainly not an emissary for Wateraid, but I do my best. I thank the crowd for their kind welcome and tell them I feel very humbled by the sincerity of their greetings.

One of my escorts relays a question from a villager to me.

"How does our village compare with villages in the UK?"

I look around at the simple mud brick and concrete houses, the goats on the dusty road, the open, friendly faces of all those that surround me. I can't begin to explain the differences. I answer,

"There are so many differences, but the welcome I have had in your village has been the best in India."

Thankfully it goes down well.

I ask about the difference Wateraid support has made to the villagers' lives. I'm told that until recently there was only one nearby water source which was shared by around two hundred and fifty households. For some people that meant a walk of over a kilometre. Now there are six water pumps in the village, which has made a momentous difference. Furthermore, in the recent past people had no toilets. Open defecation was their only choice and disease was rife. There are now numerous toilet facilities, including at the village school. I'm introduced to two local Wateraid community workers. They look after the welfare of this and an adjoining village, which includes providing ongoing sanitary education. They have earnest, gentle faces and are quite rightly proud of the difference they have been able to make to the lives of the people here.

All too quickly I have to say my thanks and goodbyes. We then ride a kilometre to a small hamlet which forms an outlying part of Pamnuur. A handful of dwellings sit next to a concrete block with a hand pump in the middle. I'm told that all the adults are farm labourers and are currently out working in the fields. A couple of shy children hide from me but a village elder comes over to say hello and demonstrate the water pump. As he cranks the handle up and down a stream of crystal clear water emits from the tap. He gestures for me to drink some. It's cool and refreshing.

"It's safe, don't worry," my escort tells me. He continues, "the bore is a hundred and sixty metres deep."

I'm told that the old man is responsible for maintenance of the pump.

"Villagers are encouraged to take ownership of their water supply. Each pump is assigned a caretaker who we teach how to maintain it," explains my guide.

The next surprise is the arrival of a TV crew. Two young men hop off a small motorcycle and join us at a trot. One carries a somewhat dated looking camcorder in his right hand, the other a telescopic boom and microphone. At least these guys, employees of a small local network, ask sensible questions about my ride and in particular, how Wateraid raise the funds in the UK that make such life-changing differences here. I spend quite some time explaining how many people like myself have set up a standing order from our bank accounts that automatically pays a few pounds a month into the Wateraid kitty. It sounds so simple explained this way, yet in action it has such a profound effect.

The interview ends on a high note. I'm asked if I have a family myself. This is no surprise as family and the extended family is so fundamentally important in Asia and I have frequently been asked about my family en route. I answer that Jane and I have one son aged six.

“Ah, micro-family” the interviewer responds to camera.

For some reason this expression really tickles me and I get the giggles. I can see how to many rural Indians, a family of one or two children would appear small, but to have a buzzword for it...

We set off again down sandy lanes surrounded by fields of diverse crops which my guide points to and names: cotton, chillies, turmeric, sunflower, maize. groundnut and red gram (pigeon pea).

We halt so that what I see can be explained...

“This area looks very arable but there have been many droughts and failed crops in recent years and most farmers are heavily in debt. The suicide rate amongst them is at record heights and one of our aims is to teach these farmers how to get more productive yields and also how to diversify into more profitable crops, including organics.”

I'm next taken to a second village, Konachalam. Around two and a half thousand people live here and their welcome is just as overwhelmingly warm as at Pamnuur. I hang the red garlands of carnations on my bike headlamp and receive, in their place, a beautifully strung together garland of yellow marigolds. Wateraid has worked on a fifty-fifty basis with these villagers to install a ten thousand litre water tank as well as eight compost pits and seven water-pumps. The transformation has been remarkable; from only ten percent of villagers having access to latrines to well over fifty percent in two years. Again I'm told that sanitary education is high on the list of priorities for the local Wateraid field workers.

"Sickness caused by poor sanitation and water-borne disease has been radically reduced," the project leader informs me. "But this is a four year project and we still have a long way to go yet."

It's a really excellent achievement and great for me to see first hand the metamorphosis Wateraid support has brought to the lives of these people.

I eat a protracted lunch with my guides, who want to have a leisurely talk with me about the UK and my bike. Unfortunately, time progresses. In the end, I have to make my excuses and leave hastily as Vijayawada lies over one hundred and fifty miles east and I am, as ever, keen to get there before dark. Before saying goodbye, the MARI workers sketch a line map that will take me cross-country to the main Vijayawada highway, a very useful tool.

My bike still lacks compression but rides magnificently. Once on the main road, National Highway 9, I find long sections of my route are just two narrow lanes wide and chock-a-block with hulking slow trucks. Again and again I rev hard and my Enfield zips past three or four of them at a time. I'm still wearing two garlands with three others somehow clinging to the headlight. The colourful sight of me in full flight causes many motorists to toot and wave as I pass.

I ride the final twenty kilometres in murky twilight. Stopping by a 'Welcome to Vijayawada' sign, I ask directions to a hotel. To my dismay, I'm told there are another ten kilometres to ride before the city centre. What's more, there's a power cut. The guys I've just asked sit astride a Bajaj Vespa scooter. When I admit that I don't yet have a hotel booked, they offer to guide me to the area by the railway station where most hotels are situated. I gratefully accept their offer.

The roads rapidly become extremely congested. Eventually we reach a roundabout that's partly blocked by crowd control barriers. One of my assistants climbs off the scooter and lifts the barrier aside so we, and no doubt many behind us, can pass. More than half an hour later I shake the hands of both my helpers when we pull up beside a large, smart-looking hotel and restaurant. They leave. I go to check in but the hotel is full.

Returning to my bike, I wonder which way to go next.

A young man pulls up on a bicycle and asks where I'm from and what I'm doing in Vijayawada? I explain I need a hotel with parking. Without hesitation he says,

"I will show you" and sets off at speed, his legs windmilling around like a cartoon character.

He's much faster and more manoeuvrable on his bicycle than I am on my weighty motorcycle and I almost lose him in the chaotic melee of vehicles that clog the streets. Three times he stops and waits for me to catch up. Finally, he points towards a hotel, waves goodbye, then pedals away before I can even thank him.

Ten minutes later I collapse on a crisp, clean bed. I once again reflect on just how deeply indebted I am to strangers for my comfort and safety before heading out for my regular evening ritual, which is to try and find a restaurant followed by an internet cafe.

Day 47 Vijayawada to Nellore, India
176 miles

To my delight I discover that my hotel is just two minutes from the start of National Highway 5, my route south. Better still, the roads are especially quiet as today is a public holiday, the first day of a two-day festival in South India called Ayudha Puja. In this Hindu festival, people worship Vishwakarma, the architect of the world. All tools, machines, vehicles, weapons etc. are cleaned, polished and where appropriate, given a lick of paint. Finally, each is carefully smeared with vermilion and sandalwood paste, and in the case of cars, adorned with large banana leaves. It's captivating.

According to my map, NH 5 is part of the Golden Quadrangle, a network of modern motorways that hugs the coast of southern India. It's been built to a very high standard and in the main I have it all to myself. After just ten minutes I see a large green road sign. In bold letters is written Chennai, 475 KM. It's the first sign I've seen for my final destination and a surge of anticipation rushes through me. From day one I've been unable to visualise my arrival in Chennai. All I've been able to see is the following day ahead. Indeed, although I have known the sequence of countries I would pass through and have had a fair sense of the general direction I would take, I've mostly planned my next day's ride the night before. Now the end is in sight. I feel so proud of my bike that I thank it out loud and give it a few strokes on its petrol tank for good measure.

I'm haunted by a snappy but immensely annoying TV advert catchphrase all morning, one of three dreadful commercials for cellphones I've seen repeatedly on hotel televisions. The first of these advertisements is for a mobile phone that plays karaoke. It depicts a hip thirty-something dancing round his slick apartment ineptly singing songs from the 1990s to the accompaniment of his phone. Next is a mobile that allows its user to draw in full colour. This is a really painful advert as the would-be artist, portrayed as a college student, makes his teacher stop writing on a blackboard three times with false questions so he can sketch a caricature of him on his 'phone.

The one that drives me nuts today, however, involves a mobile with a built-in camera that takes photos anytime someone smiles into the lens. The infuriating musical slogan, 'clicks-when-you-smile" is sung over and over in the background. It's irritating in itself but doubly so when it has become a repetitive part of my consciousness!

The near empty road and my impending finish lull me into a dangerously soporific state. In short order I have two joltingly near encounters that remind me that I've still got to keep myself safe for a further two days.

The motorway has a large central reservation planted with flowering trees and shrubs. It must be a nightmare to irrigate as so far I've ridden over fifty kilometres without seeing a break in the foliage. To my horror, an enormous adult water buffalo crashes out of the bushes, as though a tiger were at its tail, and runs directly across my path. I haul on my brakes for an emergency stop. I'm too close to swerve as at this speed I would almost certainly come off. Thankfully, the beast just keeps on running. Had it seen me and frozen I would have ploughed straight into it. As it is, I miss its galloping hindquarters by no more than a couple of feet.

I'm quite shaken by my near miss but keep riding as my destination, Nellore, is little less than three hours away. A large dumper truck, which I've been closing in on for some time, slows and pulls hard over to the left of the inside lane. I'm cruising at eighty, so ease into the outside lane to overtake it. Within fifty metres of me it swings wildly across the road. There's a gap in the central reservation; it's doing a U-turn. Again I yank on my brakes for dear life. The truck is much bigger than a water buffalo but fortunately, I have a couple more seconds in which to react. I dive for the inside and just squeeze around its rear. For the next minute the muscles in my forearms and wrists ache from the exertion of braking so hard.

Staying fully awake without any difficulty for the rest of the ride, I roll into Nellore at half past three. It's a fairly nondescript place, but for some strange reason has a grand four star hotel. Checking it out, I decide the room rate is a bit steep but make note that it has an excellent looking bar and restaurant.

I find a hotel with underground parking just around the corner for a quarter of the price but return to the swisher establishment for a hearty feed and the obligatory iced Kingfisher.

I toast my beloved motorcycle and myself. Unbelievably, tomorrow will be our last full day on the road. To prepare for it, I spend a highly satisfying hour before bed making nut and bolt checks, topping up my oil and cleaning the points. It seems unreal that this will all soon end.

Day 48 Nellore to Chennai, India
112 miles

I feel quite sentimental loading my bike this morning, thinking back to the first day of the trip and my unpractised attempt at getting things set to ride. As usual a crowd gathers around me whilst I strap on my Ortlieb tail bag, bike cover, camera tripod and tank bag. My tools are the slowest. I've taken to attaching them to the right hand side of the front crashbar as a means of putting more weight near the front of the bike, but they're awkward to make secure. Despite over six weeks of practice it still takes me close on half and hour to get the bike loaded.

Within five hundred metres of the hotel I stop at a PCO and phone Ranga, a member of the Madras Bulls Motorcycle Club. Ranga got in touch before my departure from the UK with the offer of an escort of club members and their Royal Enfields for the final stage of my journey. He tells me that a group of riders has assembled and are already heading north from Chennai to meet me. It's rather exciting.

I stop for petrol, trying to guess exactly how much to put in as I don't want to have to discard any when the bike is readied to be shipped back to the UK. Accounting for Chennai's slow city traffic that will consume fuel at a higher rate, I plumb for five litres. Finger's crossed it's enough!

As it's day two of the local holiday, National Highway 5 remains quiet and I merrily cruise along, enjoying the beat of my faithful Enfield's engine, the feel of its secure handling and the warm air in my face.

The first major signpost I see reads: Chennai 176 KM; Rameswaram 768 KM; Kanniyakumari 824 KM. This gets the blood surging through my veins with anticipation. Just a tad over a hundred miles to go. Then I start considering the other two distances. Kanniyakumari is the southernmost point of India. How cool, I think, to be able to ride there. Then it registers that the holy town of Rameswaram is also the port where, in the past, a regular ferry sailed to Sri Lanka. How wonderful it would be to ride all the way to Colombo, Sri Lanka, I fantasise... Oh Gordon, I stop myself, what are you like! I laugh as I think my friends would unanimously say "incorrigible".

About sixty kilometres north of Chennai I spot two men sitting on Royal Enfields by the roadside. They're waving their arms wildly to attract my attention. When I pull over, they introduce themselves as the club outriders, the main body are waiting ten kilometres further south. They seem just as exhilarated as I am when we set off.

It would be impossible to miss the Madras Bulls. A long line of fifteen Bullets stand resplendent beside the road. I'm really honoured that these guys have been following my journey online and taken the trouble to ride north to meet me. I walk round and shake hands with them all. They ask lots of questions and there's much curiosity from me too as I notice that many of their bikes have been stylishly customised.

The sound of our departure is deafening but thrilling. The riders all wear helmets and ride very carefully. Indeed, I'm really impressed with how they work as a team to manage the other traffic so that the bikes stay safely together, a couple of guys at the front waving aside trucks and cars so that the bulk of the riders can pass en mass. I grin with pleasure for the whole hour and a half it takes to reach the outskirts of Chennai.

Formerly known as Madras, it's an enormous metropolis of over seven million people, India's fourth largest city and the provincial capital of Tamil Nadu. It lies on the coast of the Bay of Bengal and has been a trading post for spices and textiles from the Orient for more than two thousand years. First colonised by the Portuguese then the Dutch in the sixteenth century, it became a stronghold of the British East India Company after the Carnatic Wars of the mid-eighteenth century. Known as the 'meat wars', these bloody battles resulted in Major General Robert Clive (Clive of India) and his forces driving out French colonists, who headed south to form a new colony at Pondicherry.

Chennai boasts few tourist attractions but is generally regarded as a relaxed city by Indian standards. In recent times, it has experienced a boom in IT and automotive industries which has seen the likes of Hyundai, Ford, Mitsubishi and Ashok Leyland set up major factories in the locale. Royal Enfield famously built its factory at the northern end of the city in 1955.

I have a pretty well tuned sense of direction, but navigating my way towards my hotel would have been an onerous task without my escorts. Once in the city, a further five or six riders join us on their Bullets and I can't help thinking what a magnificent sight we must make.

We reach my hotel, the Ashoka, at 2.30 pm. I've chosen it because it's one of Chennai's oldest hotels and is set in over two acres of gardens. I know my bike will be safe here and hopefully the Bulls will be able to come into its grounds with me. The gatekeeper waves us all through. I've arrived!

I park up and head for the reception. While no one is looking, I punch the air and laugh out loud. I've made it! As I check in, the club members line their bikes up for a group photo with my trusty old Enfield at the front. It's a very proud moment for me and I feel quite overwhelmed. I'm invited by the members to a club meeting at a beach in the evening. How can I refuse? The Bulls saddle up and roar out of the hotel complex, many waving to me and shouting "see you later."

I feel strangely emotionally numb when I finally unload my bike and get into my room. I wish I felt physically numb too. For most of my journey I've ridden at least one mile standing on the footpegs for every ten miles seated. It's been the only way to cope with a stiffly padded single saddle, but in India this just hasn't been possible. Driving has been so downright dangerous that I've had to sit nearly all the time to be able to react rapidly to whatever situation or maniacal driving antics I encounter. It's taken its toll. I've been constantly in the seat for up to ten hours a day for many of the last nine days. My backside throbs with pain; I've got two large pressure sores where the saddle has pressed. It would be funny if it didn't hurt so much!

I take a shower then look at myself in the mirror. What a hoot. My face and neck are well tanned despite a daily coating of sunblock. My arms and hands have coloured to a certain extent too. But the rest of me is lily white. I decide that all I need is a knotted hankie on my head, rolled up trousers and a white vest to make a decent impression of a 'cor blimey' postcard caricature. But what the heck, it's no price to pay for the adventure I've had.

The Hotel Ashoka is something else, real 1950's kitsch. The blue and white main buildings resemble a spaceship from the '60s TV cartoon, *The Jetsons*. Inside the reception area, the settees and tables are an elongated oval shape and finished in powder blue and pink. There's even a funky outdoors ice-cream parlour. I love it.

I walk to a nearby PCO. Before I 'phone my family to tell them they can stop worrying about me, I call Andy Berry, who more than anyone else deserves to know the bike has made it. I catch him at work on his mobile. Across the many miles, I can clearly hear the joy in his voice.

"That's superb, Gordon. Brilliant news!" he reiterates several times. I thank him once again for the tremendous work he's done with my bike.

"It wouldn't have been possible without you, mate" I tell him.

I'm picked up in the evening by one of the 'Bulls', Hari, on his 350 Thunderbird. It takes half an hour to reach a cafe beside the beach where the club regularly meets. Many of the riders I met earlier are seated at a long table outside, although there are several new faces and bikes present. There's a great camaraderie amongst the club members and I enjoy the conversations that ripple round the table immensely. I get to finally meet Ranga with whom I've corresponded for the last couple of months. Showing me his bike, he tells me it's a 2003 model Thunderbird. It's done seventy seven thousand kilometres, including two trips from the most southerly point to the most northerly point in India. The engine has never been touched and I'm very impressed.

To my delight, I'm presented with a Madras Bulls t-shirt, which I immediately put on. It makes a great end to a great day.

Tomorrow I'll ride the final seventeen kilometres to the Royal Enfield factory, where my bike will be crated up for its return by sea to the UK. As I lie on my bed, sleeplessly staring at the cracked plaster ceiling with its slowly turning central fan, I feel an odd combination of elation and sadness.

Day 49 Chennai to Thiruvottyur, India
10 miles

I load my bike for the very last time then alert the hotel receptionist about my plans to return in the evening... I don't want him to think I'm riding off without paying. I have a leisurely breakfast to allow rush hour traffic to thin out then don my riding gear. There's such a short distance to ride that for once I don't do a thorough nut and bolt check. I go through my usual starting procedure: turn on the fuel; tickle the carb; release the clutch; turn the engine over top dead centre and kick it over with the lightest of twists of the throttle. The engine bursts into life first kick, which once again makes me glow inside.

It's been more than three years since my last visit to the Royal Enfield factory to take photographs for the book, *The Legend Rides On*. On that occasion I flew in feeling in excellent health only to leave the city ten days later with viral meningitis, a dreadful experience I wouldn't wish on anybody. During my stay the company loaned me a Bullet to commute to and from the factory, but the route is by now just a hazy memory. I only hope I can remember my way after all this time.

I travel past the spectacular moorish-style Egmore railway station and onto Poonamalee High Road. This takes me first past Chennai Central railway station and then the magnificent Raj-era Southern Railways building, resplendent in brilliant white rendering and with a sooty black steam locomotive displayed on its well-manicured lawns. Next I see Beach suburban station followed by Chennai docks. From here it's a case of following the coast road past the simple 'thatched' houses of fishermen which are overshadowed by a lengthy queue of trucks awaiting their turn to enter the port. I turn onto Thiruvottiyur High Road. Traffic is as thick and challenging here as it has been at any other stage of my ride through India, including Delhi. Extra-wide buses make it impossible to pass, so I sit in their cloying fumes waiting for my chance to overtake when they pull in to pick up passengers.

Just as I pass one such vehicle, my engine coughs. I rev it, wondering what could possibly go wrong so close to the end of the road, only to hear the engine splutter then stop. Curses... I know what it is. Yesterday's five litres of petrol were just a thimble-full too little. I hop off and push the bike to the curbside, allowing a line of recently overtaken buses to infuriatingly pass by me. Jiggling the bike from side to side, I think I can just hear the faintest of tinkles inside the tank, although with all the city noise in the background, I suspect this is just wishful thinking. Undaunted, I lean the bike over as far as I dare towards the side with the petrol tap and am rewarded by the sight of my glass fuel filter once again full of pinkish petrol. True to form, one kick sets the engine back into a steady rhythm.

Ten minutes later I spot the sign I've been searching for. Bold red letters on a jet black background herald Royal Enfield. I turn down the approach road and pull up outside the factory gates, stopping my engine for the last time. Unlike the elation I felt on reaching my hotel yesterday, this morning I feel only a deep sense of relief.

Entering the compound is a bit like stepping into the pages of a history book. I look around at the late-colonial style office building, the two large production buildings ahead, the engine and machine shops on the right, the final assembly plant on the left with hundreds of finished motorcycles neatly lined up under an adjoining tin-roofed veranda. Between the two buildings is a long driveway where three bold yellow supply vehicles are parked and a man pushes a trolley on which a recently completed engine sits firmly ensconced.

For me, this is one of the most endearing sights at the factory. Each motor individually leaves the engine assembly shop and is pushed across to the final assembly plant where a frame is wrapped around it. The engineers note the engine number then stamp the same numerals onto the frame using a heavy hammer and various numbering chisels. Over the next seven minutes, the unit makes its way along the final assembly line at the end of which it emerges as a fully functioning motorcycle. At this point, a test rider hops on board and takes it for a spin round the company test track which is immediately to my left, somewhat poetically surrounded by tropical palms. To a motorcyclist, not least a Royal Enfield devotee, it's the stuff of dreams.

I spend the whole day at the factory under the friendly guidance of Saravana, a senior export engineer and Sachin, one of the company's senior marketing managers. There have been numerous changes in production techniques and facilities since I was here in 2005 and the resulting improvements in quality are plain to see. Most impressive is the new engine assembly line that produces the unit construction EFI engine, the company's power-unit of the future. Top of the range Japanese CNC machinery has been brought in specifically for these engines, which also benefit from the crankcase halves being joined using liquid gasket technology. These production improvements are obviously necessary to make a modern, reliable engine that will carry the company forward, but I'm pleased by the amount of highly skilled labour that is still used. The bikes are largely hand assembled by craftsmen.

We next visit the final assembly line. As I watch production, I notice a small group being escorted beside the assembly conveyor belt. Saravana explains,

"The man at the front is retiring today after twenty nine year's service in the engine shop. Those others are his family and friends. Everyone who retires is allowed to bring guests to the factory on his last day so that he can show them where he has worked and they can join in his retirement celebrations."

It's great to see that the company not only makes yesteryear style motorcycles, it has caring old-world values too.

Highlight of the day is seeing the new Bullet Classic. I'm agog when I first lay eyes on it... what a beautiful machine. Finished all over in a choice of rich maroon, dusky green or glossy black, the new bike draws so many styling features from Enfield designs of the early 1950s, but combines them with an engine that can readily cruise at 70 MPH and brakes that can safely stop from those speeds. I simply cannot wait to get my hands on one.

My bike is brought into the factory to be prepared for shipping. The front wheel and mudguard are removed, as are the screen, crashbars and mirrors. Packing experts bolt the bike to the crate base using specially made mounts that attach to the fork bottoms and footpeg spindle. It feels strange to see my much travelled friend partly disassembled in this way. Plywood sides are hammered into place and finally a lid is sealed onto the top. It's going to be five weeks before it reaches the port of Southampton in the UK. I know I'll be quite anxious until it's safely back in my hands.

I have two more days left in Chennai, both of which are spent at the factory. It's a pleasure for me to see how the ethos of the company has been enhanced by the addition of new personnel, including a very experienced and forward-thinking CEO, Mr. Ravichandran. There's a genuinely optimistic feeling amongst the staff and I believe it's well founded. There are the new retro-style Bullet models, which look wonderful and perform superbly. Production has improved too, both in terms of output and most critically, in quality. There's no question in my mind that the improvements made to the new machines come at no cost to any of the characteristics that makes the motorcycles so well loved, leaving me with a solidly good feeling for the company's future.

Although my Royal Enfield was originally made in the UK some two years before this factory was opened, it does strangely feel as though I've brought it home, well at least to its spiritual home.

In truth, I cannot think of anywhere else I would have wanted this journey to end.

Epilogue

12 October 2008

I exit the customs hall at Manchester Airport early in the evening. Setting off from the Ashoka at five in the morning, it's been a drawn-out day made longer by losing the four and a half hours I'd gained crossing time zones whilst riding. My body feels as though it's already midnight, but I'm too excited to care.

Jane's bright blue Ford sits in the arrivals pick-up area. I wheel my trolley towards it and see a small head with blonde wavy hair poke out of the open passenger window. There's an indescribable squeal of joy as the head disappears then the car door bursts open. Jacques erupts, full of six-year-old boyish energy, and runs towards me, arms wide open. He flings himself into my arms and clings to me, physically shaking as I spin us both around.

The homecoming almost turns into a minor disaster as I catch movement out of the corner of my eye. My trolley, overloaded with twenty-eight kilograms of luggage, is on the roll, heading straight for the front wing of a rather smart looking Audi. Holding tightly onto Jacques, there's nothing I can do but watch in paralysed horror as it smacks into the car.

But the good-fortune I've experienced throughout my journey to India hasn't abandoned me yet. The point of impact is the executive car's ample front wheel. Putting Jacques down, I sheepishly pull the trolley away, apologising to the concerned driver as he scrutinises his car, and, hand-in-hand with my son, walk towards a smiling (and relieved!) Jane.

13 November 2008

I arrive at the NEC (National Exhibition Centre), Birmingham at 9.30 pm, the night before the annual three-day Classic Motor Show. Finding the Pavilion Hall, I push a side-door open and am instantly wowed. In front of me is a grand vista of hundreds of gleaming, beautifully restored vintage and classic motorcycles. Some of the machines on display must be worth a fortune, I think, eyeing Vincent Black Shadows, Brough Superiors, Velocette Thruxtons and a host of other makes of motorcycle mainly now consigned to the annals of history.

In the far corner of the hall, isolated on an island of red carpet, sits a solitary wooden packing case. It seems completely incongruous next to the lustrous stove-enamel and shining chrome on all the other display stands, but to my eye there's nothing more beautiful.

With the help of one of the show organisers, Mark Woodward, I crowbar the packing case open. When the lid and four sides are removed, I take hold of a white plastic protective cover and, with relish, whip it up into the air like a magician performing his very best magic trick. Underneath is my bike, safely home.

Mark had kindly arranged for the bike to be picked up at Southampton docks earlier today, just hours after it cleared customs, so that it could be put on display at the show. I couldn't have imagined a more fitting reunion.

"It's got a certain patina, hasn't it?" he says, eyeing the thick coating of road grime and oil that covers every inch of the bike.

There are quite a few scratches too, as well as the obviously twisted forks.

"Every bit of it has a memory for me," I reply.

Together we remove all the securing bolts and put the front wheel back in. Ten minutes later, I roll it off the packing case base and lift it onto its centrestand. Mark leaves to make final preparations for tomorrow's show opening and I'm left alone with my Royal Enfield.

I'm overwhelmingly tempted to start her, no matter what the NEC health and safety policy decrees, but the empty petrol tank obviously foils me.

Instead, I swing my leg over the saddle and settle myself into a very familiar riding position, deeply and truly contented to have my wonderful, brilliant, faithful old motorcycle back again.

Suppliers: Motorcycle

Chain

Whilst running in the bike and crossing Europe and Turkey, I used a new development in roller chain technology, the **Iwis** *Nano* chain. It utilises groundbreaking nano technology on the bearing areas of the chain, resulting in a 50% improvement in chain life.

Iwis chains are made in Germany from high quality, quenched, tempered and case-hardened steels. They are pre-stretched with shouldered pins and have a high fatigue strength and superior wear resistance.

Once I reached the dry and dusty regions of Iran and Pakistan, I switched to an Iwis *Megalife* chain. This chain has a silver coloured coating that ensures it does not rust and special bushes which are sintered. This means it can be run dry or with minimal lubrication and therefore not easily pick up dust or sand. Both chains only needed one adjustment and have thousands of miles of life left in them.

Contact: www.iwis.com UK dealers: Sprockets Unlimited www.sprocketsunlimited.com Tel: (+44) 01386 831341

Powder Coating

Maldon Shot Blasting & Powder Coating powder coated all the parts likely to be subjected to rough treatment. They have a scaled approach to their work, with a choice of guarantees on finishes ranging from 1 to 10 years.

Of special note is the finish they used on the sump guard, crash bars and luggage racks. It's a new ultra-tough preparation from Dupont that the team at Maldon were confident would survive the rigours of the journey. It did remarkably well.

Contact: www.ctc-powder-coating.co.uk Tel: (+44) 01621 841100

Wheels

My bike's rims and spokes were completely rusted through. I sent the hubs to wheel experts **Central Wheel Components** who rebuilt them using stainless steel rims and spokes. The result is a superb finish that won't rust. The company provided spare spokes for the journey, which weren't needed

Central Wheels also sell motorcycle tyres suitable for classics. I chose to fit *Dunlop K70s* as they're a good all-purpose tyre with a fairly chunky tread that dealt remarkably well with some very rough road conditions. They also look in keeping on a classic bike.

Contact: www.central-wheel.co.uk Tel: (+44) 01621 841100

Oil

I've used **Penrite** oils for a number of years with complete satisfaction. They are specially formulated for use with classic bikes and cars and brilliantly stood up to the 40 degree plus heat I experienced in Iran and Pakistan.

I used *Classic 20W50* for running in and riding across Europe, *Classic HPR50*

(equivalent to a straight 50) for the hotter latter stages of the journey and *Classic HPR40* (equivalent to a straight 40) for the gearbox.
Contact: www.penrite.co.uk Tel: (+44) 01962 732601

Shock Absorbers
The original Royal Enfield shock absorbers were pretty good in their time, but certainly would struggle with the weight I carried, especially on poor roads.
I chose to fit a pair of **Hagon** classic shrouded shock absorbers because they would cope with the weight and terrain, improve handling and look great on the bike. They have a double sealed nitrogen cell, automatic compression and rebound damping control with an enclosed hard chrome piston rod. There are 3 easily selectable settings ranging from soft to firm, giving modern standards of comfort and road holding combined with classic appearance. They were absolutely unbustable.
Contact: www.hagon-shocks.co.uk Tel: (+44) 0208 502 6222

General Royal Enfield Parts and Consumables
I've bought the majority of missing or replacement parts from **Hitchcocks Motorcycles**. Hitchcocks are the world's largest supplier of Royal Enfield spares and I have to say they offer excellent telephone advice.
Several of the items I needed to complete the restoration are no longer available new (eg. gearbox middle case, clutch operating lever, RHS fork bottom tube and rear mudguard carriers), but fortunately, Hitchcocks sell used parts as well and could find 80% of what I required.
They've also provided several components that enhanced durability and performance, including forged piston, belt drive and billet crankshaft with a needle-roller big end.
Contact: www.hitchcocksmotorcycles.com Tel:(+44) 01564 783192

Cables
None of the standard Bullet throttle, clutch or twin front brake cables fit my bike. **Carrot Cycles,** a UK web-based business specialising in made-to-order control cables and quality classic motorcycle consumables, came to the rescue. They provided me with custom-made cables that fit perfectly. They also supplied a new BAP fuel tap, classy braided fuel hose and a glass bowl fuel filter which proved very useful.
Contact: www.carrotcycles.co.uk Tel: (+44) 01522 595975

Crash Bars
I've fitted Indian army front and rear crash bars which were supplied by UK Royal Enfield distributors, **Watsonian Squire**. Originally painted olive green, I've had them powder coated black. They did an invaluable job protecting the bike the two times I dropped it, and both it and me when I crashed in Pakistan.
Contact: www.royal-enfield.com Tel: (+44) 01386 700907

Magneto
The magneto is probably the most vulnerable part of my motorcycle. I toyed with carrying a spare but they are exceedingly heavy. **Tony Cooper of TC Motorcycles**, magneto and dynamo restoration specialists, came up with a great solution. He made me a spare armature, complete with bearings and spacer ring. If the magneto had failed, I could have replaced the main components in one go. Most importantly, the armature weighs only a fraction of a complete magneto body.
Contact: (+44) 0121 559 2405

Alarm
Peace of mind is priceless. I chose to fit an alarm to act as a deterrent to potential thieves, especially at night. **Acumen**, a British electronics company, make a range of very high quality alarms. I fitted the CAT 3.1 DIY alarm into my off-side toolbox. The alarm comes with a key fob remote and has both a nudge sensor and a proper movement sensor. The current draw is very low; less than 5mA, and it's fully waterproof.
Contact: www.acumen-electronics.co.uk Tel: (+44) 0870 240 32 57

Mirrors
I tried to fit stainless steel fittings to the bike where possible. **Halcyon Design & Manufacturing**, famous for their aviator and motorcycle goggles, produce beautiful stainless handlebar and bar-end mirrors. I fitted a pair of their *Stadium 850* handlebar mounted mirrors which look authentically classic and were surprisingly untroubled by vibration. They also manufactured the excellent stainless tax disc holder that I used.
Contact: www.classicpartsltd.com Tel: (+44) 01920 486032

Number Plate
In the UK, pre-1973 cars and motorcycles can use an old style numberplate with silver or white letters on a black background. Mine was made by specialists **Tippers Vintage Plates**. The numerals are die pressed, highly polished aluminium on a stove-enamelled black background.
It looks stunning; far superior to the stick-on white letters you often see applied to the rear numberplate of many classic bikes. Tippers recommended I use a 7 1/4" x 5 3/4" plate with curved sides, which fitted perfectly onto my numberplate carrier.
Contact: www.tippersvintageplates.co.uk Tel: (+44) 01702 549830

Battery
I chose a **Yuasa** battery as engine-builder Andy Berry swears by them. His experience is that they hold their charge far better than other battery makes he has tried. I concur, it was excellent on the trip. We upgraded the electrics on my bike to 12 volts, so I fitted a Super MF YTX7L-BS battery. The Yuasa website is

well worth a look as it has some useful information on battery maintenance and how to select a battery for your bike.
Contact: www.yuasa-battery.co.uk Tel: (+44) 08708 500257 (sales); 08708 500259 (technical)

Indicators & Light Bulbs

I'm usually very happy to use hand signals whilst riding my classics. However, for this journey it seemed prudent to fit indicators; especially for use in Europe. **Paul Goff**, a specialist supplier of classic motorcycle electrical parts, provided a pair of bulls-eye indicators and matching relay as originally fitted onto the handlebar ends of 1960s BMWs.
As I wanted to run the bike all day with good lighting, I chose an LED tail light. Not only is it brighter than a standard lamp, it also lasts longer and uses very little current. At the front, I used a quartz halogen 12V bulb as a daytime running light, fitted into the pilot light hole. For the main beam, I installed a British pre-focus quartz halogen 12V 35W. These were also supplied by Paul Goff.
Contact: www.norbsa02.freeuk.com Tel: (+44) 01494 868218

Fuel Cat

My motorcycle was originally built to run on leaded 4-Star petrol. To cope with poor quality, low octane unleaded petrol, I installed a **Formula Power** *Fuel Cat*. This helped my engine run cooler, protected the exhaust valve and assisted power output when the fuel was low grade. You just drop it in your petrol tank and forget about it.
Contact: Tel: (+44) 01403 754173

Suppliers: Rider Equipment

Jacket

I was really proud to wear my **Barbour** *International* jacket. Made from 100% waxed cotton, the jacket has been in production since the 1930s when it was used by a succession of British teams in the Olympics of motorcycling, the International Six Days Trial. Johnny Brittain wore one on a Royal Enfield 500 Twin in 1953, the last time a British team won the event. His father, Vic Brittain, also sported one in 1930s events and when riding a 350 Bullet to victory in the 1948 competition held in Italy.
I already have a well-worn black *International* jacket which never seems to be off my back. Barbour kindly provided me with a new sandstone coloured one for my ride to India. Its light weight and breathability was perfect for the hot climates I rode through.
Contact: www.barbour.com Tel: (+44) 0191 455 4444

Helmet
I entrusted my head protection to a **Cromwell** *Spitfire*. Now made in Italy, these beautifully designed helmets are light, comfortable and exceed the latest EU standards. - it even has a stainless steel outer shell. It looks in keeping with my bike and I've been thrilled with it! Mine was supplied by **Barry Vincent**. Barry has many years experience working in the crash helmet industry and is a regular sight at major UK motorcycle shows, where he sells Cromwell helmets alongside his other well-known line, **Vac-Bag**, which I also highly recommend. Barry is a friendly and helpful chap who offers great service as well as excellent prices.
Contact: www.vac-bags.co.uk Tel: (+44) 01832 733 115

Body Armour
I've tried hard-shell armour in the past and always found it too stiff and uncomfortable. I simply couldn't believe just how light and easy-to-wear **Forcefield** gear was when I first tried it on; I could hardly tell it was there! And unlike any other armour I've encountered, it's even reusable after an impact.
I used a Forcefield *Sport-Lite L1* back protector. It's soft, light and breathable and was perfect for long distance riding. I also used Forcefield *performance upgrade inserts* which I slipped into pockets sewn into my jacket's shoulders and elbows and also in the knees of my trousers.
I was fortunate to land quite softly when I crashed in Pakistan (except for my ribs and twisted knee), but felt reassured at all times to be wearing such high quality protectors.
Contact: www.forcefieldbodyarmour.co.uk Tel: (+44) 01933 410818

Boots
I used **Alt-Berg** Original Hogg Lites. They were absolutely superb.
They're designed as a dual purpose bike and walking boot, making them ideal for touring. The beauty of these boots is that they are made to measure, so the fit is perfect. For a fitting you can visit Alt-Berg, as I did, at their premises in Richmond, Yorkshire. It's a bonus that their shop is surrounded with great motorcycling countryside. Alternatively, you can see their stand at one of the UK's major bike shows.
I was very impressed to meet a fellow biker in their shop who had brought his 6-year and 120,000-mile-old Alt-bergs in for a resole. Now that's longevity!
Contact: www.altberg.co.uk Tel: (+44) 01748 850615

Gloves
Lewis leathers have a proud heritage of making leather clothing for aviators and motorcyclists and their quality is just as legendary as their styling.
I've always owned thick, chunky biking gloves, which would have been far too hot for this journey. The Lewis gloves are unlined and made from the softest hide imaginable. Now I know what it means when people say 'it fits like a kid glove'. Surprise bonuses were the increased sense of feel and control of the handlebars

and how easily I could get them off, even on the hottest days. The company have now opened a specialist shop in London, which sounds like a great place to meet other motorcyclists as well as checking out their classic riding gear.
Contact: www.lewisleathers.com Tel: (+44) 0207 4020863

Riding Clothes
I wear **Icebreaker** pure New Zealand Merino wool clothes just about every day, summer and winter. They're just so practical and very comfortable.
The beauty of Merino wool is that it's super warm when layered, yet remarkably cool in hot climates. It naturally breathes and resists body odours; you can wear it day after day in tough outdoor conditions without getting whiffy!
Icebreaker are especially good for motorcycling. I wore a *BodyFit 150* t-shirt under my biking gear, with a *Go Tiger 220* top to layer when necessary. These are great biking tops as you can zip the neck up and pull the sleeves down using thumb loops on colder days. I also used Icebreaker Merino socks for the same reasons.
I went for days on end in 40 degree heat wearing the same *BodyFit* t-shirt. Not once did I detect a hint of body odour. Amazing!
Contact: www.icebreaker.com (list of UK and international dealers available on the website)

Travel Clothes
I only had enough room in my luggage for one change of clothes. **Rohan** travel clothes were inimitably suitable. They are extremely rugged yet very packable and easy to care for. They also look smart however tough the conditions.
I took a pair of *Bags*, Rohan's iconic multi-function travel trousers. They weight just 335 grams and have a lightning fast drying time of 3 hours. To keep me looking presentable, I also packed a classy short-sleeve shirt made from a mixture of cool bamboo and cotton.
Rohan specialise in very well-designed travel accessories too. I wore an *All Terrain Money Belt* that from the outside looks just like an regular belt for holding your trousers up.
Contact: www.rohan.co.uk (list of UK stores available on the website)

Trousers
I went straight to **Draggin Jeans** for my motorcycle trousers. Leather trousers would have been too hot and I don't like wearing synthetics all day, which ruled out nearly all Enduro pants.
I chose a pair of Kevlar-lined *Draggin cargo pants*; the perfect combination of safety with easy to wear trousers. They look great, are supremely comfortable and were cool to wear in the extreme heat of the Iran and Pakistan deserts.
Contact: www.dragginjeans.net Tel: (+44) 01732 834 888

Rain Suit

I packed a **Jofama** *Wet Stop Rain Suit* just in case the weather turned against me. The suit is exceedingly well designed, with zippers that come up to the knee for ease of getting on and a main zip that runs diagonally across the chest, almost down to the knee. The waist is elasticised for comfort and there is a fold-away hood hidden in the collar.

The large Hi-Vis stripes that run across the sleeves, back and chest area are a very nice touch. It was invaluable in Britain whilst running the bike in and was priceless when called on for two days when crossing Europe. Jofama are made in Sweden to the highest standards and much of their gear looks in keeping with classic motorcycling.

Contact: www.jofama.se (list of UK & international dealers available on the website)

Goggles

I've been riding with **Halcyon** goggles for roughly 15 years; they are comfortable and allow great peripheral vision. In my opinion, the style of their split lens goggle compliments a classic bike perfectly. For the trip I used a pair of soft leather *MK49 Deluxe* goggles with tinted lenses to cope with the bright sunshine. I removed the visor from my helmet and I wore my goggles all the time as they provide great protection from dust. After 9000 very tough miles, there's still not a scratch on the lenses.

Contact: www.classicpartsltd.com Tel: (+44) 01920 486032

Hydration System

Some days I drank up to 8 litres of water. Finding room to carry that volume of liquid, as well as stopping frequently enough to drink it, could have been problematic.

A lightweight backpack-type hydration system was the perfect answer. UK distributors **Zyro** supplied me with a **Camelbak** hydration pack. The company are market leaders in these products, whether they be for motorcyclists, bicyclists, walkers or general sports use.

I used a *3 litre Classic*, which is simple in design and style and didn't look too out of place on the back of a classic motorcyclist. With my open face helmet, it was very easy to drink on the go as well.

Contact: www.zyro.co.uk Tel: 01845 521700

Suppliers: Bike Equipment

Tools

After years of fiddling around with secondhand tools of average quality, I now have a set of the best, thanks to British manufacturer **Britool**.

My bike uses Whitworth fixings exclusively and the Britool combination spanner set and 6 piece socket set covers every nut and bolt on it. Modern Bullets are mostly metric, although they still have some Whitworth fittings. Obviously, Britool cover all metric sizes too. I have never used such superbly made tools and they feel as though they will last a lifetime. When some serious spannering was required in the Baluchistan desert after my crash, it was extremely reassuring to have such fine tools to do it with.

Contact: www.britool.com Tel: (+44) 01142 917266

Bike Cover

A good cover not only protects your bike from the elements, it can act as an extra deterrent to prying eyes and hands. Being able to securely cover your bike when you want to explore a new place gives peace of mind and makes for a more enjoyable trip too.

My cover was tailor made for my bike by experts **Specialised Covers**. I have to say that the quality is excellent and the company have gone to great lengths to accommodate my panniers and fly screen. Watching their expert pattern-maker at work was an education and my cover fits like a Saville Row suit. One feature I really like is the brass eyelets that allow a padlock to secure the cover in place.

Contact: www.carcoversuk.com Tel: (+44) 01943 864646

Tank Bag

Using a tank bag to more evenly distribute the weight of my luggage seemed essential to safe riding. I chose to use a **Pacsafe** *Tanksafe* tank bag. It's constructed with a high-tensile stainless steel mesh 'lock-and-leave' security system that makes it slashproof, snatchproof and tamperproof. You lock it closed then secure it to your bike using a coated heavy duty cable. I've used a variety Pacsafe travel security products for several years and they have never let me down. The bag is capacious at 26L and it looks very much in keeping on a classic bike.

Mine came from UK motorcycle accessory distributors **Motohaus**. Amongst other goodies, their website features the full Pacsafe motorcycle range including an equally secure tail bag and helmet bag.

Contact: www.motohaus.com Tel: (+44) 01256 704909

Rack Pack

I needed a versatile holdall bag to carry equipment including a spare 5L fuel can. **Lyon Equipment**, of Sedbergh in the Lake District, provided me with the perfect solution; an **Ortlieb** *Rack Pack*. Ortlieb make superb outdoors equipment, tried and tested by travellers for over 25 years.

I chose the large (49 litre) *Rack Pack*. It has a full-width roll closure which allows fast access. Although initially designed for touring bicyclists, the *Rack Pack* has been awarded 'highly recommended' and 'top-product' status in several European motorcycling magazine tests. It was superb on the journey, never once letting rain, dust or sand in to my equipment.

Contact: www.lyon.co.uk/ortlieb.html (list of UK dealers available on the website)

Waterproof & Dustproof Travel Bags

Aquapac is a highly creative UK based company that won the Queen's Award for Innovation in 2007.

They produce waterproof bags with all manner of applications, from protecting your mobile phone, iPod, GPS or camera to keeping valuable documents and money safe.

I took an Aquapac *Camcorder Case* on my ride to India. It has a specially hardened clear lens which you can film through and is waterproof down to 5 Meters. It's also dusts and sand proof... an essential on this journey.

Contact: www.aquapac.net Tel: (+44) 0207 7384466

Earplugs

I never considered earplugs to be technology until I had a pair of *Pro Guard* plugs custom made for my ears by experts **Enhanced Listening**.

An appointment was made for me at a local specialist who took impressions of my ear canals. The resulting earplugs are supremely comfortable and I was able to wear them all day (once I learned not to push them in too far!). Small filters were added so I can still hear the sounds I want to hear.

In case I lost one of the plugs, Enhanced Listening also kindly provided me with a back up pair of Alpine Motosafe Earplugs. These are specially designed for bikers and are a quality, cost effective solution.

Contact: www.enhancedlistening.co.uk Tel: (+44) 0208 1440370

Satellite Navigation:

Garmin Zumo 550. A great piece of kit. It fits easily on the bike and draws a maximum of 15W which is important when your dynamo produces a meagre 60W! The unit came with street-level maps that guided me all the way across Europe. A world map to cover main roads for the rest of the journey was relatively inexpensive. A really great feature of the Zumo 550 is that it comes with a car mount and speaker so I get maximum use year round from the equipment. I bought mine from **GPS Warehouse**. They supply a wide range of GPS accessories and their prices beat high street retailers hands down.

Contact: www.gpsw.co.uk Tel: (+44) 020 8893 939

Luggage Straps

Made in Australia, **Andy Strapz** have so many benefits for motorcyclists over bungees: there are no metal hooks so there's virtually no risk of eye injury; they don't roll off or cut into luggage; gear can be packed and unpacked in seconds; they hold firmer yet under less tension due to their width and they are kinder to paint and bodywork. They also fold away into a very small package. It has to be said; they're the bees knees! I chose a pair of 1250mm long *strapz* to hold my rack bag onto the rear luggage rack.

Contact: www.andystrapz.co.uk Tel: (+44) 01202 744599

More Luggage Straps

I've tried many ways to hold awkwardly shaped odds and ends on bikes in the past, with only limited success.

Rok Straps do the job superbly; they're specially designed for motorcycles. The larger pair I took can hold up to 40KG. They're adjustable and can be fitted a number of ways. I also used a pair of smaller straps which were a neat way to add extra items onto my crashbars. The product is excellent and the company great to deal with.

Contact: www.rokstraps.com (list of UK and international dealers available on the website)

Lock

It's reported that over 100 motorcycles are stolen on average per day in the UK, yet more than half are left unprotected. As my Bullet has no ignition key, a good chain and padlock were essential.

The 10mm Barrier chain lock from **Oxford** met my needs perfectly. It's relatively light but also tough, heat treated to resist attack and the lock is pick resistant.

I especially like how the padlock is integrated into the chain - it was one less thing to remember or fiddle about with.

Contact: www.oxprod.com Tel: (+44) 01993 862300

Thread Locker

British singles are notorious for losing nuts and bolts due to vibration. I liberally used **Loctite** *Lock N' Seal* on all fixings and didn't lose a single one.

On visiting the Loctite website I was very surprised to see the company make everything an overland motorist could possibly wish for in a emergency repair kit.

As well as the essential *Lock N' Sea*l, Loctite manufacturer, **Henkel**, very kindly provided me with a whole range of products including *Duck* tape, epoxy glue, instant gasket, chemical metal, silicone sealant and even a magic metal compound that would plug a hole in the crankcase if necessary!

Contact: www.henkel.co.uk

Cleaner and Polish
I've spent a considerable amount of time and money restoring my motorcycle so I wanted to protect the paintwork as well as possible before my ride to India.
Autoglym is respected worldwide as a manufacturer of leading car and motorcycle care products.
I used their *Motorcycle Cleaner* product, which is safe on all surfaces including polished alloy. Tough polish protection was then provided by a coat of *Super Resin Polish* followed by a coat of *Extra Gloss Protection*, a tough protective sealant that contains a blend of hard resins and waxes.
Contact: www.autoglym.co.uk Tel: (+44) 01462 677766

Solar Battery Charger
Jonny Krause's tip was a good one and I just loved being able to charge my numerous batteries on the go!
Online solar power specialists **The Solar Centre** kindly supplied me a *Freeloade*r portable battery charger plus an additional velcro-mounted solar panel that made the charging process 3 times faster.
The Freeloaded comes with multiple power adapters so it was easy to use with my mobile phone, PDA, digital camera, film camera and even my Sat Nav!
Contact: www.thesolarcentre.co.uk Tel: (+44) 0845 0941250

Wind Up Radio Torch
This eco radio torch, designed by legend **Trevor Baylis**, was just the ticket for both late night spannering and musical entertainment. It has two powerful LEDs and best of all, no batteries are required. One minute winding gives 25 minutes of light. Furthermore, it also has a red LED map light and doubles up as an emergency mobile phone charger. The entire unit is compact and has a tough rubber coating too.
Contact: www.tclproducts.co.uk (list of UK dealers available on the website)

Charity Contacts:

JBF (Scotland)

East Newton Farm,
Foulden,
Berwickshire,
TD15 1UL

www.jbfscotland.org

Tel: + 44 (0)1289 386720

WaterAid

Supporter Services,
47-49 Durham Street,
London,
SE11 5JD

www.wateraid.org/uk

Tel: +44 (0)845 6000 433